THE GRAIL JOURNEY
THROUGH WALES

THE GRAIL JOURNEY
THROUGH WALES

Megan Wingfield

ATHENA PRESS
LONDON

THE GRAIL JOURNEY THROUGH WALES
Copyright © Megan Wingfield 2007

ISBN 10-digit: 1 84401 829 6
ISBN 13-digit: 978 1 84401 829 1

*Every effort has been made to trace the copyright holders of
works quoted within this book and obtain permission. The
publisher apologises for any omissions and is happy to make
necessary changes in subsequent print-runs.*

First Published 2007 by
ATHENA PRESS
Queen's House, 2 Holly Road
Twickenham TW1 4EG
United Kingdom

Printed for Athena Press

This book is dedicated to the old path

Also by the author

Light is the Rainbow Bridge
by Megan Wingfield and Olive Hesketh,
A 'thought for the day' art book,
obtainable from the author.
Privately published. ISBN 9533 1910 5

Preface

This is a true story that came about as the result of my visiting a high altitude lake in Mid Wales. It is one of three sister lakes and this one is called Llyn-y-Tarw (the Lake of the Bull). We were later to discover that its name referred to a connection with the Bronze Age people who once lived there, and with the Pleiades star system. I was introduced to Merlin himself, who told me, 'You were a pupil of mine in the old time.'

This was the start of a series of adventures, and information was given in meditation that was written down in the form of a diary, and was never intended to become a book.

It was discovered that the lake was a crown chakra, and gradually the other land chakras revealed themselves to us, until we had found thirteen, all taking their energy from 'the Pathway of the Beloved', a feminine energy line running from the Scilly Isles to Whitby.

When we went to find the sites we respectfully introduced ourselves to the spiritual guardians of the places and their genius loci. I was given messages and was able to write them down from their dictation to me, and many times was able to confirm the information given, through books and sometimes news programmes on TV. This is why there is so much information in this book.

How could this be? I asked myself frequently. How can I do this? Where does this information come from? It comes with the ancient Celtic gift of the seer (called *gweledydd* in Welsh). This is similar to the mediums who connect to and through the human spirit, but the gift of the seer is through a connection with the spirit of the land itself. The '*awen*' was known by the Druids as the 'spirit of the muse', a poetic gift of eloquence, bestowed by the Goddess Brighid. This is also an attribute of the seer.

I believe there are other ways of accessing information through this contact with sacred sites. One of these is genetic encoding, because I have known and used these sites before in former lives, which brings with it an ability to read their akashic records. The debt that I owe to the guidance of my friends and teachers who are in the spirit world, and have guided me at every turn of the pathway must be acknowledged.

I have had a deliberate policy of not reading any book or accessing any information until the site had been visited in order to be completely open to the etheric energies. This was so that no one could accuse me of fabricating the whole thing based on prior research.

These places, which have been used for possibly hundreds and thousands of years, leave a very strong impression on the Earth's energy field. The Druids' tests for their students leave a dramatic imprint, like the initiation pit at the heart chakra. Similarly there are two waterfalls in Mid Wales known as 'Water Break Its Neck'. One is near New Radnor and one on the River Severn (its Welsh name is Hafren) at Hafren Forest. Jumping over these waterfalls was a test of strength, agility and courage for the students.

I went to the sites with an open mind and a positive expectancy, which is not anticipating anything other than simply 'tuning' into the energy. In this way the mind is not used to imagine things or set limitations. If you go and don't receive any messages except a feeling of peace, be aware that peace is your message.

This story is not just about Wales: all of Britain was Celtic once – this is our inheritance and it belongs to us all. It was meant to be shared, so that others can reconnect with, and honour once again the sacred feminine energy of Mother Earth, and that we will once more walk gently on her face.

Megan Wingfield

Acknowledgements

A big thank you to my husband Bob and those friends whose destiny it was to walk this pathway with us, and for their contributions (they know who they are). I would also like to thank friends and family for their superb photos, and Rhiannon of Tregaron for a photo of her craftsmanship. Most importantly, I would like to thank my proof-reader for her hard work (made a lot harder because I am dyslexic) and my son Ian for putting this story on the computer, because without their contributions this book could not have happened.

I would like to acknowledge the contributions that the members of staff of Athena Press have made in helping me to bring this story to print.

Contents

Crown Chakra at Llyn-y-Tarw

This Sacred Isle

This island of Britain is the sacred isle, the mystic isle of the ancients; there are many sacred places yet to be discovered. It is of vital importance to the whole planet that these places are rediscovered and honoured, so that they may be rebirthed into the present age. All of us can do this. We can all go on a pilgrimage to be 'tuned' in to the vibrations of these places; the choice is yours! You can look for a stone circle or a standing stone on your local map and visit them; there are so many of these sites. You may want to visit the ancient Ridgeway, the Uffington White Horse, Avebury, the Rollright Stones or Stonehenge, etc.

These are places where the ghosts of communities linger on in the ether, taking eternal possession of the landscape, giving a purpose to modern pilgrims. You might like to visit some old churches around you, remembering that they were built on ancient sacred sites. You might want to go on a Celtic pilgrimage to Brittany, Wales, Scotland or Ireland. You may want to create a sacred place in your own garden.

All you need is a sense of respect, and to ask the guardian for permission to enter, remembering that it is a holy place. You may honour it in whatever way feels right to you: singing, dancing, saying prayers or leaving biodegradable gifts for the elementals. You may both give and receive healing. Be aware that if you are visiting an Earth chakra, it will affect your own corresponding chakra also, so do take care to allow for this. It is a good idea to make the pilgrimage to the base chakra and work your way up to the crown if you can, although this is not essential. We didn't do it this way because I was unaware of the other chakras until after the discovery of the crown. If you can do this, you will be performing a service to this sacred land. Bless the Earth and ask for a blessing on yourselves also.

The Importance of Sacred Sites

Where did they come from? From the beginning of Planet Earth. What are they? They are Mother Earth doorways to other dimensions. Earth was part of a star before it became a planet. We are children of the Earth but we are also children of the stars. All of the many peoples and cultures have stories of the Creation. They are pieces of a jigsaw from before recorded time.

From long before recorded time there were places – sacred places – that were seeded with information containing universal consciousness, the ether, or the 'flow' as we are apt to call it. On these sites there were stones that formed at this time, so that through these portals our ancestors can communicate with us. Many of us are Celtic. Most of those people who originated in Western Europe have Celtic roots, and so do those from this continent who crossed the oceans to other lands. This is why there has been a revival in learning once again the ancient ways and secret places of our land.

Each circle of standing stones has a different purpose, which you can discover for yourselves. There are earthly and stellar libraries that can be accessed, information on what has been and what will be, as we are more and more able to come into harmony and balance, and to use this balance to create wholeness within ourselves. It is through visiting these sites that your living energy field can exchange states of resonance with the ancient stones. You need do nothing more than just be there.

You may wish to know the purpose of the place and consciously speak to the guardian of the site. You may need several visits to become attuned to the energy. To go in a group to meditate and say prayers for peace and healing, or to perform a simple ceremony, will open up the site and yourselves. Many of the sites have been shut down and are just waiting for you to awaken them. Some, however, have been closed, never to work again, but you will 'know' whether your site is working or not. All you really have to do is to approach with a sense of respect for its ancient lineage, its spirit guardians and its elementals. Leave flowers as gifts for them, to show your respect, for as you give so shall you receive.

HOW IS IT POSSIBLE TO MAKE THIS CONNECTION IN THIS WAY?

We all live in a dimension of space–time that is composed of energy and light. This space–time is a fourth-dimensional holographic field through which energy appears and disappears, moves, grows and changes. We ourselves are multidimensional beings. We are an energy field within a particular dimension. We have energy fields that surround and penetrate the physical body.

The planets, stars, Earth and moon, the animals and plants, also have these fields, which can be seen by psychics, intuitives and mediums, and can be photographed by Kirlian photography.[1] There are connections, pathways or conduits between these physical and non-physical bodies. They are called chakras, or energy vortices, which spin at different speeds connected to the different energy frequencies of light and they connect to different dimensions. Our planet also has chakras on her body, and meridians interconnecting with other frequencies and dimensions throughout the cosmos. They are connected by an electromagnetic system of ley lines and crystalline grids. Where these lines meet they form the power centres or the sacred places of the Earth – the chakras of our planet. They can be major or minor, but each one is of vital importance to our Earth and its inhabitants. They are sited all over the planet in every country. They emanate certain types of energy that can be measured and categorised. There is electric, magnetic, electromagnetic and crystalline energy at these sites. The power is measurable and can be sensed through meditation, prayer or attunement. It is possible to

[1] Kirlian photography is a method of photographing the energy field or aura around people, animals and plants.

connect with or travel to other dimensions, to contact other dimensional beings, to receive psychic impressions from the past, present or future. You can connect with your past lives, your higher self, your spirit guides and your guardian angel.

All sites have a special guardian who protects it and protects you when you are there. Always acknowledge this guardian and ask permission to enter the site. You may bring a gift that will not harm the site. State out loud your intention and include the elementals who also guard and protect it. White Eagle[2] says that when we visit ancient, sacred places, although the ceremonies on an outward level may be gone, we can still sense the impression these wonderful rituals have left upon the ether and we can be aware of how they are still being performed in spirit. The isle of Britain is called the mystic isle because it is full of these centres of pure spiritual power. The ceremony that was once performed can be celebrated again in the ethereal world, with our help. Please honour the sacred site and approach it with the greatest respect, for it is the 'stairway to heaven' that the ancients knew.

The First Discovery of an Ancient Sacred Site

In 1997 my husband Bob and I had gone to live halfway up a mountain in Mid Wales. There we met a farmer's wife who was also an artist, and who was part-owner of some land and a lake at the top of this mountain. One day she said to me, 'You must go and see this lake where the black-headed gulls breed. There is a standing stone as well. You will like it there. It is reputed to be the last place in Wales where fairies were seen. People at one time used to go up there to see them.'

It did not prove easy to find either the lake or the stone because they cannot be seen from the lane. We found the stone on our second attempt. It is a magnificent stone and we wondered how far it went into the ground. It seemed alive. When Bob leaned against it he said it seemed to lean against him, and he could feel a pulse or the heartbeat of the Earth. We said some prayers and took some photos and returned home.

---

[2] White Eagle: the spirit guide of Grace Cooke, a well-known medium (1892–1979). See White Eagle Publishing Trust for more information.

One of the photos of the stone was amazing. On the right of the stone was a bull's head, and on the left a gnome's head could clearly be seen, inscribed by nature, and not by man. I thought I had found them, but of course it was no accident. In meditation I was told that it had revealed itself to me because of my respect for its ancient lineage. We were never able to photograph this again so clearly. It depends on the light, the time of day, and time of year, so that we never got it quite right again.

The standing stone

I meditated about this stone and this is what I was told.

'This goes back to when the Earth was young, and everything had a spirit, a consciousness that was known by all. It was easier then for

elementals to manifest when it was known that they existed in stone, Earth and sky. This shape was one which manifested at the time because it was easier then to be surrounded by sympathetic souls and spirits who understood that there is life in stones and rocks.'

'What is the meaning of the bull's head?' I asked.

'This is power. It is male energy, procreation and protection. A bull is like a chieftain among men. It represents strength and wealth, many calves and great herds. There is no difference then and now, in the understanding of an agricultural society of the importance of the bull.'

I asked how we might approach this stone.

'With respect, as always. You may bless it. It has shown its face to you as a response to your respect for its ancient lineage. It wishes you to know that it has a consciousness, that it is alive, and that it understands that within you is a sense of its ancient energies. You may speak to it if you wish.'

A photograph was sent to a friend, Joan Fugeman, with a request for her to meditate with it.

This is her meditation.

THE STANDING STONE

Many rocks and stones in this area of the mountains were scattered by gigantic upheavals of Earth disturbances, of earthquakes and volcanic eruptions, millions of millennia ago. When the Earth settled, the rocks formed patterns of geometric shapes. Much later, the ancients living in the mountains re-erected the mass of rock and stone into circles with light energy, keeping them in their geometric forms. When the correct formation had finally been placed, devas from the Mineral Kingdom entered the circles and took guardianship of that area of land. Their images they implanted on the stones in protection of the sacred land of the goddess. Some of the stones were not included in the building of the circles and therefore were not given the sacrament of the light, but were, nevertheless, guarded by the lower elementals of the nature kingdom. I believe this is one of the stones that was scattered by itself and became separated from the mass. The standing stone is holy, protected by the gnomes and crystal fairies; their images appear on the rock face: it should *never* be removed by man from the place where it stands. It sends out much love to its parent *Mother Earth*.

Joan

THE PLANET AND ITS CRYSTALLINE STRUCTURE MUST HARMONISE, VIBRATE AND SING!

Standing stones are the acupuncture points on the surface of the Earth, where energies can be accessed. Accessing this energy will link with a grid which has been placed deep within the Earth. Wakening these stones will bring this energy to the surface where it will facilitate the process of clearing and uplifting energies to the next dimension.

'There is a master who is responsible for this process, and he is known as the crystal master, a master who is able to link energies for the greatest good. Love is the link for this master to do his work, and it is the way to access the information which is required, which will be for the furtherance of Aquarian energies and the working of this planet. In one sense the crystal master is an Earth master, for the planet is itself a living being, and it is necessary to coordinate the energies of this being, in order that a vibration of harmony may be induced. This means that all structures must be involved and included in the harmony strategy. This includes the humans on the planet harmonising within their own living systems (physical body and aura), and then with the planet. The planet with its crystalline structure must harmonise, vibrate and sing.

'Life itself must be brought into balance, and the crystals are only the beginning, but they are structures which, by responding to the new energy, will commence to bring the vibration of light into physical form. To work with the crystals is very important now, to concentrate on them and work with the crystal master. The crystal master is pure light energy, and is yet another form of it, of which there are many forms.'

ACKNOWLEDGE THE ELEMENTS

The elements of earth, air, fire and water are vital to us on Earth. We are children of the Earth, and she is our mother. Like a mother, she nurtures us and cares for us, but we have lost our connection with her. This loss proved tragic for both us and her in the twentieth century. To honour the Earth is to recognise this connection, to recognise the sustenance that she gives us and return it with love and respect. Honour your connections with the Earth as the ancients did, for we cannot own her, we can only hold her in trust for our lifetime, as a trust for future generations and for the Earth herself.

WHAT ARE ELEMENTALS?

Elementals are energy with a consciousness at another level of vibration, which some people can see and most of us cannot. They have always been here on our land, trying to work with us. The Western analytical mind denies this knowledge, while those who do not analyse have always known them. Elementals are the reason why some people have 'green fingers', for it is through a person's love and respect for the Earth and its fruits, through their labour and vibrations, that nature spirits can work with them, even if they do not know it.

Whenever we recognise a place that is 'magical', where flowers bloom and fruit and vegetables grow, where there are animals both wild and tame, and birds and butterflies can be found – then you will know the elementals are there also. So speak to them, invite them into your garden. They need to know that they are welcome and acknowledged. This, and respect, is all they require to do their work. It doesn't matter if you cannot see them; you will see and feel the difference in your enhanced surroundings.

The Lake and the Island

It took three attempts to find the lake. It is well hidden, and has remained so as a sacred and undiscovered site for at least 1,000 years. We do not know how old it is, but it was known to the Druids, and there is evidence of Celtic roundhouses and stone circles. It would seem that the land was flooded at a later time when the climate changed. On a clear day, you can see so far that it feels like the roof of Mid Wales.

It is a large lake in a hollow above the tree line in a rocky, stony landscape. It has two small islands; one is flat and feature-less, the other has small willows. This is where the black-headed gulls nest. The grass on the island is always short, as if cut by fairy lawnmowers. The energy of the place is very beautiful – quiet, peaceful and somehow powerful. The wind at this height can be cruel, and is described by country people as lazy: it does not bother to go around you, it goes straight through you! After my first visit, I meditated at home to link with the energy of the place. I received a personal message of welcome from the elementals.

Llyn-y-Tarw

A MESSAGE FROM THE ELEMENTALS

'All that we are is light. There are many, many forms which we can take and our joy is that of light. We are in service to the light, this is our work. We welcome you. Welcome, welcome, welcome. It is a long time since anyone has been to visit us – too long! It is our wish that you will come again soon. We recognise you from long ago. You have been before. This is why you were drawn here, on the pathway of the Little People, "Y Tylwyth Teg" [the fairies].

'There are many colours in us for we are made of light as you would expect. Have regard for all our forms; we know you see only one. You have been blessed with second sight. Come again and we will talk some more. You are an artist. You may paint us. We are light.'

We made several visits to attune to the energy and nothing else happened. We then decided to perform a ceremony at the site with a friend. We were saying Celtic prayers for peace and healing, and intended to honour the site by scattering some flowers on the surface of the lake. I was reading the prayers, so was looking at my book, when Pat, my friend, said, 'Megan, look!'

I looked and saw bright flashes of very bright white light, just like camera flashes. They appeared to be going off inside the breaking waves. This took place only in the waters between ourselves and the island, nowhere else. There was no sun. Pat saw the flashes in colours of red and gold, and described them as 'sparkly bits'. Bob saw them as I did: flashes of white light. We all agreed on where we saw them. As I stopped saying the prayers they stopped also. They only happened as I was reading, so that I did not see them as much as the others. We went home that day knowing that something magical had happened. It had now become apparent that this was a very special place indeed.

A little later Joan was sent a photo of the island and asked if she would meditate with it.

JOAN'S MEDITATION

The island is beautiful and sacred. There is a lot of peace and love. I felt that where there is now water, there was once land which was a valley between hills. Cattle grazed and animals roamed freely. There was, I feel, a farming community and the people lived in peace and harmony. Violent storms hit the country and water poured in and destroyed the land. I felt it was at the same time as Avalon, and Merlin was here. There may have been a Druid temple on the island that never went down. There is a stone amongst the trees, I feel, which is the place where religious ceremonies took place. This stone holds a lot of power, and protects the island.

Later Joan was able to visit the lake. We are unable to get to the island because there is no boat, although there used to be one for the use of the fishermen. The lake has fish that are only found at high altitudes. Looking from the shore there is no sign of the stone that Joan saw in her meditation. However, three psychic friends have independently stated that there is a stone on the island. It must be lying down or beneath the ground.

THE CEREMONY AT THE LAKE

Without any planning on anyone's part, it just so happened that we went to perform a ceremony of prayers and meditation, ending with an offering of flowers that we were going to strew on the water on 21 September. This was the time of Lugnasadh, on the date of the autumn equinox. We put the flowers on a flat, square stone as a makeshift altar, and began our prayers. We were soon joined by a huge butterfly, a red admiral, which is not normally found at that altitude. It was the largest of this species that I have ever seen, twice the size of a normal one. This butterfly alighted on each one of us in turn, finally resting on the brightly coloured flowers. By this time we had stopped the ceremony and were watching it, when it flew over the water towards the island, dipping down in flight, almost touching the surface of the lake as it did so, until it was lost to our sight. The following day I read that the Celtic ancients used to teach their children that butterflies were the souls of fairies, and it seemed to us that this was true.

On the altar stone with the flowers I had placed some white quartz pebbles, which I had intended to throw into the lake as an offering, because quartz has a special connection to the Celts. On an impulse, I left some on the stone. Bob asked me if I had counted them.

'No,' I said. I had no idea how many pebbles I had left there.

'Did you realise there are seven?' he asked. 'Do you realise there are seven of us?'

I did not. This was another very special day, and it was after this that things really began to happen. The butterfly is a symbol of change, colour and joy. In early Christianity it was the symbol of the soul. It awakens a sense of lightness and joy, to remind us that life is a dance, and growth and change do not have to be traumatic, but can be as gentle and joyful as we wish. After this we were often to see a red admiral on our visits and at our ceremonies.

Merlin

This is where Merlin (Myrddin) comes into the story.

When King Vortigern wanted to build a fortress in Gwynydd, in the mountains of Snowdonia at a site known today as Dinas Emrys near Beddgelert, a strange thing happened continually. All the building materials disappeared overnight. So Vortigern asked his advisers what should be done. His advisers told him to find a child without a father, kill him, and sprinkle his blood around the site. Vortigern sent messengers throughout Britain to look for such a child. After some time, when they were in the town of Carmarthen, they overheard two quarrelling children; one child said to the other, 'O fellow without a father, no good will be thine.' They searched for the boy's mother and she was asked who the father of this boy was. She was the daughter of the King of Dyfed, and a nun at the Church of St Peter. She told them that she did not know who the father was because she had been raped by an unseen force. The idea of a supernatural birth was not unknown in the ancient world.

The boy's name was An ap y Lleian (An, son of a nun). After this time he was known as Myrddin ('myriad' in Welsh), and translated into Latin as Merlin. He was also known as Myrddin Wyllt (Merlin the Wild). It must have been difficult for him to become incarnate and he had many difficulties to overcome.

When he was taken before Vortigern, Myrddin challenged the king's Druids so that they had to admit that they were out of their depth. He then began his most famous prophecy. He told them to dig in the middle of the site where they would find two sleeping dragons, one white and one red. When the dragons awoke they began to fight, and Myrddin declared that the red dragon, representing the Welsh, would eventually defeat the white dragon – the Saxons. This is why there is a red dragon on the Welsh flag, the symbol adopted by the Welsh nation. Myrddin then ordered Vortigern to leave the site because he would never be able to build on it. Vortigern was obsessive about his own safety because he had introduced the Anglo-Saxons into Britain when he had hired them as mercenaries. This did not make him very popular with the native Britons. The rightful heir to the throne, Ambrosius Aurelianus, was smuggled to Brittany after his brother Constans was murdered by Vortigern, so when he returned he laid siege to Vortigern's tower and killed him.

Myrddin's next involvement was with Uthyr Pendragon, and his part in shape-shifting Uthyr to look like Gwrlois, so that Eigyr would think he was her husband. It was from this union that Arthur was conceived. When Gwrlois was conveniently killed in battle, Uthyr married Eigyr. Since Arthur was born out of wedlock, Myrddin asked for the baby to be given to him to find foster-parents for the child, and this was done until Arthur was fourteen years old.

Arthur became king when he was fifteen years old 'in the year of the Lord 498',[3] after pulling the sword from the stone. The sword was called Caledfwlch (Excalibur). Myrddin was not present when Arthur pulled the sword from the stone. He was with Bishop Blasius, his confessor, and the scribe for his prophecies. His advice had been sought on finding Uthyr's successor, and he had told the nobles to 'come together to the church, and pray to God in all innocence that he may make clear who is worthy to reign over you'.

So who was Merlin? He was a priest of the Druidic order, and they had a standing that was on the same level as the magi, the Egyptian priests and the Indian Brahmins. The Druids concerned themselves with divination and all branches of wisdom. They were not pagan priests. On the contrary, Joseph of Arimathea came to Britain because of them. They were steeped in the religious traditions of the Egyptian mystery schools, on the same level of understanding and training as the Essenes, of whom Joseph was a member. The Egyptian monks lived in desert communities, and as there were no deserts in Wales, the monks chose wild, lonely and 'deserted' places, called in the Welsh language '*dyserth*', meaning wilderness. They also chose islands, as in the tidal island of Lindisfarne, and Bardsey Island, Caldy Island and Puffin Island.

Merlin was the greatest arch-druid of all time, and his advice was always sought by Arthur. He was born, lived and died in Wales, circa AD 480. There are two versions of his birth: one that he was born in South Wales, and also somewhere in the Conwy Valley in North Wales. His grave is on Cader Dinmael. In the centuries between then and now, he has been much maligned. Perhaps we should take another look and begin to reassess Arthur's wise and trusted counsellor.

---

[3] Geoffrey of Monmouth, *Historia Regum Britanniae*

Merlin as the planetary guardian

IN A MEDITATION I FOUND MYSELF TALKING TO MERLIN

I found myself at the top of the mountain in the Bronze Age. I was met by the chieftain who took me into his house. He was tall and slim and wore a short cloak fastened with a large round brooch. He had a large spiral painted in dark blue on each cheek, and wore a short sword on his right side. I think he had a punk-like hairstyle, and wore brown boots that looked home-made. Inside his roundhouse, I sat by the fire. It was dark and smoky and very uncomfortable. There were other people milling about but it was too dark to see – I could only hear them. He told me he would take me to the Druid. I followed him out and along a little path through the birch trees until we reached the Druid. He had white hair and a beard, and his eyes were sapphires that flashed light.

'I am Merlin,' he said. I somehow understood that he was an immortal and felt a connection with Egypt. He is an immortal with special responsibility for Wales and the Celtic nations. The Druids and the Essenes both practised the old mystery school teaching and the true teaching of the cosmic Christ. This is why both were destroyed by the Roman Church, while other religions were assimilated. The Welsh nation is carrying the genetic blueprint of the Druids and the ancients. This was due to Merlin's care. Quite a feat to preserve such a small nation for thousands of years!

The teaching can only be brought through if the genetic inheritance is intact. It is like a password to key into a computer, which is probably what it is. It is about incarnation, plus genetic inheritance, plus spiritual guidance through what is sometimes known as second sight or inspirational means. I understand that the story of Merlin and the red and white dragons has a further twist. As already mentioned, when the sleeping dragons were awoken by Vortigern's men, they began to fight. At first the white dragon, representing the Saxons, was winning, but in the end the red dragon of Wales would be victorious. The Welsh have always enjoyed a friendly relationship with their red dragon, seeing it as the guardian of their land. Wales has been ruled over for 1,000 years, but in the coming Age of Aquarius the Welsh nation will rediscover their Druidic inheritance and lead the world in the true understanding of the native Christian teaching and the universal ageless wisdoms. The red dragon will win in the Aquarian age, with wisdom and light. This has always fallen under Merlin's jurisdiction and protection.

ON MEETING WITH MERLIN FOR THE SECOND TIME IN MEDITATION

For one moment I was standing at the lakeside, and in the next moment the water had gone and I was met by the chieftain who is the guardian. He took me to Merlin, and this is what I was told.

'Merlin is with you for protection and teaching. The connection between you is very strong. Be brave. All is well with you.'

I was getting a sense of a very ancient lineage – ancient energy, pre-Earth, a guardian angel of the Earth.

Merlin: *'I am one of the planet's guardians and you have always been aware of me. You were one of my pupils in the "old time".'*

I asked him what he thought of the failure of the world summit talks on global warming which had happened on that day.

'It is too late for that. This is about will. It is about making things happen, but it is already too late for the physical Earth because the third dimension will fall away. Fear not. All is well. Look!' he said, and he passed his hand over the air. I looked, and we were up in the cosmos, looking down on a beautiful Planet Earth. Merlin was made of stars, with lines of light between them, like joining up the dots. The Earth was in its light body. I was looking at the Earth in the next dimension. It seemed to be made of light, and was very, very beautiful. It seemed to be light in weight, not solid at all. There was a great sense of peace, tranquillity and beauty. All is well. I afterwards learnt that Joan had had the same meditation in the same week. The only difference was that Merlin was not present in hers.

A MESSAGE OF REASSURANCE THAT I RECEIVED FROM MERLIN (STARGATE, 5 FEBRUARY 2005)[4]

'Today is a very important day because this is the day and night when there is an opening in the stargate which will allow in friendly beings from above the stars. These beings are energies which left the Earth to its own devices many aeons ago and they are coming back in order to give their guidance to the people of the Earth. Would you understand that they are coming in particular to the women of Earth?'

Question: Can you tell me what they want from us?

'They want nothing for themselves but it is their intention to give guidance for the love of the Earth. In many ways, this is the only really important thing that is required now. Love for, and of, Mother Earth. This is the energy behind Imbolc, this is the connection and the meaning. Mother Earth needs this love. This is the most powerful and unassailable energy in the cosmos. Now is the time to connect with the energy, for the Earth is ready at last. These beings are a part of a hierarchy of cosmic beings that are a part of the Cosmic Spirit's wish and intention for the Earth. They are a part of the original blueprint for this planet and its people. They are very elevated beings and it is not possible for you to comprehend with your mind, only with your heart; but you will feel the change in the energy. We thank you for your efforts to usher in this change. Continue with your work. Blessings.'

---

[4] Stargate: a cosmic portal or gateway to other galaxies and star systems, used by beings from these star systems and galaxies, and some spiritually advanced humans.

The Mistletoe Flower Remedy Opens Another Doorway

I was given some drops of a flower remedy that was very special. It was made by a man who had a vision that he should make a mistletoe flower essence from a plant that grew in an oak tree. Mistletoe does not grow on oaks; it is usually found in apple trees, so he searched for this tree for a long time.

One day, as he was driving along a road, he saw a man coming towards him. Something made him stop and ask him if he knew of such a tree.

'Yes,' said the man. 'I will show you.'

Unfortunately the plant was far too small to harvest, and a few more years passed before it was ready. He was 'told' that it was to be cut as the Druids had done, with a sickle made of gold. As he did not possess such a thing, he set about making one himself. When it was ready, he was made to understand that the plant was to be cut without being touched by a human hand. Well, oak trees are known for their height and girth, and this one was no exception. So that no one would see him, he climbed that tree at night, with his partner standing below with a blanket! Eventually, a few drops of this precious liquid were given to me, and were mixed with water from Chalice Well in Glastonbury. Some of this water was poured into Llyn-y-Tarw during a ceremony of prayers, healing and floral offerings.

The next time we went to the lake was the week after the tragedy in America in September 2001, and we spent time in prayers for healing and peace. We said the Celtic prayer, 'Deep Peace', which had been set to music, and we played it on a tape that we brought with us.

As the wonderful music and the roses we offered spread out over the water, suddenly, from out of the blue, we were joined by a flock of swifts, who flew around us seemingly enjoying the music as much as we did. Two dragonflies also came, the ones with huge brown wings that look like helicopters. We have never seen either the birds or the dragonflies there before, and they vanished as the music died away and all was quiet again. The gifts of flowers and music were given and received with love. One of our group walked to the other side of the lake and sat down to meditate. When she came back she told us that she had 'seen' two Druids. They each carried a staff. One had a ram's horn on the top of his and one carried a staff with a golden sickle. The Druid with the sickle was of a higher status. At home the next day I was visited by this Druid who had a message for us.

FROM THE DRUID WITH THE GOLDEN SICKLE

'This is our land and we are its people. This land has never changed from being our land. We are always here in the ethereal realms. We are the guardians and protectors of the light. We would wish that you will open up this energy in the service of the planet and of the light, and we understand that this is what you wish to do also.

'There is much healing needed and there is a great deal of energy here for that healing. Here, there is peace, healing and light. You are under our guidance and every time you visit us, more guidance for your spiritual pathway is given to you. We have performed many spiritual and sacred ceremonies here on this land. We observed the Celtic calendar and fires were lit on our sacred festivals. We are pleased that you have begun to observe our sacred times of the year. These are the times when the energies for learning and access to our knowledge is greatest. We thank you for your gifts and for your reverence for our sacred place. All that is really necessary is to bring your special respect to our place and be open, for many blessings will come to you. Each time you come, the gap between the worlds narrows. It is only a thin veil. The ancient presence that presides over this land is an angelic being of light. You are in its service. Continue in this way. Go in peace. Tangnefedd *[peace].'*

The Rainbow Crown

One night, unable to sleep, tossing and turning and thinking about the lake, suddenly I was able to see it clearly. Around the island was a rainbow in the shape of a crown. How beautiful! I thought, and fell asleep. In the morning the realisation dawned that this lake and island together form a crown chakra of the land.

While painting the picture and using horizontal brush strokes, I found myself using short, vertical strokes around the island for some reason unknown to myself. However, it 'felt' right, but I did not know what it was. It later came to me that it looked like many pairs of wings, and that is what it is – the wings of the fairies who attracted those people of long ago. When people close their eyes at the lakeside, they can sometimes 'see' many pairs of wings over the water, the elementals of water and air. They had told me that I could paint them – and there they were. There was no conscious thought in my mind of painting them – they just happened.

The rainbow crown

The Chakras Revealed

After the vision of the crown at Llyn-y-Tarw, I knew I needed to get some help and feedback about sacred places. So it was that I was guided to make contact with a friend, Roma Harding, who later came with me to Bryher, in the Scilly Isles. When she was told about the crown chakra, she suggested that I should look for the other chakras, but I had no idea where or how to begin. After this, Roma bought a map of Wales, and began to plot a line. The line went from Llyn-y-Tarw to Strata Florida, a Cistercian abbey in west Wales, straight through to Carmarthen Bay. However, I was still feeling very unsure of my dowsing ability, especially as I had been the only one in a dowsing class who couldn't get the pendulum to work!

Some months went by without any attempt on my part to do anything, when one night I 'felt' that I should draw a line on the map and dowse for the centres. This was done the next morning. I moved the crystal down the line, asking, 'Show me where the third eye, throat, heart, solar plexus and sacral chakras are.' The pendulum swung at the third eye, a mountain called Bryncrugog. Next it swung at Blaenycwm in the Ystwyth Valley – the throat. The heart chakra was Strata Florida. The solar plexus was Tregaron Bog. The sacral was under the water in Carmarthen Bay, and I couldn't find the base chakra because the line just went out over the sea, missing Cornwall and Brittany. Roma said, 'I knew you could find them'; I wasn't so sure.

What followed was a voyage of exploration that is still ongoing, and synchronistically has led to more and more discoveries. At every chakra on the map there was archaeological evidence of the Bronze and Iron Ages: cairns, roundhouses, stone circles, standing stones and tumuli. Sometimes the place names gave a clue, e.g. Bryncrugog: a *crug* is Welsh for cairn and *bryn* means hill, Bryn Brân (hill of Brân), a Bronze Age hero. When we began to visit these sites and experience the energies, happenings, visions and information, it proved that we were on the right pathway.

One day a friend arrived, and I told her about the line. 'Where does it go to?' she asked.

'Just out over the sea.'

'Perhaps it goes to the Scilly Isles?'

And so it did, ending at the island of Bryher. On this island recently, archaeologists found a grave containing a sword and a mirror, the only known Iron Age example of both found in the same grave from north-western Europe. The 'Welsh Line', as we have come to refer to it, is much more than a chakra line. It is a Grail journey, leading us to synchronistically make contact with people and places that have begun to reveal ancient wisdom waiting to be activated. What follows is a record of the experiences and channelled information which arose from our visits to these chakras. I found myself researching the early Christian Church and the religious life and practice of the Druids and the priestesses of Brighid, after meeting some of these spiritual guardians and teachers at these sites. The Druids were the magi of the Britons. The term 'magnus' among the ancients did not signify a magician in the modern sense at all, but a superintendent of sacred and natural knowledge.

While working on this chakra system, I have used the analogy of a puzzle, slotting the pieces into place to see the whole picture. But a better analogy would be the weaving of a tapestry, following a clue which is a strand as tenuous and as delicate as a silken thread, and weaving it into a tapestry which is stretched across a framework made from time itself, into a fabric of unbelievable depth, richness, colour and light. Such has been the guidance from the realm of spirit.

This is the substance of our lives, and this is the substance of the Grail journey, of the inner and outer discoveries that we make. We are all blessed with this richness; we are all touched by this beauty of spirit, which is their gift to us at this time.

The Silver Voice of the Lake Communicates With Us

It was eleven months before we were able to visit the lake in the mountains again, and we had explored the throat, heart and solar plexus chakras in the meantime. We said prayers and scattered flowers and rose petals on the water. I emptied some water that was brought from the throat chakra of Blaenycwm into the lake.

Afterwards, as we sat quietly by the lake, its lapping seemed louder and more urgent. There seemed to be a pattern to the rhythmic sound. It seemed to be talking to us. The sound of its voice had the quality of silver: very calming, very gentle. Wishing that I could speak to it, I began to talk to it. The only thought-form that came through was, 'We are very happy.' The lapping became louder and louder and then gradually died away, and then continued quietly, as if to itself. Since our visit to the throat chakra, we were tuned in to the voice of water and had become more aware, but it wasn't until the next day that it was remembered that water from the throat chakra had been given to Llyn-y-Tarw. Intuitively, I knew that it was important to give the lake's water to the other chakras, but this was the first time I understood that it was important to exchange the energy in both directions.

This year (2001) was the first year in living memory that the black-headed gulls had not nested on the island. This is because the waves are gradually eroding the island and there was a visible hole in the middle and yet another willow had fallen into the lake. The two islands cannot last for much longer if nothing is done, and people visiting in the future will wonder where the islands have gone.

Taking a Photo of a Statue That Isn't There

In the summer of 2001, when we visited the lake and poured the mistletoe and Chalice Well water into it, the weather worsened and it became pretty dark for mid-afternoon. We continued to take photos although the camera was flashing 'TOO DARK'. When the photos were developed there appeared to be a statue where no statue existed!

What could it possibly be and what could it mean? There seemed to be a white shadowy figure near it and a faint white ball of light to the left of it. Thinking that it could be seen better if it were enlarged, this was done, but there was no statue on the enlargement. When looking through a magnifying glass (x10), different people saw different things, and it seemed to move and look directly at them. I saw a female head and shoulders made from creamy Cotswold stone, on the shoulder of which was a dove with wings outstretched about to take off. This dove was pure white and seemed to be made of marble. It looked very, very solid.

When I tried to connect with it in meditation, it was not willing to talk to me. I was told that it had revealed itself to me because I was a 'way-shower' and it thanked me for this. This would seem to relate to the chakra system that was later spoken of as 'the Pathway of the Beloved', but perhaps the time was not right, or I was not ready. I was told it was a guardian spirit of the land and it could take many forms, sometimes a white horse, sometimes a bull. I asked if there was a connection with Egypt, and was told, 'Of course it is to do with Egypt.'

It was not until we had begun to attune to the sacral chakra in Carmarthen Bay that the statue was willing to talk to me. This was because we had tuned into the rose and its link with the Madonna. We had understood its symbolism for the feminine energy, and the statue represented and embodied the feminine energy of the seven stars of the Pleiades. These stars are: Alcyone, Celaeno, Electra, Maia, Merope, Sterope and Taygeta. The statue was Pleiadean, hence the dove on its shoulder.

The lake, with statue in distance

The statue (pixilation restricting clarity)

Planetary movements during Taurus 2002 reached a climax in May, which must have had a direct relationship with this statue and Llyn-y-Tarw. First there was the alignment of the five planets, Jupiter, Saturn, Venus, Mercury and Mars. The new moon fell into the earthly sign of Taurus on a degree that carried the symbol of a white dove flying over troubled waters. Its meaning is that spiritual inspiration will overcome crisis. The dove is associated with the goddess of love and the ruler of Taurus is Venus. The dove is also associated with the coming of peace and the Holy Spirit.

From about 9.15 p.m. until 11.20 p.m. on 12 May 2002, Saturn, Mars and Venus clustered within the Hyades, the V-shaped stars forming the head of the Bull. On 14 May, the moon passed in front of these planets, making planetary eclipses in the third eye of the Bull.

On 14 May, the crescent moon appeared as an upturned crescent or bowl and was seen as if holding Venus, an image which can be seen on the flag of Islam. The white dove of the Pleiades flying over the Earth's troubled waters is the symbol of the angel of peace.

SOME ANSWERS ARE GIVEN IN MEDITATION

'Many, many moons ago, there was a community of monks and nuns who lived in this high place. At that time, it felt as if it were high above the world itself. Above the clouds, so to speak. These people set about their lives in a healing way. They practised healing and divination for the whole of the surrounding area. They were handmaidens and officiates of the Celtic goddess Brighid. They were quiet but joyous people.'

I found myself looking at the statue but I seemed to have gone a long way back in time, it is impossible to know how far. There were women (the sacred handmaidens) who were laying flowers on the grass in front of the statue, as we had done on the lake.

'It blesses all who do this. Honour it in your own way. It can take many forms. It has revealed itself to you to honour you as a way-shower. It is not angelic, it is a guardian.'

THE STATUE SPEAKS

Question: 'What is your connection to the stars? Are you connected to the Pleiades?'

'Yes, I am connected to the Pleiades and this is the reason that you can see a dove on my shoulder. This represents Britain and this sacred isle. Britain is sacred to the Pleiades and this line is laid down by the Pleiadeans in preparation for this time. Here is the place of the moon and the feminine energies. These energies have been isolated and now is the time to create their flow again. This is why you must mix the waters one with another, for the flow is feminine.

'The Pleiades represent feminine energy in this land. They are Daughters of the Moon. Have respect for the moon goddess, bring her into your thoughts and ceremonies. You will be guided. At this point in time you must give more thought to the feminine, silver, water, side of the balance equation. There is much work for you to do; you have made an excellent start. With love you may continue, blessed be.'

It was not until April 2002 that we were able to go to the spot where the statue had appeared. There were seven Canada geese on the water, guarding the site. Two of them kept an eye on us, occasionally honking, as if in disapproval. The Druids used birds and animals, their number and the direction they came from, in divination. In numerology seven means wisdom – a seeker after truth. The geese were coming from the west, which means a vision, dreams, a quest or journey with a spiritual renewal at its end. Geese are important in ancient mythology. They equate with the figure eight and the infinity symbol – a figure eight lying on its side. They are associated with stories and storytelling. Maybe they are helping with this story. Their incessant honking seemed to be calling us to follow them on a great spiritual quest, as they stirred the imagination while leading us towards new travels in different places in both the physical and spiritual realms.

Taurus the Bull and the Dove of the Pleiades

I began to walk over the area where I knew the statue had appeared but could not find it, so we decided to perform a ceremony for peace and healing. A blue glass bowl with a pattern of dolphins around it was placed on a square-shaped rock, cushioned by sphagnum moss that had tiny bright pink flowers. In the bowl, water from the lake was mixed with water from Ffonnyn Ddrain (Thorn Well) and Saint Anthony's holy well in Carmarthen. Special crystals were placed in the bowl. We stuck five roses into the moss for the five planets in the alignment.

Prayers were then said, some of them in Welsh. Then one of us 'saw' an elderly Druid with a circle of flowers in his hair, a white calf and a rider on a white horse going in the direction of the statue. We both 'saw' a dove that turned into an angel, the angel of peace. I saw this bird become so large that it spread its protective wings over the entire lake. When the ceremony had finished, the rock which formed our makeshift altar was giving off enough heat to warm our hands and ourselves, and the water in the bowl, which was then returned to the lake, was warm.

The geese had become quiet and I set off again to try and find the place where the statue used to be. This time I found it easily by dowsing. Some of the sacred water was poured onto the spot and the roses were left there. When standing on the spot I received a vision of the Egyptian goddess, Hathor. It was very quick and there was no time to have a good look, but she was standing in front of me and looking at me. I saw her horned headdress with the solar disc between the horns. In pictures and statues, goddesses who wore the horns of a cow usually embodied the lunar aspects. The bull is masculine but is sometimes depicted as lunar because its horns resemble a lunar crescent, giving it a link with the feminine. This had a connection with the crescent moon on 14 May 2002 when the moon was seen cradling the Planet Venus. This was a sign that the feminine energy of the universe was flooding into the Earth on a giant cosmic wave. It has re-energised the crown chakra at Llyn-y-Tarw and flowed through all the other chakras in this system. Ultimately it flowed into the crystalline grid and re-energised the entire planet with its feminine energy.

CONNECTIONS WITH THE BULL AND THE SEVEN SISTERS OF THE PLEIADES

There are many people who are now aware that the pyramids at Giza are connected to the constellation Orion, but how many know that all sacred sites have a star connection? After finding the bull's head on the standing stone, and realising that the lake is named after a bull, it was understood that this sacred place came under the star sign of Taurus. What was puzzling about this is that Taurus is associated with the throat chakra, but this site was a crown chakra.

So what was the connection? The answer lay in the Greek myth of Europa and the Bull. This story has been handed down through Greek legends but is much older in origin. Europa was the beautiful daughter of Phoenix, the king of Phoenicia and Atlantis, with whom Zeus fell in love. In order to get close to her, he took the form of a shining white bull and mingled with the herds of Phoenix. While she was gathering flowers one day, Europa saw this beautiful, gentle animal. She placed flowers around his neck and horns, and when he knelt down she climbed onto his back. He then spread his wings and flew with her across the heavens carrying her to a secret place on Earth where they made love. When Europa gave birth, it was to Mercury, the golden child, bringing in a golden age of wisdom and peace, the Age of Aquarius.[1]

However, there is another version of this story without a happy ending. In this version, the bull has no wings and has to swim across the cosmos with Europa. She is unwilling to go with him and so he kidnaps her and rapes her. The result is not a golden age but a hurt and barren land. These two alternative versions are about what might be. The bull is Europe and Europa is the dove on the bull's back. In the ancient star maps there is a dove sitting on the neck of the bull. This dove is composed of the Seven Sisters, or doves. They were the daughters of King Phoenix and Pleione. They are the seven principal stars of the Pleiades. This sacred site is dedicated to Taurus and the Pleiades. The astrological sign of Taurus and the Pleiades is associated with the establishment on Earth of the Age of Aquarius.

THE DOVE LINKS WITH THE PLEIADES AND WITH THE GODDESS

The key messages of the dove are the feminine energies of maternity, prophecy and peace. This bird symbolises traditional motherhood and the feminine. The symbol of Europa represented by the bull and the Pleiades star system is the symbol of the dove resting on the bull's neck. Aphrodite, the goddess of love, was born from an egg brooded by a dove. The bird has been associated with female sexuality through goddesses like Hathor and Isis. It is because of this association with many goddesses that it is considered to be the embodiment of maternal instinct. Its song was considered to be an invocation to water, showing where the pools or springs could be found, because the dove would come back to drink at them at dusk. The dove is a ground-feeder, which shows the importance of contact with Mother Earth. Its voice is said to be the rain song, reminding us that new waters and new life are always possible because the Earth is a female planet;

---

[1] Peter Dawkins, 'Europa and the Bull', *Grail Kingdom of Europe*

the possibilities of creation and new birth are always there.[2]

The dove is a bird of prophecy. It awakens the promise of the future so that we can see how to create a new world, and unfold our own wings of spirit and magic. It tells us that we can all fly. It is not surprising, then, that the visionary dove was seen flying over the lake of Llyn-y-Tarw at the time of the planetary alignment in May 2002. Or that the strange statue, seen in the photo at the side of this lake, seemed to have a white dove on its shoulder about to take flight, or that we have two collared doves in our garden!

THE GODDESS AWAKENS

'The alignment is the beginning of the changes in the heavens which will manifest here on Earth, like a birth into another house of light. There will be many changes, some of them small and unnoticed, some of them of astrological significance but all are shifting, moving and changing this planet as you know it. All of this is heavenly in impetus and design. People will know this. They will see the connection between Heaven and Earth for themselves. Even those who have never believed will believe. All of this is to come very soon. It is starting already. It is here! The goddess has now awakened and this is for the greatest good. There are energies snaking through the Earth's crust and none are more powerful or more important than Llyn-y-Tarw. Awakening these energies must be done now as the planetary alignment focuses and distributes the heavenly energies – so must the Earth be ready to accept and channel them. It is the energy of humans who must do this. It will bring much joy and re-alignment to this planet. This is walking the pathway of the Pleiadeans who have laid out this path that you are walking now. Enjoy your Earth-walk. All is well.'

My spiritual teachers have spoken to me about this Earth-walk before, and their invitation to enjoy it applies to everyone on this planet at this moment. If you were on the moon it would be a moon-walk; when you are here you are on an Earth-walk.

CONNECTIONS

The connections came, slowly at first, then they began to tumble over themselves in their hurry to be recognised.

---

[2] Ted Andrews, *Animal-Speak*

Is there a connection with Egypt? 'Of course it is to do with Egypt.'

Finding the Link with Egypt

On my first encounter with Merlin, I somehow felt a connection with Egypt. How could this be? On top of this wild mountain in the middle of Wales – was I dreaming? Were the Druids Egyptian priests? When I asked, I was told, 'Of course it is to do with Egypt', and again at Strata Florida, 'We do wish to tell you about Egypt because this is where it all begins. Egypt is the centre of the teaching which is being discussed at this time. Of all the places in the British Isles, we would say that Strata Florida was most influenced by the mystery schools of Egypt.'

This was pointing to the historical link being in ancient Egypt, which might be too far back in time to be found. This was not the only connection to be traced. There was the link with the zodiac constellation of Taurus, and the dove on the bull's neck – the stars of the Pleiades. The task seemed impossible, until I was lent a book written by Emil Bock, a contemporary of Rudolf Steiner, who wrote *Genesis, Creation and the Patriarchs*. One of the chapters concerns Joseph (of the coat of many colours) and his Egyptian destiny.

Jacob had twelve sons and one daughter. Joseph was the youngest child to be born in Babylon. He was the first-born son of Rachel, Jacob's favourite wife. He was different from the others; he was a seer and a clairvoyant. He dreamed of the twelve constellations of the zodiac, one for each of the brothers, who founded the twelve tribes of Israel. Joseph's constellation was Taurus, the bull.

Because they were jealous of him, his brothers decided to throw him into a small cave which resembled a grave, and they left him there for three days and nights. In this way, and without intending to, they put him through a period of initiation similar to that of the sun-priests and the Druids. They then decided to release him and sold him as a slave to Ishmaelite merchants who were on their way to Egypt. From 2907–747 BC, Taurus was in the position of the vernal equinox, and the Egyptians' lives were dominated by the cult of the holy Apis Bull. Since his zodiac sign was Taurus, he had a star relationship with their temple world. The title of the high priest signified 'priest of the holy bull' – Potiphar. As Taurus rules the throat and communication, it is no surprise to find that Joseph 'mastered all languages'.[3]

When he was thirty years old, he married Asenath, the daughter of Potiphera. By giving his daughter to Joseph, the sun-priest of the sun-city acknowledged him as the rightful co-guardian of the secrets entrusted to himself. He was initiated into the Egyptian mysteries.

Joseph used his gift of clairvoyance with understanding and intelligence. It was through Joseph that the Hebrew nation, who still partly remain on the path of the moon, were gently led even closer to the sun, and the great sun-archangel, Michael.

Heliopolis, the city of the sun, was to the north of Memphis, and retained the mysteries of ancient Egypt in a pure form into the late ages. Plato himself was a disciple of the priests of this city for thirteen years.

This is going back to the beginning of time, to the blessing of Moses – 'His glory is like the first-born of a bull' (Deuteronomy 33:17) – and to the blessing of Jacob – 'Joseph is a fruitful bull' (Genesis 49:22). I believe that the connection with Llyn-y-Tarw and the chakra line goes back this far.

Llyn-Y-Tarw is a Very Different Place Now From the Early Bronze Age

There are three lakes on a raised plateau that forms part of the Cambrian Mountains on the north edge of the Upper Severn Valley, four kilometres to the west towards Carno. The pass of Bwlch-y-Carreg (Stony Pass) runs north–south, dividing the plateau into two areas, with the rocky side to the west and the more gentle slopes to the east. In the centre lie three lakes, sister lakes representing the sacred three of Celtic mythology, linking with the goddess Brighid and her two sisters also named Brighid. They are Llyn Ddu (Black Lake), Llyn Mawr (Big Lake) and

---

[3] Emil Bock, *Genesis, Creation and the Patriarchs*, p.168

Llyn-y-Tarw (the Lake of the Bull). All of the three lakes are of seemingly post-glacial origin and have been used as water supplies in more recent times. Both Llyn Ddu and Llyn-y-Tarw have been dammed for this purpose. The damming of Llyn-y-Tarw has caused the water to rise and huge waves driven by the winter winds have almost washed away the two islands since we first saw them in 2000.

In prehistoric and historic times the lakes would have been an attractive source of food, providing fish and waterfowl. Way back in the Bronze Age there would have been bears, wolves, wild boar and beaver in the area. The village was there before the climate change that flooded the hollow in which it was built.

There are areas of coarse grass with heather and bilberry, and bracken grows on the better-drained slopes on the east side, with sphagnum moss and cotton grass on the boggy areas. In previous times, there were trees around the lake; their remains can still be found.

Ownership of the land is divided between several farmers, and the land to the east is owned by the Crown. Evidence of ancient people is all around: there are two standing stones, two ring cairns, a curb cairn, five other cairns, two stone circles, three hut circles and two medieval or post-medieval hut foundations. Much of this evidence has been broken up by the farmers' land improvement. The area is scattered with cairns (barrows), where the people buried their dead. The history of this sacred place goes back to the time of the ancients.

LIFE IN THE VILLAGE

The early Bronze Age was a time of the greatest agricultural use of upland sites, the people living in villages of roundhouses. They are known today as the beaker people, so named after their beautifully decorated pottery that accompanied cremations. This pottery has been dated to 2500–1600 BC. These people worshipped the goddess Brighid, and her priestesses led them on her sacred days. They were consulted about anything and everything, from the right time to plant crops, to personal problems. People came from all over the area for their services. They were oracles: by scrying in a mirror, a pool or a bowl of water, they were able to receive an image of themselves, which was like looking inside themselves in a spiritual way, seeing the aura and reflections of their spirit.

The high priestess was responsible for the ceremonies that were performed around the Egyptian statue which had many sacred days in its honour (this is the statue in the photo which isn't there in reality). The people observed the sacred days with singing and dancing. There were fire festivals and mead was drunk at their feasts. The land was sacred and so was the water. They had a close relationship with the Earth as if it were their mother, close and loving, respecting its power over their lives and treating all living things as their brothers and sisters.

Avebury Temple was the largest in Western Europe at the time and the high priestesses of Llyn-y-Tarw travelled there many times in their lifetimes, as others would have done from the rest of the country, bringing back with them a sense of a far larger community nationwide. As they journeyed in this way, they created spirit-paths that are still present on the etheric patterning of the planet. There were regular trackways serving the Severn Valley along the Kerry and Clee ridgeways that would not only have served the local community but would also have linked with the long-distance routes. These trackways led the people along energy lines which helped the traveller to walk further than they would otherwise have been able to do, using the Earth energies. Opposite the gate to Llyn-y-Tarw, on the left, is another gate that leads along an ancient trackway used by them to reach the highest visible point. Walking along this ancient roadway after hurting my back, I could feel the energy helping me. I was able to walk much further than normal and had to restrain myself in case I couldn't get back. This energy can be dowsed and enabled the people to drive their chariots faster and further. Once the road is paved, this doesn't work, and, of course, the Romans paved the roads.

The drovers' roads followed these ancient tracks and this is where to look for them in the present. These trackways would have skirted around bogs, heavily wooded areas and rocky crags, always finding the easy path. Travellers along them would have needed to journey from one well or rivers to other sources of water to fill their containers and allow the animals to drink. These wayside wells would have been dedicated to the goddess Brighid. In Wales these roads would have carried people over the mountain passes. The highest pass in Wales is Bwlch-y-Groes (the Pass of the Cross) from Mallwyd to Bala – a drover's route.

This trade brought beads of Whitby jet and Baltic amber to Mid Wales, as well as changes in the fashion of clothes. At the beginning of this period buttons were used on leather garments, but around 2000 BC leather gave way to woven garments which were fastened with pins. Mid Wales's resources of gold, lead and copper made it an important region for trade, and must have made it a wealthy area in which to live. The area's prosperity was represented by the bull, both as a symbol and as an animal. The bull was very important to the people living there because it was necessary for the continuing of their herds. They understood the importance of fertility. This was why they worshipped the goddess Brighid and served her as a mother and fertility goddess. They lived a peaceful life in the hills and they were blessed in their work and celebrations, of which there were many. They lived sacred lives, being conscious of every being, from each blade of grass to each other – everything was honoured. From time to time when they had a problem, they dealt with it by appealing to the Earth Mother and all was well.

When they buried their dead they preferred cemetery mounds where no single person was given priority of place, regardless of wealth. This suggests that family membership remained the basis of local tribal power. The people lived in peaceful farming communities, which is why very few weapons were found in their graves. The dagger, distinct from a small personal knife, is a rare find. The warrior does not seem to have been the admired ideal and it is fitting that the most spectacular symbol of power in Wales at this time was the gold cape from Mold that belonged to a priestess (not a warrior), who lived 4,000 years ago. The cape is a work of extraordinary skill and beauty, and is one of the top ten treasures of Britain.

It is fashioned from 28-carat gold and illustrates technical and stylistic innovations that sprang up in Britain, dispelling the once-held idea that all key developments from prehistory came from continental Europe. It clearly shows that north-east Wales played an active and vital role in the substantial economic and social changes which marked the beginning of the metal age in Europe. Analysis shows it to be typical of the period 1950–1550 BC.

The gold cape of Mold

The cape was found in 1833 in a stone-lined grave under a substantial cairn of stones and earth which was known as Bryn yr Ellyllon (Hill of the Goblins). The local folklore tells that some time before the cape was found, a woman had seen a spectre in the form of a large man cloaked in gold, at the 'witching hour'. The figure passed in front of her and disappeared into the mound! This means that the mound must have been a *sidi* (*sidhe* or *sidh* in the Irish tradition). These cairns were believed to be the homes of the fairies, or Tylwyth Teg (the beautiful family) in Wales. In Ireland, it was said that the children of the goddess Danu were given the underground half of the realm and an earthen barrow for each to live in. They became leprechauns, which shows a link between these two nations' myths.

The cape could not have belonged to a single person but would have been owned by the whole tribe and handed on through the generations. Its value would not have been in wealth but in its purity as a metal, which was believed to come from the sun and held the sun's energy, just as silver was understood to hold the moon's energy within it. All of this was reborn in the fire of the furnace under the skill and direction of the alchemist who could perform the magic of recovering this energy from the Earth. This is why metal workers were so revered, and why one of the three sisters of the triple goddess Brighid was a smith.

A MESSAGE FROM A PRIESTESS WHO WORE THE GOLD CAPE

'You will find everything that you are looking for as you follow your guidance in visiting the sacred places as they are revealed to you in sequence. The gold cape of Mold is the key to the higher vibration that will bring this through. You have understood correctly that the incorruptible property of gold (meaning that it is pure and remains pure) was the reason for us valuing it so much. So much time and care was taken in finding, smelting, creating and using this precious metal. Love your gold. Treat it as you would a precious crystal; it has its own properties which will infill and inspire you. Work with it in this way and you will find it easier to embody the higher energies that you aspire to.

'The golden energy links with Sirius, whereas silver links with the Pleiades. Wear both for balance. Remember that the sun energy is held in the gold – this is its strength – this is its beauty – this is its value. I am happy that you have made these connections since you went through the gateway on Anglesey. I, too, went through this gateway; we all did. Blessings.'

The invisibility of earlier Bronze Age settlements indicates that farms or hamlets were undefended. It is only at the end of the period, possibly after an increase in the population, together with a deteriorating climate, that protective walls and fortifications became necessary. At about 1000–500 BC the climate changed and severe weather became the norm. The higher rainfall and lower summer temperatures damaged the economy of the area and caused the abandonment of much of the uplands and coastal regions.[4] This must have been the time when the water rushed in and the village was drowned under the lake of Llyn-y-Tarw. The people were forced to take refuge on the lower slopes, and they were never able to return. In Wales, the evidence for climate change comes from the peat bogs that show a rapid peat growth

---

[4] Lynch, Francis, Stephen Alderhouse Green, and Jeffrey L Davies, *Prehistoric Wales*, Stroud, Sutton Publishing, 2000

caused by higher rainfall as early as 1250 BC, which includes Tregaron Bog in the middle Bronze Age. In some areas of the British Isles, blanket bog began to form over abandoned field systems that led to a loss of soil fertility, and tree cover failed to regenerate, leading to the extension of moorlands that characterises so much of the Welsh uplands today. Late Bronze Age clearance or loss of woodland through changed environmental conditions probably corresponds to a time when there was an acute shortage of land for cultivation or grazing. This was a time when the environs of Tregaron Bog were cleared c. 400 BC, and there was extensive burning of the sissile oak and alder woodland on the lower slopes of the Ystwyth Valley and the Ystwyth Forest plateau in the third and second centuries BC.

My intuition tells me that most of the myths, legends and fairy tales of Wales, including those in *The Mabinogion*, began life in the Bronze Age, and were added to later. Their leaders must have been very colourful characters who led extraordinary lives. Some of these myths have been found to be based on fact, and new information is literally being unearthed today, like the story of the flooding of Cantre'r Gwaelod, the Lowland Hundred. This is a land which was said to be beneath the sea in Cardigan Bay. The story goes that there was a gatekeeper whose job it was to close the floodgates and keep the sea out. However, there was a big celebration at the king's court and everyone got drunk, including the gatekeeper. He forgot to close the gates and the sea flooded in and everyone in the kingdom was drowned, except one man, who rode away to spread the news of the disaster to the area. This man was the poet Taliesin.

Cantref is Welsh for hundred. Each kingdom was divided into *cant* or hundreds, which in turn were divided into *cymwds* or *commotes* (a province or region). The only remaining link with these ancient divisions are the Hundred House inns, of which there are two in Mid Wales. The princes or kings who ruled Wales were peripatetic, travelling around on a royal circuit, and within each commote they would have had a royal hall or *llys*, where they stayed when in residence in the hundred. A place name, Henllys, means ancient court, and would have been a home of a Welsh prince or king.

For the last twenty years archaeologists and dendrochronologists (who study and date ancient trees) have been examining the remains of an ancient forest which can be seen at low tide on the beach at Borth. They believe that this flooded forest was growing five thousand years ago, in the Stone Age. This indicates that our tribal memory goes back much further than we ever imagined, and lends weight to the stories of sunken lands around Britain's coasts and the sunken church bells of Cantre'r Gwaelod and Aberdovey ringing in wild weather.

A MESSAGE FOR OUR WORLD FROM THE BRONZE AGE

They worshipped the energy of life itself in the solar father and the lunar mother. This was their way. They understood the connections that we do not understand today. They knew all was connected in the ether and there were no divisions. They understood this, and it is my ability to see connections, which is a gift brought forward from that time. The more we immerse ourselves in the sea of connectedness the more we can do and the more we can see.

'Vibrations are connected, all is energy and all flows. There are no divisions in the spirit world and there are no divisions in this world either. The future lies in the dissolving of these perceived divisions which exist only in the mind of man… (therefore they exist in reality, but they are man-made). Dissolve the divisions. Ask that they be dissolved. Be they walls or barriers composed of differences of race, religions, schisms, ideas, different scientific disciplines, etc., they are barriers! Humanity is banging its head against these barriers. Ask that they be dissolved, keep asking and it will be done.'

The beautiful artwork of the people of the early Bronze Age flowed from one thing to another, and this is how they perceived their universe. Their message to us is that we must learn to do the same. It is how we must see our universe, our relationships, our lives, our Heaven and our Earth. We must concentrate on what unites us and not what divides us. All energies flow, one to another. There are no divisions.

THIS IS THEIR CONCEPT OF THE TREE OF LIFE

'The tree of life is an ancient pre-Celtic concept which goes back to the beginning of time and cannot be homed in on because it is a concept which

has been lost in time. However there were many ancient peoples who accepted this idea and took it into their awareness and into their national psyche. They brought forward the idea of a world tree from which everything grew. Its roots were deep in the cosmic "Earth" and its branches were across the cosmic "sky". These ancient people were aware of the cosmos and the creator of the universe. Their way of describing their cosmic world was that of a great tree, shaken by storms, bending before the winds of change, but always surviving, sometimes damaged but always repairing itself, always growing, always producing fruit – forever.

'Their God was like this tree, He or She was this tree. This was how they understood their lives. Living in the shelter of their God who provided for them everything they needed. They had faith in the abundance and divine order of things, and their lives were divinely ordered.

'If modern mankind could only get back to this kind of living they would find themselves under far less stress and they would live kinder, healthier lives.'

Bronze Age Déja Vu

At the crown chakra at Llyn-y-Tarw, in meditation, I found myself in the Bronze or possibly Iron Age village, and was taken inside the house of the chief. I had never had the opportunity to visit a Celtic roundhouse and was very interested to check on the validity of this experience. In May 2002 we were able to go to Castell Henllys, an Iron Age village which has been reconstructed just south of the town of Cardigan, and featured on TV in the programme, *Surviving the Iron Age*. This village has been rebuilt on the original foundations, leaving the energy of the place intact. It has some Iron Age-type sheep that can jump seven feet over fences and can reach a top speed of thirty miles per hour. They do not need shearing; the wool is simply pulled off. They were kept for wool and for milk. The villagers had a garden where they grew vegetables and herbs.

Going into the house was exactly as I remembered! It was too dark to see much. The only light came from the open door and the central fire. There was a kerb around this fire and around this were seats on which I remembered sitting. They seemed to be made of huge logs and had some kind of fabric on them, possibly sheepskin. The place of honour was the seat in front of the fire. It was very smoky. The smoke hung in the air and prompted the thought that the people living here must have smelt of smoke all of the time. There was no hole in the roof because the draw from the fire would have burnt the thatch. The smoke produced a kind of tar that helped to waterproof the roof, and it fumigated it so that the house was kept insect-free.

The only difference was that the walls were made of mud and wattle, whereas the walls of the other Welsh house in my meditation were made of stone. Stone would have been stronger and more able to take the weight of the roof timbers. A staggering amount of wood and rushes would have been needed for the roof, the building of which would have taken a lot of skill and organisation. Once built it could be in use for 200 to 300 years, with a little repair occasionally. The roof was pitched at 45 degrees to allow the rainwater to run off and was completely waterproof. I experienced some physical discomfort on being there. It felt as if my aura had wobbled off centre and I experienced a nauseous feeling in the pit of my stomach. This made me feel certain that this was a former life experience. The meditation was a flashback to a former life.

The village at Llyn-y-Tarw has been there before the lake, on the site now occupied by the lake. The weather was warmer then and there were once trees growing there. This has been proved because some of their remains have been pulled out of the boggy ground. I have a photo of one of them; it looks like a dragon. The people would have needed this wood for houses and fuel. There would have been plenty of rushes; there still are. The stones from some of their walls have been made into present-day sheep shelters.

First Visit to the Third Eye

Our First Visit

This is the chakra that was visited last of all, when the system was completed after a visit to the base chakra at Bryher on the Scilly Isles. It was from here that the whole chakra line could be seen and understanding would, hopefully, be apparent. It is the link with the cosmos and the intuitive energies. It is from here that it should be possible to get an eagle's eye view of the landscape, and on an energetic level, the Pathway of the Beloved may be better understood.

In order to find it, guidance was asked for before we set off. Climbing the mountain is a single-tracked tarmacked road with a very steep gradient, and, at first, finding Bryn Crugog seemed an impossible task. There was a great deal of mountain and it was difficult to know where to go without a visible marker of some kind. The lane kept climbing, as we went higher and higher and we really did not know where it was. 'We need to ask someone,' we said, if there was anyone to ask. Turning a corner we met a Land Rover leading a flock of shorn sheep, followed by a white van. So we asked the driver of the Land Rover if he could tell us where Bryn Crugog was. 'We own it,' he said, pointing further up the lane to the left, so we asked him if we could visit it. 'Well, there is a bull on it right now.' The driver of the white van got out to speak to us. We told him that we would like to photograph the views and asked when the bull would be taken off. 'Not until September,' he said. He told us that he would take our phone number and let us know when the time was right. He began to talk about the effects of the weather at this altitude. He said that he had stood on Bryn Crugog when the mountains were under snow, and he could look around for miles and see the fascinating sight of the snow line, where the valleys were clear and the mountains were covered. There were times in the winter when the wind was so strong that he could not get his vehicle door open.

Although this was a setback it seemed entirely appropriate that there was a bull in residence, both here and at Llyn-y-Tarw. It was a reminder, if one was necessary, that this system is under the constellation of Taurus. There is a wonderful sense of continuity in that bulls have been on this land for thousands of years, which gives a tingle down the spine. It is a living link with the ancients and their belief in the power of this land and the power of the bull. Since the cattle are put out to pasture in late spring and brought in again in late autumn, the best time to visit would seem to be in Taurus. But this is the high country and here, the weather has to be respected also. Feeling a little daunted at having left it too late for this year, we followed the lane, climbing further still. A beautiful spring was now running by the side of the road, and the views were breathtaking from every side.

At last we reached the top where the mountain flattened out for a long stretch and the lane straightened out and ran across the top into the distance. The view was superb. An eagle's eye view for miles and miles and miles! It was exactly what could have been expected for the third eye chakra. For the first time, looking towards the north-east, the rocky outline of Mynydd Clogau, which shelters Llyn-y-Tarw, could be seen. When we held up our hands with the palms turned toward this mountain, a tingle or heat could be felt as the crown chakra gave out its energy.

The Arrans from Bryn Crugog
(Photo by April Henderson)

It was here that prayers were said and thanks were given for the guidance that had been received. Water from all of the places of the system was added to the little stream at the side of the road, taking this energy through the land and adding its own energy to it. A deep respect comes, literally, with the territory. A respect for the ancient spirit guardians, for the present-day animal guardians, for the weather and the elements of wind and water – all of this is a re-acquaintance with the 'Old Earth'.

As the planet changes its vibration, we humans can get out of step and find ourselves caught out. The water from the springs, wells, streams and rivers comes from deep within the Earth's body and carries this attunement to the surface where we can access it. When you are visiting these places, ask for a blessing on both them and yourselves, and having asked permission, take a little of the water with you when you go. Put some of it on your own chakras for balancing.

The mountain of Bryn Crugog is more accessible than Llyn-y-Tarw, and is slightly higher by thirteen feet. It has a good road with passing places, and there are several directions to take when you are there. One of them will lead across the next valley to Llyn-y-Tarw.

A forest in this area has been cut down recently; it was used for the Welsh section of the Round Britain car rally. This forest had been planted on a section of the mountain called Gors Goch (red bog). This is a connection with Tregaron Bog and the solar plexus chakra, which was once known as the 'red bog of Caron'. The outlet from the lake at the crown chakra forms a tiny waterfall before disappearing into a small bog. Both the rivers Wye and Severn, which rise not far away from here, are born from a bog, perhaps bringing with them a reassessment of the life-giving energies of our ancient bogs and strengthening the call for their conservation.

When guidance is asked to find a place, it is also equally important to ask what time is the right one to visit. The tapestry from which this story is woven has many delicate threads and colours, the weaving of which takes time. Each person reading this story will have their own unique understanding, their own timing, and each one will have their own unique experience as they visit the sites – and so the woven tapestry will be a little different for us all. This is the message of the third eye chakra: you are weaving your own beautiful fabric as you go on your pilgrimage. Please remember that pilgrimages are not always meant to be easy. Sometimes a degree of difficulty is a part of the whole.

As it was said at the beginning of this story, a sacred site is an inter-dimensional gateway to other worlds. It is also a place where former lives can be accessed and healing and attunement to the Earth's vibration can be given. All of this has happened to people who have been on this pilgrimage, and will continue to happen to others. Sometimes, a flashback to a former life can be something that you need to take into account as a part of your own healing process. Sometimes, simply going to the chakra site can bring about a healing change. This is all part of the ongoing methods of healing the planet and ourselves.

A pathway is often used in the ancient Hebrew mysticism known as the Qabala. The paths depicted in the Qabalistic Tree of Life are symbolic pathways to various levels of the mind, the spirit and the cosmos. They link the *sephiroth* (different levels of the mind) with the energies available to us at these levels. They can be used for inter-dimensional travel, healing and invocation and manifestation of specific energies in your life.

The water from the rest of the chakras was given to Llyn-y-Tarw on Midsummer day 2002. It was important to do this at this time, because this was the moment for the release of the feminine energy. It was the time of the full moon, when she was giving her soft and gentle light to Planet Earth and the people of Earth were concentrating on the rising of the sun. Throughout this adventure we have been guided by the stars and the planets, as we all are, and it was time to remember and honour this guidance. On our way back we were startled by a curlew, with its wonderful call, so evocative of high and wild places. As we went through the village of Aberhafesp a flock of white doves flew over us. We counted eight of them, the number of infinity and the dove.

Throughout this journey of the pathway more and more birds entered our lives, bringing their special magic with them. They are symbols of the initiation of air; they reflect a period of opening to higher knowledge and wisdom, a time of opening fully to divine ideas and guidance, to develop and manifest a higher wisdom and sensitivity. Birds have been used as symbols and signs by people from all of the ages and nations of this Earth. This is why they have been given their place in this story, and if you allow them to come into your awareness as you walk your pathway, they will guide you also.

The important element in this story has been water: water that has been responsive to the efforts that have been made to communicate with it. It is known that it has elemental beings within it, and now it is known that it can respond to us. It has a voice and is capable of talking to us when we are willing and able to listen. It is a liquid tape recorder that can receive, store and transmit vibrations. This is how homeopathy works. Its constant communication with the cosmos makes it act as the Earth's sensory organ, conveying this information to all living organisms on the planet. This, then, is our precious element of water.

Throat Chakra at Blaenycwm

The Throat Chakra at Blaenycwm

This is a very narrow valley with only room for a road and the stream. It is exceptionally straight; valleys usually wind and twist with the stream. Where it opens out enough for there to be fields, there is a tiny village. This village is called 'Blaenycwm' on the map, but the sign in the village says 'Cwmystwyth'.

The valley represents the throat, which opens out at the site of the chakra. There is a bridge where three streams meet, and the whole is surrounded by high mountains. The streams under the bridge are very beautiful. The river is the Afon Ystwyth ('*afon*' is Welsh for river). It flows on to Aberystwyth (which means 'mouth of the Ystwyth'). This mountain throat brings energy and nourishment to this part of Wales in the form of the river leading into the harbour in Cardigan Bay.

Could it be that all river valleys are the throats of the landscape? When we talk about the song of the river, are we perhaps recognising that the valley has a voice? If this is so, then should not this voice come from a throat?

> I give you the waters of the Earth, with the right to listen to the whisper of the stream as it rises in the hills, to the chatter of the river as it gathers and widens, and the shout of the cataract as it splashes through the rocks.
>
> Arthur Mee, *New Children's Encyclopaedia*

THE MOUNTAIN STREAM

> '*Can you feel the joy of the stream, the power of it?*
> *Can you hear it singing its song as it splashes and flows along its*
> *bed?*
> *Its power is such that nothing can withstand it.*
> *Its power is to heal and cleanse.*
> *To "go with the flow" is like the stream.*
> *Nothing can withstand the power of the flow as it gathers*
> *momentum.*

> *There is healing in giving yourself up to the flow, for it means*
> *that you have put yourself in the hands of the cosmic spirit –*
> *for the flow is love.'*

When the river ends in the sea, we call it a mouth!

It is the water that creates the valley that carves and forms the landscape. Water has the tremendous power to shape and to change it. Water also has a voice – a sound. This voice has a healing effect on us. It brings calm and is often used in meditation, either as a gurgling stream or rhythmic ocean waves. Celtic rivers were feminine. Water represents the feminine principle, creating and bringing life to the Earth. The water is the voice of the land.

The Ystwyth Valley

Following the Ystwyth to the top of this valley, the road traverses a plateau by the side of Afon Elan until it comes to Pont ar Elan ('pont' or 'bont' means bridge), where the river flows into Craig Goch Reservoir. This area is rich in ancient history.

The road then passes Maengwynweddw (white widow stone), a white quartz boulder from the Bronze Age, and a little further on there is a standing stone called Maen Serth (stone on the steep slope).

Between these two stones there used to be two cairns, where a Bronze Age hammer from the Preseli Mountains was found.

Near Pont ar Elan there used to be a Celtic monastic community, and one of the ancient trackways of Wales crosses the Elan and continues across the mountain in the direction of Strata Florida.

As the road descends into Llansantffraed Cwmdeuddwr, it passes an area of land once held sacred to the goddess Brighid, and her feast of Imbolc was held there every February. This was on the site of the present church that means 'the church of Saint Bride in the valley of the two waters' in Welsh.

(Left) The River Ystwyth
(Photo by April Henderson)

It was in this valley that some beautiful gold Celtic jewellery was found, which is now in the British Museum. In December 2003 a piece of Bronze Age gold was found at the lead mine in the valley and was declared to be a treasure trove. It was a golden disc that would have fitted into the palm of a hand. It was believed to have been a decoration for a bridle.

SPIRIT OF PLACE, GENIUS LOCI

One day I stopped at this chakra to try to find out whether any harm had been done by an invasion of a fairly large group of people. I saw a lady dressed in white, exactly as I was later to see the goddess Brighid dressed at the crown chakra. She had long, very dark hair. She was standing, holding her arms above her head with her hands uplifted so that her whole body formed the shape of the letter 'Y'. I explained that I had come to see if any repairs were needed to the energies and she replied, 'All is well, but thank you for your concern.' I asked this question to the ether, 'Who is she?'

'She is the spirit of place,' was the reply. This was the only time on the line that I have been privileged to meet the genius loci.

A Message Received at the Throat Chakra

A friend who has joined us on this pathway received this beautiful message while visiting the throat chakra in the Ystwyth Valley. This was after we had made the connection with the base chakra and were on a pilgrimage to link up all of the chakras.

'It is with great love and gratitude that I welcome you today, a welcome that extends to all people who walk the ancient pathways, and who are awakening to the old energies. These energies that have been here since time immemorial – forgotten, hidden. Now is the time to awaken the old energies, to allow them to course and flow through the land, to enrich this land, to bring it back to the way it was before. We do not turn back the clock, we release the flow that has always been here waiting for this time. Its time is now. You can feel it beneath your feet when you touch the rocks, and you can hear its gentle sound in the water, as everything awakens once more. This awakening will re-energise the land. The free-flowing of these energies will enable everyone to connect with them. They will feel it within themselves and these energies will change and flow like the river before you today, flowing as rivers have always flowed, something long forgotten but now remembered. You have come here on the fifth stage of your journey. A journey on which both ends form a circle, and only when the connections are made will the realisation be found. Go in peace upon your pathway knowing that your feelings and intuitions have brought you to this place and will carry you forwards, flowing like the river, always flowing forwards in the direction you were meant to be. Allow yourselves to be, my children, and allow yourselves to flow and awaken every centre within your being.'[1]

THIS MESSAGE WAS TO THE RIVER

'I have brought these children who are intrinsically a part of you, as they are a part of the energies, so that we can all flow together now and forever.

'We are all this, we are all one.'

The Song of the River

The river is flowing, flowing and growing.
The river is flowing down to the sea.

---

[1] By kind permission of Dee

Mother Earth, come carry me, a child I will always be,
Mother Earth, come carry me down to the sea.

You are the land. The land is you.

Merlin

'Be Still', by Ginny Edwards

Be still and know that you are God, and from that infinite space
let trickle the whisperings of the ancient sages.
Let the wisdom of the heart dictate across the winds of time, as
oceans move in undulating form so does form ever change.
The soul sits and looks upon the face of ancient knowledge, as it
slowly rises, to also take form through the stillness and power
of the heart.
First one, then two, then four, and eight, until thousands feel the
beauteousness of creating the new Earth.
Oh mortal being, dost thou not know how truly beautiful and
wondrous you are?
The rainbow colours weave their patterns in glorious harmony to
the music of the spheres.
Awaken, beloveds, to the drumbeat. The time is now. Listen, and
listen carefully, as your cells awaken to the cosmic dance
which is unfolding before you.
Be in your joy and in that moment of listening know that you are
one with all, and all is one with you. Namaste.[2]

To Mankind

The water of the Earth is the life-blood of the Earth.
It is your life-blood too,
For you are its children.
You are privileged,
O, children of the Earth.
Honour her,

---

[2] By kind permission of Ginny Edwards

> *Love her,*
> *Guard her waters,*
> *Share them with all living things*
> *For you are its caretakers*
> *And the Earth is in your hands.*

A Prayer for the Waters of the Earth

Divine cosmic spirit, we ask that the yellow ray of wisdom will surround and penetrate our planet and ourselves.

We ask that wisdom will uplift us, and fill our hearts and minds with understanding, so that we may know what we must do.

We ask that the red ray of love and determination, strength and courage, will be our support.

That the blue ray of inspiration will guide us in the way of purity and peace.

We ask especially, that the healing waters of our Planet Earth shall remain forever pure, clean and free from taint, and that mankind shall enjoy the pure water, and will come to understand that it is there to share with all other creatures on Earth, who are as dependent on the life-giving waters as we ourselves are.

The Connection Between the Christ Consciousness Grid and the Crystalline Grid

'The Christ consciousness grid around the planet is an energy grid of love and protection through which the love of cosmic beings and the people on the planet can connect.

'There is a circuit of energy between it and the crystalline grid which is underneath the surface of the Earth. This grid is the Mother Earth grid and needs to be fed with the loving energy of the people of this planet. This can be done through all the ancient sacred places. People in towns and cities can find this connection through the ancient churches built with the sacred alignment of the ancients in mind. An awareness of this when you visit is necessary; send your love for the Earth through your feet. Consciously link with the grid under the ground at your feet, and the underground streams which will carry the imprint of your thoughts through the Earth's crust. Be more aware of water – it is the flow – the life blood of the Earth. Link the grid system with love and all will be well.'

The spiritual teachers who are showing me the pathway have given me the above message. They want to ask for your help in further activating the crystalline grid with the energy of love. The symbols for this are red roses for the Mother Earth energy, and the dove of peace. Please use these symbols when you convey your loving thoughts to our beautiful and precious planet. Visualise it surrounded in a loving pink light, because this is the colour associated with the Christ consciousness. I am told that there has never been a greater need for this energy than now. *Thank you.*

Meditation of Fountain International[3]

Many readers will be aware of the work of Fountain International.

> This is a network based on an idea which really works. The concept is that communities, like people, suffer from disease and may be healed. This 'community healing' will affect people, places and ultimately the planet. Every person can now play their part in the improvement of the quality of their own lives and their own area. The technique is beautifully simple. All it needs is an individual or group to relax into a peaceful frame of mind (a meditative state) and send healing thoughts to any focal point within the community, recognising its problems. There is a positive reaction in the Earth's field to this movement of energy, which will have a profound influence on the quality of life. The extension of this on a world scale will produce a network of light around the planet. This is the meditation used by us in opening the chakras once again. I would like to invite you to add your own healing energy to this planetary network of light, and if you could, to join in sending light to this chakra system also, so that we can help in lifting the vibrations of our Earth.

THE MEDITATION

Take a few moments to quiet the mind and shed the busy thoughts of every day. In a group, let someone slowly guide the meditation.

Let us each focus on our own inner light.

[3] By kind permission of Fountain International, www.fountain-international.org

Then extend this light and become one united being.

Picture the place chosen and visualise the brilliant spiral of energy from the centre of the Earth flowing up into the focal point, and golden light pouring down.

As the energies meet and merge, the focal point becomes a beacon.

As the energy increases, so it radiates out, sweeping through the streets, buildings and landscape of the area above and below ground, enfolding everything in its loving light.

As the energy spreads beyond our (name your place) we link to all Fountain centres and others who are working to raise the consciousness and vibrations of the Earth.

It sweeps through the energy lines and so joins the vast web of light surrounding the world. Now we see the (focal point) radiating love and light.

We bring our focus back to this room and our awareness of each other.

Anyone can begin to use the Fountain concept with this simple meditation focused on a significant point in their town, village or local area.

The daily input of a few moments of thought and focus is the nub of the whole Fountain concept. You do not have to join a group. Start today, alone or with a friend and the work is begun!

Pilgrimage of the Lady Mary

With my gift as a seer, I was able to discover that the Lady Mary, the mother of Jesus, came to Wales. I was able to tune in and follow her energy. I have been privileged to 'see' her once on Bryher in a meditation and also on Anglesey when she gave me a message that is on page 205. I have no doubt that she once lived here, and friends who are psychics have also sensed her presence. There always seems to have been a folk memory of her, which is one explanation for the existence of so many churches dedicated to her in Wales (Llanfair).

When I began this journey, I had no knowledge of this, but after tuning into her vibration, I read *The Marian Conspiracy*, by Graham Phillips, in which he set out to discover what happened to Mary after the crucifixion. By following a series of clues, he ended up in Anglesey, and so did I. This was confirmation for me, and it is important to know that reading this book came after my intuitive discovery and not before! Another author, Michael Poynder, in *The Lost Magic of Christianity*, says that Mary, accompanied by Joseph, Jesus's brother, brought Christianity to the land of the Silures, South Wales, in AD 36. My own experience would agree with both these writers – that Mary came to Wales.

Later on in this journey it became apparent that the Lady Mary had travelled up this valley, on her way from Brighid's shrine at what is now Strata Florida, to visit an important shrine to the same goddess at Llansantffraed Cwmdeuddwr at Rhayader. No man was allowed to set foot in this temple. Here, Mary was able to consult the priestesses of Brighid, the Divine Mother, the embodiment of whom she was destined to become. This was a place of administration for the entire area, which had grown up around the shrine where the priestesses, the Daughters of the Moon, officiated as they did at Llyn-y-Tarw.

The Sacred Land Between the Two Rivers

On the outskirts of Rhayader lies the village of Llansantffraed Cwmdeuddwr, 'the church of Saint Bride in the valley of the two rivers'. The two rivers here are the Wye and Elan, and this valley in turn lies between the two rivers of the Wye and the Severn, both rising from Pumlumon Fawr, which is 2,468 feet high.

In ancient times the country was divided into four quarters, north-west, north-east, south-west, and south-east, in a similar way to Ireland, with the fifth province of the high king at the centre. Each tribal land was ruled over by a dynasty of kings or princes, consisting of a ritual court, a high priest, a chief justice and a ceremonial bard. There were three lesser kingdoms in each of these four quarters making twelve divisions, which were subdivided into cant (or hundreds), commotes and family holdings. The commotes were made up of fifty landed families with their own courthouse and place of assembly.

Twice a year the king and his court made a ceremonial journey to all his provincial courts and assemblies, spending three days in each. In this way the rulers would have been very close to their people and would have known what was happening throughout their lands. The king presided over a judicial council of twelve elders. In Glamorgan, the tenth century King Edgar appointed twelve judges to settle disputes, and later the Normans administrated this district through twelve knights. It is thought that this ancient Welsh law is the reason for the 'twelve good men and true' on the jury system.

All this gives some idea of the organisation of the ritualised Druidic society which was designed to keep tribal order, and was confirmed in the code of Welsh law which King Hywel the Good (Hywel Dda) established in the tenth century. He appointed a committee of twelve jurists who were presided over by a doctor of law. It is from this code that the information on land measures gives a glimpse of the esoteric code of Druidism.

The number system is based on twelve. There were twelve realms of Wales, three to each quarter, roughly marking the old counties of Wales. Each was 120 square miles, making 1,440 square miles for the entire country. This represents the cultivated land only, and does not include the wilderness part, which is five times larger. This is sacred Wales, corresponding numerically to the 1,440 acres of Saint John's New Jerusalem, and the 1,440 acres which formed the twelve hides of Glastonbury, a hide being 120 acres. So it was that the Welsh tribes had received the laws that were the numerical expression of paradise and were enacted through the music of the perpetual choirs.

WELSH LAND DIVISIONS

> 4 acres = 1 allotment (*tyddyn*)
> 4 allotments = 16 acres = 1 rander
> 16 allotments = 1 garael
> 64 allotments = 256 acres = 1 farmstead (*tref*)
> 4 farmsteads = 1,024 acres = 1 maenol
> 50 farmsteads = 12,800 acres = 1 commote (*cwmwd*)
> 100 farmsteads = 25,600 acres = 1 cantref
> 3 cant = 120 square miles = 1 realm
> 3 realms = 360 square miles = 1 quarter
> 4 quarters = 1,440 square miles = sacred Wales

It is believed that Cwmdeuddwr was the centre of the four quarters, and was the equivalent of Tara in Ireland. This is where the palace or '*llys*' of the high king of Wales could be found. It was from this centre that lines of energy like the spokes of a wheel radiated out to where the ancient perpetual choirs were sited. These were probably Saint David's, Llandaff, Llantwit Major, Bangor-is-y-coed, Bangor and Saint Asaph's. Perpetual choirs were first mentioned in print in an old Welsh triad. Parties of monks chanted in unbroken succession day and night through the year (24 hours of the day, 7 days of the week, 52 weeks of the year). This raised the energies of their monasteries to such a level that the grass was lush and the crops could be grown without fertiliser, so that production exceeded modern levels. Its power is such that even to say the words 'perpetual choirs' lifts the energies; in fact, it could be used like a mantra in the present time.

The magical number 2,400 was the total number of saints in the three perpetual choirs of Britain. One of these perpetual choirs was at Llantwit Major, where Saint Illtyd founded a monastic college in the sixth century called Bangor Illtyd. In the Iolo Manuscripts it is written:

> Illtyd founded seven churches and appointed seven companies for each church, and seven halls or colleges for each company, and seven saints for each hall or college. Prayer and praise were kept up, without ceasing, by twelve saints, men of learning in each company.

This meant that the total number of saints in the seven churches came to 7 x 7 x 7 x 7 = 2,401, which was one more than the number of members of a perpetual choir. The early Celtic Christians preserved this knowledge and custom from a time when there was a sacred rule of perpetual choirs covering the entire country. The Romans destroyed all this, but the early Christians hung onto these traditions so that the lapsed choirs were restored and the ancient music was once more heard in Christian plainsong.

These people were versed from the cradle to the grave in the understanding of the numerology and sacred geometry of the universe. They wished to make their own land a part of this sacredness, and so they imposed its blueprint on the Celtic regions as an act of connectedness with the divine source. It was an act of worship, and the ritual centre of this precious land was Cwmdeuddwr, the legendary heart of all Wales. Its sacred valleys have been flooded to give water to Birmingham, and it is now known as the Welsh Lake District. It is very beautiful, a place of awesome atmosphere; sometimes darkly brooding, at other times sparkling with light.

As you would expect, it was fiercely defended against the Roman invaders, and many centuries later the white-robed monks of Abbey Cwmhir and Strata Florida held a procession along its ancient trackway, chanting as they went. It was along this route that the Lady Mary travelled from Strata Florida to Cwmdeuddwr, on her way to visit the shrine dedicated to the goddess Brighid, and we can now better understand her reason for doing this, and the importance of this sacred place.

Heart Chakra, Strata Florida

The Heart Chakra Connections

When we first visited Strata Florida, the story seemed simple and straightforward. But as we tuned in to the other chakras and they, rightly, connected back to the heart, the tapestry's weaving became more and more intricate. In the analogy of a tapestry, it follows that the thread must not be broken. It cannot be woven with a thread that is full of knots from joining up the pieces. It must be a continuous line. The challenges of this story is to find the link between apparently unrelated happenings, people and places. Things that seem as unrelated as the ruins of the Cistercian Abbey of Strata Florida and the Egyptian mystery schools, the Hebrews and the arrival of Joseph of Arimathea and Mary in Wales, are all in fact one continuous thread, unfolding over thousands of years.

There is a connection with Hathor and the Temple of Kom Ombo in Egypt. This is where the Pleiadean guidance becomes apparent and Merlin appears again, together with the Welsh spiritual leaders, the Druids. The ancient feminine Earth energy in the form of the goddess is shown, linking with the symbolic rose. There is the story of the Welsh Grail leading to Joseph of Arimathea and Mary, the mother of Jesus. Then there is Lord Rhys and the Cistercian monks. Finally there are ourselves in the present day, awakening this sleeping pathway and helping in the grand plan to raise the planet's energies as we ascend into the Age of Aquarius. This shimmering tapestry has been woven over millennia. It is here now for all to look at, marvel and enjoy.

A Pleiadean Connection for Strata Florida

A MEDITATION ON THE CISTERCIAN MONASTERIES IN WALES, ASKING THE QUESTION: ARE THEY CONNECTED TO THE PLEIADES?

It seems that they themselves (the Pleiadeans) seeded the holy places with what they call 'star seed'. My feeling is that there is much more to discover if you go to these places and link with the Pleiades in your mind and heart. This connection is particularly important in this chakra system when we remember that the crown chakra at Llyn-y-Tarw is dedicated to the Pleiades.

'Yes, indeed they are connected. When the star seed fell to Earth it was like a gardener planting his seed. Some seeds were placed here and some were planted there. All was working according to plan. The Cistercian monasteries were built where the seeds fell, and this was part of our plan and followed in the footsteps of the master. In many ways a seed it was, for it grew to flower and then to fruit. We know that all that is left is stone but we say that the energy which we planted was nurtured and has flowered. If you go to these places with our star sign in your mind you will understand much more.'

'Was Joseph here at Strata Florida?'

'My dear child, of course he was! This is a very holy place. It was holy long before Joseph and the monks. At one time there was an island at this point which was the focus for the whole area. There were crystals here. We have placed quartz crystals under the ground and this was done in the pattern similar to the Coptic cross. Ancient peoples walked in these walls before there were walls. They gathered flowers and made a temple of trees.

'It was a tree temple of the Druids. The energies are there still. This is why it is so easy to reawaken them for the good of the Earth. These people tuned in to the Earth and the stars and knew that one day there would be a coming of greatness, a coming of the Aquarian Age.

'We are going back beyond the Age of Pisces to the Age of Taurus and beyond. We have guarded this spot. It is our temple of peace on Earth. Tune in to it. It is hallowed ground. It represents love, our love for those on Earth who wish to devote themselves in the spiritual sense to the brotherhood of mankind. We have charge of the initiation into this brotherhood.

'This is our special task and our part in the awakening of mankind. Our guidance is forever with you. Go in peace.'

Message from the Pleiadeans, July 2001

Initiation Chamber at Strata Florida

Strata Florida means 'a covering of flowers'. There is a strange 'pit' inside the abbey which is unknown anywhere else. It has steps down. You walk through the water at the bottom, and up the other side. No one knows what it is for.

'It is part of an initiation ceremony in which the monks passed into a new life or were "reborn". You must do this yourself and you will understand. The energies are still there and they can be re-energised by people born of the light. Some of the monks understood this connection but because of the fear of Rome they said it was a baptismal font. It was one of the ways in which an underground covert religion was practised. Welsh religion was practised as the Druids would have done. Try it. Test the energies and you will know.'

The initiation chamber or pit at Strata Florida

On 9 July three of us visited the abbey, and were very fortunate to find ourselves alone when we got there. We took it in turns to walk down, through, and up the other side of this strange pit, which must be done facing towards the altar. I did it first without stepping into the bottom which should have held water but didn't. Stepping over this pit made me feel very queasy. It hit me first in the solar plexus and made me feel sick, then it hit me in my head and I felt very faint and had a headache. This is not recommended! It is necessary to stand in the pit in order to ground yourself. However, it still seems to get you in your solar plexus and crown chakra. We all felt this in different degrees, but we found it powerful and a little disturbing. This is an initiation chamber, similar to those found in Egypt. As you walk through it, it changes your vibration to a higher level and you are transformed! On the other side you find yourself at the high altar, where you could both give and receive a blessing.

In fact it is a Celtic initiation chamber taking the temple at Kom Ombo as its model. This Egyptian mystery school taught the Left Eye of Horus, the feminine side. This deals with the emotional body and the heart chakra. It is to do with freeing the heart. Afterwards a red kite flew low over the copper beech tree, telling us to trust the bird's eye view and guidance of our higher selves.

The Initiation: How Does It Work?

We poured water from Llyn-y-Tarw into the pit at Strata Florida, and on the altar. We left a rose on the altar as a mark of our deep respect. It seems that both novices and initiates, and all those in between, can use the initiation chamber at Strata Florida. Somehow the energy is balanced to be in tune with the person. So how can this be? It doesn't seem possible that the energy itself alters; it is more likely that it is guided and balanced by the higher self and some other factor.

I believe this other factor is in the shape of the angel guardian of the chamber. After I had been through, I 'saw' this angel. He looked very Celtic, as if he had come out of the Book of Kells, with brown curly hair. He wore a cream and gold robe. Both the monks and the Druids before them would have spent many months in preparation for this event. They would have spent their time in prayer and meditation. They would have linked with the Earth, sky, air and sea. They would have been aware of the heavenly connection and respected it. It would have been, perhaps, their most sacred moment. They would have known that the energy moves the spirit forward, but the body lags behind and needs time to catch up again. This causes a sense of disorientation, which is what happens when the physical body is not aligned with the subtle bodies. This disorientation can take as long as a week or more to settle.

In our busy, busy world we are unable to take the time to meditate and rest after initiation, but we should try to rest and take our time to adjust. It is better to let someone else do the driving on the homeward stretch, or at least to be aware that you may be disorientated. Those who came before us were so much wiser than ourselves, and their lives were much more ordered and peaceful. The angel wished me to understand that they protect all those who walk through the chamber, and that one could ask, and receive, their blessing.

THE MESSAGE FROM THE ANGEL OF STRATA FLORIDA

The angel

'You have opened up a well of energy in this abbey which has been dormant for many centuries. Although it has been dormant, it has been very much alive, like a sleeping serpent. It is in the form of a spiral and adjusts to the energy focus of the novice or initiate. This is mainly through our help. We are the guardians and guides of this site, and of this energy. You have guessed correctly, that the body lags behind the transformation.

'The monks knew this and spent much time in meditation and prayer both before and after, as did the Druids. A time of initiation should always be prepared for, and followed by a long period of rest and prayer.'

'How long?' I asked.

'About three months of the lunar cycle. Awareness is sharpened and heightened. The ability to communicate with evolved beings of the higher levels is also within this energy. You need not worry about the after-care and protection of those who go through this, for we are with them and they are safe under our protection and light.

'We are very pleased with the energy, which is being directed in a very beautiful shape and form in the centre of the heart chakra of this system. Many people will come to this system over the coming years. They will all contribute to the opening of the planet to the will of the cosmic spirit, and to the energies of the angels and beings who will be able to influence the planet's movement into the golden age. All of these people are equally important and have a vital role in the present and the future.'

'Is it a dimensional gateway?'

'Yes it is. These gateways have been guarded since the beginning of time by the spirits of light. They have been used before in the old time, and will be used again for the new age. A sense of reverence, a sense of joy, a sense of new beginnings, will be with all those who understand this, and their lives will be blessed with new understanding and guidance. You may liken it to a torch that has been lit and will spread the light to all who visit it. You will all find great joy in this service to the light.'

A QUESTION ABOUT STRATA FLORIDA

'How long has the initiation pit been there?'

'Since the beginning of time itself. It was a seed thought in the mind of God, a chamber for the new age of the world of man.'

THE IMPORTANCE OF WATER IN THIS CHAKRA SYSTEM

'Energies have begun to flow. These energies are unstoppable. There is no one who can divert these energies now, although many might have tried, had they known. There is water at these places – a connection with the source of all being and of all life. The connection is through the water. This is an all-powerful force running through, cleansing, healing and living. It is the very flow itself. Take a hallowed view of water. It must be given and exchanged one with another. Do not miss any source, for this will break the chain and stop the flow. Work with the water and remember the angel of water, as well as the elemental beings.'

I linked with, and spoke to, this angel. She was blue in colour with a silvery laugh. She seemed very happy, light, airy and joyful. I was told that I must take water from the lake, the holy wells and the rivers in this chakra system, and give the water from each to the other, so that none are missed.

Visiting the Chakras

THE ANGEL SPEAKS

'All is well. There is a code that is partly DNA, partly karmic and partly earned knowledge. This does not mean that you must not be discreet or guarded in your words or deeds; of course you must. But the overlighting angel is keeping watch on this system. You have been told of the sequence and the necessary work to be done. You have received many lifetimes of training for this. This means that you have the necessary coding within you to perform this task. Those people who do not have this coding will be unable to perform it, but this does not mean that they will not be helped and healed through their contact with it. This is an opportunity for us to reach them and open their chakras, their doors into themselves. What will be given will be according to their needs. What is inappropriate will not be given. This chakra system is not to do with them – it is to do with us. Sometimes people who come will not be prepared. This is no matter. They will receive whatever is appropriate for their highest good. We are able to look into their hearts and minds across time – previous lives, present and future lives. It is in the light of this knowledge that we are able to work for the highest good of all concerned. The reason they come is not important. We are the light.'

A Covering of Flowers – the Meaning of 'Strata Florida'

'THEY GATHERED FLOWERS AND MADE A TEMPLE OF TREES'

At their sacred ceremonies, the ancients laid flowers as offerings on the altar at the end of the tree temple which stood on this site. There would have been a 'covering of flowers'. The ancient altar stone was later Christianised with a cross, and now stands at the back of the present church.

Shortly after beginning their monastery, the monks began to build another one a couple of miles away. Why was this? It was not because the Normans had been forced out of the area, because we know that Prince Rhys actively encouraged them. I was 'told' that the land they were given was 'a holy place long before Joseph and the monks. Ancient peoples walked in these walls before there were walls. They gathered flowers and made a temple of trees. It was a tree temple of the Druids'.

The Druids believed that words were holy, too holy to be written down. It had to be memorised and handed down from generation to generation, through stories that were remembered with great accuracy. There was no room for deviation or embroidery. They were told and sung by storytellers and bards around the fires in the evenings, at *eisteddfodau* (*eistedd* means 'to sit') and at celebrations. They knew what the place was for. They knew about the initiation pit, and they saw no contradiction between their holy places and the Christian ones because there wasn't any. So they decided to give their most holy place to the Cistercian monks, and in doing so, they ensured that it would remain protected as hallowed ground, as it still is today. They may well have been spiritually guided to do this.

It is strange that the pit is on a direct east–west line, whereas the abbey is a little askew, but it is not surprising that, centuries later, they forgot its original purpose, and had to invent one. After all, it was there, wasn't it? It must have had a reason. So they used it for the ceremonial washing of feet, following the example of their master, Christ. Soon after its reawakening, a friend entered the pit and 'saw' himself standing in it as a monk, having his feet washed by a brother. He was aware of an order of procedure and the position which the monks took at the altar, and at the initiation pit at that time. In April 2003, the Archbishop of Canterbury, Dr Rowan Williams, performed this ceremony of washing feet for others. This was the first time it had been done for 400 years.

Stargate

The initiation pit under the watchful eyes of the Druid guardians

Another friend met the guardian of this sacred place in the abbey ruins. She had her dowsing pendulum with her, and was about to enter the pit, moving in the direction west–east towards the altar, when the chain holding the crystal was broken by the guardian. He was about seven feet tall, with wide shoulders. She sensed he had tremendous power. He was not a monk, but a Druid with white hair. She felt that if he could break her chain, there was no knowing what else he might do! He was one of the Druids who exist in the fourth or fifth dimension, in their *merkaba* or light body. We felt he was Merlin. When we were talking on the phone about this, the line went dead. She phoned back, laughing. 'He cut me off!'

He would not allow her to enter the pit west–east direction! She was made to enter east–west, from the altar side. While on the steps, she felt that she could 'step off the world', stepping off the three-dimensional Earth into the fourth or fifth dimension. At a later date, the angel told me that it was a dimensional gateway used before in the old time, and will be used again in the new age.

Other friends found themselves pushed back by the energy when they tried to enter the pit. They waited for an adjustment to take place, and then were allowed through. We are wondering why different people should be made to approach from different directions, but we don't really know. I felt very strongly that I should go towards the altar.

One explanation is that it depends which era or age of time they are tuning in to. By 'seeing' what is going on around them, people are able to understand where they are in time. If they are tuning to Druid time, the pit is walked west–east. The west was 'the land of the dead', so they walked away from the west towards the east. The most sacred rivers were considered to flow in this direction also. As the monks forgot the purpose of the pit, they invented one, which was the washing of feet, and at that time, they entered the pit from both directions. Some people may be tuning in to former lives here, which would explain their etheric vision. It may also be that east–west is following the sun's course, because the Druids walked in sacred circles from east to west as the sun rose and set.

We have met Merlin at the crown chakra, the heart chakra and the sacral chakra. We all found him frightening! When I first met him, not only were his eyes flashing light, but lightning was flashing all around him as well. I believe this powerful guardian is in overall charge of this pathway, and both it and he must be treated with deep respect. He is telling us to be careful and thoughtful in all that we do.

THE EXPERIENCE THAT DEE AND JOHN HAD WHEN THEY WENT THROUGH THE INITIATION PIT

On 27 June 2002, we went to Strata Florida carrying a white rose and a yellow rose which I had been asked to take with me. I said a prayer and explained that I was continuing my journey which had started at Saint Anthony's Well at Llansteffan, and continued through Saint Caron's Well and Cors Tregaron. I walked through the pit and was welcomed by females in white, and asked to place my flowers. There was tremendous energy on my hands from the altar as I placed the flowers. I was asked to go through a rite of passage, back down the steps, through the pit, and up the steps again to reach the altar. There I was asked to dedicate myself to the goddess, and for the first time I truly felt that I could do this from my heart. I was then asked to move to my rightful place and found myself walking to the left of the altar, and then to the centre back, and it felt as though I was back where I belonged. I was aware that I had stood there before when initiates had gone through the same rite of passage and that at that time, there was holy water on the altar that they anointed their foreheads with. On my way back to the altar, John was standing in front of me and he moved to the right as I came close. When I moved to the other side, he was standing behind me. I felt this was symbolic in that I was releasing my own male energies in service to the goddess.

Following this, I felt very strongly that John needed to go through the pit, and he, too, went forward towards the altar and dedicated himself to the goddess. When we eventually moved to one side, I was told, 'All is well.' I felt very strongly that I had been in the presence of the Priestesses of the Moon, who had been there long before the abbey was built, and they also predated the Druids.

We were firstly aware of the Priestesses of the Moon at Llyn-y-Tarw, laying flowers before the statue which appeared in the photograph. This was another meeting with them, and on Bryher in the Scilly Isles they had a temple, and there is a grave of a high priestess of their order. Our sense is that these priestesses are a very ancient order, possibly the original people of this chakra system. This is the feminine line of the grid system, representing the Earth Mother energy.

As each age surrendered itself before our wondering gaze, yet another age would appear from an even more distant past. Like a little boat piloting itself through the sea mist, more and more islands kept looming up. This is an appropriate analogy – as the Druid said, the past is an island in the sea of time. We have been privileged to be asked to connect some of these places, with this awareness in mind, to bring them into the present.

So it is that the unbroken thread leading from the Age of Taurus through the Age of Pisces and into the Age of Aquarius has been traced. It has even gone back beyond Taurus to the Atlantean goddess Brighid and her Priestesses of the Moon, who once officiated at the Temple of Light. This ground is indeed sacred, more so than we could ever have imagined.

The cross in the rose of the heart chakra

This rose was named after Saint Cecilia, the patron saint of music. It has a cupped shape and a powerful myrrh fragrance.

The Rose of the Heart

The Rose of the Heart
Brings forth Love's perfection
Distilling the dewdrops
Of Divine grace outpoured
Tenderly embracing creation
In compassion's scent
Revealing the knowledge
That all are one.

Felicity Boden, 2003[1]

This poem was given to Felicity when she went on a sacred pilgrimage to Israel. Copies were handed out to the group in the setting of the original Upper Room in Jerusalem, which is now at basement level under the Syrian Orthodox Church of Saint Mark's. Felicity feels that it therefore carries the blessing of the Christed energies.[2]

---

[1] By kind permission of the author
[2] Christed energies: a universal energy of love that we all carry within us to a certain degree, but Christ carried a great deal more than the rest of us.

Connections to the Heart Chakra

Connections to Strata Florida Abbey

The revelations began to appear, as inspirations from the past gathered momentum and shone a clear light onto the present. It illuminates the ancient people, events and countries of Europe and the Mediterranean.

The gateway to Strata Florida

Meeting a Knight at Strata Florida

After the discovery of the initiation chamber at Strata Florida, other people began to visit it as well. One of our friends said that she had seen, clairvoyantly, two hands holding an old-fashioned fully blossomed pink rose. She also saw a man riding a horse through the abbey towards the east. She knew he was an important person, a knight, although he was not wearing any armour. After doing some research, I thought that he might have been the abbey's founder, the Lord Rhys. Neither of us had even heard of him up to this moment. Through dowsing, we established that it was him, and on her next visit, our friend saw him again, firstly wearing armour, and the second time without. He had injured his leg, probably in battle. This was Rhys ap Gruffudd (died 1197), prince of the ancient Kingdom of Deheubarth, Yr Arglwydd Rhys, Rhys the Good, Rhys the Great, the unconquered head of all Wales, who restored the political, military, cultural and religious prominence of Deheubarth. Lord Rhys became patron of both Whitland and Strata Florida, but he 'loved and cherished Strata Florida'.[1] So much so that when the monks moved to a new site two miles away, where the abbey now stands, it was to become the burial-church for the Deheubarth dynasty of princes. (Wales did not have kings; it was ruled by princes, and it is still a principality today.) Lord Rhys was buried in Saint David's Cathedral, where his fourteenth-century tomb effigy is believed to lie.

Gerald of Wales, Giraldus Cambrensis, was a relation of Lord Rhys, and visited Strata Florida in 1188 to try to persuade the family to enlist for the crusades. He came upon Rhys's third son, Cynwrig, in a wood, leading his war band of lightly armed young companions. He was tall, handsome and curly-haired, dressed in the traditional thin Welsh cloak and shirt, without boots or shoes to protect his feet from the thorns. Gerald said he was 'a man adorned by nature and not art, having a natural, not artificial dignity'.[2]

He met Rhys and three of his sons, so he preached them an instant sermon. Cynwrig preferred dignity to action, and Gruffudd was more interested in getting rid of his brother

---

[1] David M Robinson and Colin Platt, *Strata Florida Abbey and Talley Abbey*, Cadw, 1992, p.11

[2] Charles Knightly, *A Mirror of Medieval Wales: Gerald of Wales and his Journey of 1188*, 1988

Maelgwn than in going himself. After a lot of argument, Maelgwn agreed to go with them on their mission but would not take the crusading vow. What struck Gerald about the Welsh princes was their militarism. They travelled the country in armed retinues and believed in military glory and a heroic death above all things; they were highly skilled in guerrilla warfare and loved liberty. In defeat they had shown resilience and a capacity to make a comeback. Lord Rhys had learned the art of cavalry warfare from the Normans and the importance of castles, which he either built or captured.

However, the Welsh had one fatal flaw, 'they obstinately and proudly refused to submit to one ruler'.[3] Sometimes a powerful ruler might unite them and Rhys was one such ruler. Gerald came to the conclusion that the only hope for the Welsh was that they unite behind 'one prince and he a good one'.[4] Astutely, Gerald made his own prophecy. The Welsh, he wrote, were often harassed and weakened by various attackers, not least the English. But, he declared, they would survive. 'Nor do I think that any other nation than that of Wales, nor any other language shall, in the day of severe examination before the Supreme Judge, in any case answer for this corner of the Earth.' This is because the country is fortunate to be under the protection of Merlin (this is what I was told).[5]

Strata Florida and the Fight to Preserve Celtic Christianity

The native Celtic priests, the Druids, were slaughtered on Anglesey by the Roman Army. Why were the Romans so frightened of them? Was it because their spirituality had no place in the world of Rome? Their understanding and vision of spirituality within nature was one of the elements of the Celtic faith, and lived on in the early Christian Celtic Church.

Pelagius, a Celt whose real name was Morgan, as one of their exponents, was teaching in Rome in 397. The essence of his

---

[3] Ibid. p.60
[4] Ibid. p.61
[5] Ibid.

teaching was that evil and sin are external to humanity, and through the exercise of free will, we can gain salvation. His opponents, the most influential of whom was Saint Augustine, asserted that salvation is entirely dependent upon the Grace of God and the power of the Catholic Church, and that all human efforts to attain perfection must fail without it. Pelagius taught that:

> We put in the first place, power; in the second, will; and in the third, manifestation. The first of these comes from God, Who has given it to His Own creatures. The other two are related to the human condition, because they stream forth from the sources of the human will.[6]

He taught that it is within our own power to live a blameless life. This means that we can be self-reliant in religious matters, and attain perfection. The same idea appears in Druidic philosophy. His teachings were addressed to social justice. Pelagius was persecuted for his ideas. He eventually ended up in the Holy Land, supported and protected by John, Bishop of Jerusalem.

There were two different groups of Christians – the Celtic Christians and the Roman Christians. The Roman Christians obviously looked to the Bishop of Rome as head of their Church. The Gospel of Thomas in the Nag Hammadi scrolls indicates that James, the brother of Jesus later known as James the Just, had been put in charge of all of Jesus's followers.[7] James adhered strictly to the Jewish law and was only concerned with Jewish matters. Paul, on the other hand, wished to carry the message of Christ's teaching to the Gentiles.[8] This was the beginning of the split between the two groups and explains why the Celtic Christians believed that the Jerusalem Church was the true Church. Since Pelagius was given sanctuary by the Bishop of Jerusalem when he was persecuted by Saint Augustine, it seems logical that this was the Church that the Celtic Christians followed.

The fathers of the Church of Rome believed that they could

---

[6] Nigel Pennick, *The Celtic Saints*, 1997, p.76
[7] James D Tabor, *The Jesus Dynasty*, 2006, p.231
[8] Michael Baigent, *The Jesus Papers*, 2006, p.262

legislate away all knowledge of the spiritual world, and with it the freedom to gain access to the knowledge and beliefs that lead to the spiritual growth of the seeker. There were many differences between the Celtic and Roman churches.

The Celtic Church was a truly spiritual body; they were not interested in the trappings and benefits of temporal power. They recognised that the Roman Pontiff was the successor of Saint Peter, but had a firm conviction that the Patriarch (or Bishop) of Jerusalem was the true successor of Christ.

The Roman Catholic Church could not allow this to go un-challenged as it clearly ranked the Pope beneath the Bishop of Jerusalem. Saint Augustine of Hippo began a series of doctrines which led to a foundation of repression and persecution. Pelagius was condemned by the mainstream Catholic Church as a heretic and his works were destroyed wherever they could be found. This one sentence seems to be all that remains: 'Should there be one law for the rich and another for the poor?'[99] So he never became Saint Morgan or Saint Pelagius. But his ideas were so widespread in Britain in the 420s, during the so-called 'Dark Ages', that Rome sent Germanus of Auxerre to suppress them. Vortigern, himself a Pelagian Christian, kept Britain independent until 442, when he invited in the Saxon mercenaries.

Meanwhile, Romanised Britain collapsed completely, and it was after this that Saint Augustine, the first Archbishop of Canterbury, arrived. His mission was to convert the Saxons and Angles, who worshipped Woden and Frea. 'Converting the natives' to Romanised Christianity had been done successfully in Europe, but in Britain there was a complication. In the north and west, there already was a Christian Church that was not under the control of Rome and had a significant following!

So it was that both Churches came into competition for con-verts, the Roman Church being concerned with status, land and money. The Celtic Church first came up against the Roman Catholic Church in Northumbria, where, at the Synod of Whitby in 664, it met its end.

King Oswiu was a Celtic Christian, but his wife Eanfled was a

---

[99] Nigel Pennick, *The Celtic Saints*, 1997

Roman Catholic. The celebration of their feastdays at different times caused their court some inconvenience. So they asked Saint Hild to organise a meeting between the two Churches. The king told them that as they all expected to go to the same heaven, they should have the same celebrations on Earth. However, he had been told by the queen that the Roman Catholics would not change, so he asked Abbot Colman of Lindisfarne to explain the Celtic tradition. He explained that he had been given his dates for Easter from his elders, who had been given it in direct line from Saint John the Evangelist. A convincing argument, you might think.

Abbot Wilfred of Ripon countered that he had travelled far and wide, and that only the Celts had Easter at a different time from everyone else. Wilfred said that Saint Columba was not a true saint because he did not follow the Catholic practices, and that the Celtic Church was a false church built on the foundation laid by Columba and not Saint Peter. His church was founded by Saint Peter, and was the true Church. King Oswiu was afraid that he would not get into heaven unless he followed Saint Peter, because he believed Saint Peter held the keys to heaven and would not let him in otherwise.

One of the leading figures of the Welsh Church who attended was Saint Cadwaladr from Anglesey. He had been the King of Gwynedd but became a monk when his wife died. He, too, refused to accept the ruling, and set out immediately for Rome to challenge Pope Vitalian. On reaching Rome, he died in mysterious circumstances. His body was brought back to Llangadwaladr Church (Llangadwaladr: church of Cadwaladr), on Anglesey, where he became the island's most revered saint, being known as 'The Blessed', Cadwaladr Fendigaid.

These then were the grounds under which the Celtic Church was forced to give way to the Roman Catholic Church. Those priests who would not give in were expelled from Anglo-Saxon lands, and Abbot Colman travelled to Scotland where the Celtic Church did not recognise the Synod of Whitby. The Celtic Church continued in Scotland, Ireland and Brittany. It continued in Scotland and Cornwall until 1069. The religion was suppressed but the bardic tradition remains unbroken in some parts still, e.g. in Wales.

What Happened to Saint Hild?

She was a lady of noble birth who was helped by Saint Aiden to set up a monastery and in 657 she was abbess of a monastery for both monks and nuns, which became a centre for learning and the arts. This creative monastic rule, which was a part of the life of the Celtic people, fell foul of the Catholics and was suppressed by them after she had organised the Synod of Whitby.

The story of Celtic Christianity in Britain is relevant to the Abbey of Strata Florida. I was told in my meditation, 'Of all the places in the British Isles, we would say Strata Florida was most influenced by the mystery schools of Egypt.' How could this be? It was through the teachings of the Druids, which became a part of the Celtic Church.

The first Cistercian communities in Wales were those at Whitland (1140) and Margam (1147), both taking their marching orders from Saint Bernard of Clairvaux. Both these communities were Anglo-Norman, and were not popular with the native Welsh. In 1164, Whitland was offered a modest endowment by Robert FitzStephen within the Anglo-Norman lordship of Ceredigion (Cardigan). FitzStephen greeted the monks on the banks of Nant Ffur, and this was the site that they chose and is now known as Yr hen fynachlog (the old monastery). But within the year, the Welsh chronicle *Brut y Tywysogyon* (*Chronicle of the Princes*) records, 'all the Welsh united to throw off the rule of the French'. The Norman Clare family was pushed out of Ceredigion in 1164, and the following year Robert FitzStephen was captured. There was a resurgence of Welsh supremacy in the south-west, the kingdom of Deheubarth. It was Rhys ap Gruffudd, the prince of this fertile kingdom, who captured FitzStephen and restored his own kingdom. The Lord Rhys was intelligent, cultured and showed great leadership. He also recognised the value of the monks in holding on to his kingdom.

The Power of the Church in the Twelfth Century

Why Lord Rhys found it important to invite the Cistercians into his kingdom of Deheubarth is difficult for us to understand now, but the twelfth-century Church was all-powerful, not only in Britain but in Europe as well. It dominated not only religion, but culture, public life and politics. The bishops and abbots were among the ruler's wealthiest and most influential tenants-in-chief. They were a source of men and money to the kings. The clerics were the best educated men of the age and acted as advisers and administrators to rulers. There was a constant round of worship in Latin in all cathedrals, monasteries, and parish churches.

On Sundays and holy days (every day in monasteries) mass was offered. Public health, charitable giving, solemnising of agreements, and disposing of property after death, were all done by the priests. They provided education, and their scribes preserved, stored and copied precious manuscripts, such as the beautiful psalter written by Rhigyfarch at Llanbadarn Fawr, at Aberystwyth, which was kept at Strata Florida. Such all-pervading influence made it vital for rulers to enlist the aid of churches. Since the end of the eleventh century, the Church had been used by the Norman kings, barons and archbishops of Canterbury to overcome native resistance in Wales. Any attempts by the Welsh to claim autonomy had been quickly snuffed out by the Norman Church and state.

These policies had not gone unresisted. Welsh princes tried to prevent Welsh bishops from bowing to Canterbury, and endowed Cistercian monasteries, which had lost their Anglo-Norman associations. These monasteries, with their holy life, strict discipline, pastoral farming, the giving of education, patronage of literature, culture and patriotism, won the support of the princes. They also supported the rights of Saint David's as an independent archbishopric, but of all the monasteries, Strata Florida was their most holy place. Many of the abbots, with names like Deiniol, Cedifor, Rhys, Morgan, and Dafydd ab Owen, were as Welsh as the land itself. It was under such men that a major history was written in Latin, which is now lost. This formed the basis for at least one translation into Welsh, *Brut y Tywysogyon*, that was written by the monks of the abbey in the late thirteenth century. The monks of Strata Florida became the custodians of native culture and traditions. In the beginning when the monks built the abbey, I feel sure that they knew the purpose of the initiation pit which survived with its Druidic traditions and understanding.

Maintaining these traditions was very dangerous for them and they were sometimes risking their lives. In 1212, King John decided that Strata Florida 'which sustains our enemies should be destroyed or as far as possible wasted'.[10] The king was prevented from doing this due to other troubles in his realm, so he fined them £800, which crippled them until 1248, when a remission was granted.

Joseph of Arimathea and the Cup of the Welsh Grail

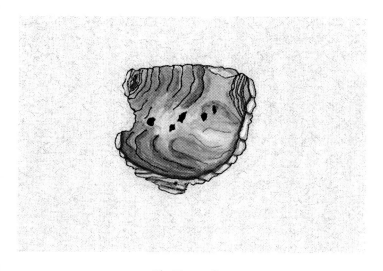

The Nanteos Cup

'Nanteos' means the stream or valley of the nightingales. This is the story of the Nanteos Cup, believed to be the Cup of the Last Supper or Grail.

Joseph of Arimathea is said to have arrived in Britain in AD 36. This seems to be the only thing there is agreement about, but this is the story of this cup.

---

[10] David M Robinson and Colin Platt, *Strata Florida Abbey* and *Talley Abbey*, Cadw, 1992

In AD 1200, three monks set out from Glastonbury, just before the monastery was sacked. They were on a mission to carry the precious cup to the monastery of Strata Florida. The cup was safely housed at the abbey, where it was known as Saint Mary's dowry, until they heard that troops were on their way to remove the abbey's treasures.

The three monks set off once more, to take the cup to safety across the Irish Sea, planning to leave it in the Abbey of Mellifont, in County Meath. When they were halfway to Cardigan Bay, they were in danger of being overtaken by their pursuers. They asked for refuge at Nant Eos, the home of the Stedman family. It was here they remained until they died. When the last monk was on his deathbed, he called for the head of the family. The monk explained that he was the last 'Keeper of the Cup', and asked that Stedman and his heirs would take over guardianship of the cup, 'until the Church shall claim her own'. This cup was guarded by the Stedmans after the dissolution of the monasteries. Later, the Stedmans married into the Powell family, who built Nanteos House in 1739. The Powells are the guardians still. Richard Wagner, the composer, was a visitor to Nanteos and was aware of the cup. While he was there he was inspired to write the opera *Parsifal*. He was a guest of George Powell, himself a poet and a friend of Longfellow and Swinburne.

This broken little wooden bowl, a wine cup made from olive wood, remained at Nanteos House for over 300 years. It was placed into a glass bowl, and the family used to pour water into it, which was then bottled and given to people to drink. Many hundreds of people came from all over the country to seek absolution from it. There is an extensive record of the healings which took place. It was even lent out to people, and many pieces were broken off as talismans. Numerous cures were documented and accounts were kept which still exist today.

> 23 January 1857: Two half-sovereigns deposited in drawer, library table to Ebenezer Vaughan for the use of his wife, left £1-0-0-. Cup returned 5 October 1858. Cured.[11]

---

[11] Michael Poynder, *The Lost Magic of Christianity*, 2000

The cup is still in the possession of the family, but I believe you can only see it if you are invited to, and its exact location is a secret, although it may be in a bank vault in Hereford. I do know that it is not at Nanteos House in Aberystwyth. When it was at Nanteos it was kept in a walk-in cupboard, according to a friend. A visiting medium was convinced that it was the Cup of the Last Supper, because when she went into the cupboard she 'saw' Joseph of Arimathea and Peter. Later in this story I too 'saw' Joseph, to my great surprise, but that was at the sacral chakra in Carmarthen Bay.

The head of the Nanteos family was a member of the 'Sea Searjeants', an eighteenth-century secret society that used the dolphin as their symbol. There is a connection between dolphins and whales and the crystalline grid that I was told about at Llyn-y-Tarw. They will carry the song of the singing crystals, when 'the planet and its crystalline structure must harmonise, vibrate and sing!'

As might be expected for a story that has been around for many hundreds of years, there are other versions. Laurence Main writes in his guide book, *The Spirit Paths of Wales*,[12] that the cup was moved from Glastonbury in the sixth century and not the sixteenth – a thousand years earlier. It was brought by three warrior saints, Sir Galahad, Sir Percival and Sir Bors, the three knights of the Round Table who achieved the Grail quest. This was done by the full moon in December 537 or 539, after King Arthur had been mortally wounded at the Battle of Camlan,[13] and Glastonbury was expecting a Saxon attack.

Two of our friends were taken to Nanteos House in the 1960s, and were privileged to drink water from this sacred object and can verify its existence. Richard Wagner's great-great-grandson Adrian Wagner, himself a composer, has made a CD with a story of this cup called *Sought and Found*.

The Ancient Symbolism of the Rose

The rose was the symbol of the Lady Mary, mother of Jesus, who came to the ancient temple of Brighid, which predated the abbey.

---

[12] Laurence Main, *The Spirit Paths of Wales,* 2000, p.62
[13] Laurence Main, *Camlan, the True Story*, 1997

Oh, no man knows
Through what wild centuries
Roves back the rose.

Walter de la Mare

Fossil studies have shown that wild roses bloomed 40 million years ago. The world's oldest painting of roses is a mural on the wall of the palace of Knossos in Crete, which is 4,000 years old. A wreath of five-petal roses was discovered in an Egyptian tomb dating from about AD 26. They were a species known as 'the holy rose of Abyssinia', because they were a feature of Coptic Christian churchyards in that country. The rose was sacred to Isis, and it is known that Hathor was identified with Isis, so I suppose that it was sacred to her also. Roses were recorded in Ur around 2648–2630 BC.

Among the Sufis, the experience of the sacred is intimately associated with the form and scent of the rose. They call it a messenger from the garden of souls.

> There is a heavenly rose garden, with roses of every colour, not just the ones on Earth. In the centre is a fountain of white roses, but every colour is reflected in their petals like pearl. Mankind is not yet aware, that here on Planet Earth is the manifestation of that garden.

Megan Wingfield and Olive Hesketh,
Light is the Rainbow Bridge

In Ancient Greece the rose was dedicated to Aphrodite. Legend says that the first rose grew out of the white foam that covered her at her birth. The word 'rosa' comes from the Greek word '*roden*' meaning red. Venus, the Roman version of Aphrodite, is also closely linked to the red rose. While she was rushing to help her dying lover, Adonis, who was mortally wounded by a wild boar, she tripped over a thorn and cut her foot. Her blood spilled out onto the petals of a white rose, staining them a deep shade of red. The Romans worshipped the rose; no other culture has been so obsessed as they. Alhenaeus says that the petals were eight inches deep on the floor of the private rooms where Cleopatra first met Mark Antony. It was because of this that after the fall of their empire, the Roman Catholic Church condemned the rose as a heathen flower. It was particularly contemptuous of the pagan custom of offering wreaths of roses to the dead. But they could not win the battle of the rose, so it was gradually incorporated into early Christian mythology. It became the symbol of the blood of Christ, the five petals representing his five wounds.

A rose was given to Cupid as a bribe to Harpocrates, the god of silence. It has been the symbol of discretion from Roman times. At Roman banquets a rose was suspended above the table to indicate that anything said below it was not to be repeated outside, and this is the origin of the expression 'sub rosa'. It means 'in secret', under the rose. Merlin warned us in a meditation with a friend, that we must remember 'sub rosa'. It was a warning to be discreet, and not to disclose anything until we had been given permission to do so. This flower was carved over the doors of confessionals in the churches as a sign of secrecy.

To early Christian mystics, the white rose associated purity and divine love with the Virgin Mary. According to tradition, the Virgin appeared to Saint Dominic wearing a string of roses, which led to the first rosary being made, from 165 dried, carefully rolled up rose petals. By the twelfth century, Rosa Galilea was grown in the Christian 'Marian' gardens, planted only with red roses. The symbol of purity was no longer appropriate as man had 'fallen'. Although the five petals were thought of as the five wounds of Christ, the 'gnosis' or ancient wisdom was deliberately buried as part of the Church's desire to become the only intermediary between man and God. The rose as a symbol went into decline as a result.

Each wild rose petal forms a perfect heart shape. The two sides of the petal represent not only the two chambers of the heart, but also the two worlds (above and below) of cosmic extremes. The breath that unites them pumps the blood around the body in a figure of eight, the infinity symbol, creating a dance between the oxygenated and deoxygenated blood. This symbol also connects the individual soul with the cosmos, and was found to be the way the energy was flowing through the chakras and the higher chakras after the crown, crossing at Strata Florida. Saint Bernard of Clairvaux (founder of the Cistercians), had his monasteries all dedicated to women. There were twelve feminine houses plus Strata Florida, making thirteen in all, the number that begins a new, higher spiral. This heart chakra of Wales was intended as a Druidic heart link to the esoteric.

At the Druidic ceremonies long before the abbey was built the most likely flowers for the 'covering of flowers' would have been the wild rose. There is a wild red rose bush in the abbey car park. Does it come from the time when the initiation pit was used by them?

The pattern of the rose coming into our dreams means that we are beginning to acknowledge the spiritual aspects of our country. Now the lost knowledge is beginning to unfold and the rose emblem of the Mother is merging with the mother country. The heart chakra for all of this, as the ancients knew well, is Strata Florida. Mary and Joseph of Arimathea knew this too, which is why they came here, guided by the crystal in Carmarthen Bay.

The Druids were the Magi of the Britons

They taught an awareness of the cosmic Christ consciousness before the Master Jesus was born. They carried the burden of high priest, king and prophet. When Jesus came to Britain, he studied at the Druidic branch of the ancient schools of the universal ageless wisdoms on Anglesey.

The Origin of Christian Monasteries in the Deserts of Syria and Egypt

Some Christian priests retreated to the desert to live the contemplative life. Their aim was to recreate paradise on Earth by reunifying the body and the spirit, which they believed had become separated. Through techniques that brought the mind, body and spirit into realignment, they strove to re-establish the human body as a point of contact between heaven and Earth. This would have been done through spiritual discipline, meditation and an understanding of the chakra system and the alignment of the subtle bodies. They would have sought to develop the celestial body through the awakening of both the *pingala* and *kundalini* energies, which rise up the spine allowing the person to become surrounded in a 'light body'. This was seen by those with clairvoyant vision as a fountain of light which flows from the crown chakra in three separate streams or feathers, and is the meaning behind the symbol of the Prince of Wales's feathers, and the fleur-de-lys. If this seems familiar to you, it is because this teaching and spiritual practice was reintroduced to the Western world in the twentieth century. As the saying goes, 'There is nothing new under the sun!'

Saint Paul of Thebes (died 314) and Saint Anthony (died 356) both believed that the fallen state of humanity was no more than an aberration from what is the natural state of grace. They taught that once this grace was restored humans could regain their true condition as the image of God, in harmony with all creation. Man was made in the image of God. Once this had taken place, the separation between the physical world and the spiritual world would be at an end, and the Kingdom of God would be here on Earth, and in Heaven.

So, this was the teaching of the Celtic Church. Nature is the manifestation of God's creative power and love. This teaching and philosophy was very similar, if not the same, as the philosophy of the Druids, who were familiar with the Copts of Egypt and the ancient mystery schools. Celtic Christian intellectuals recognised that humans were a part of the whole. Saint Ninian taught that the aim of Christian study is to 'see in each herb and small animal, every bird and beast, each man and woman, the eternal Word of God'.[14]

The Church fathers delved into mythology in order to reveal the beginnings of the Gospels. Saint Augustine made Hermes Trismegistrus, an Egyptian priest identified with the god Thoth, whose writings were believed to contain the remaining ancient wisdoms, a descendant of God. But although he admired him, he rejected the magic revealed in his work, and Clement of Alexandria liked to compare Hermes's Logos with the Christ Logos.

---

[14] Pennick, *The Celtic Saints*, p.55

Alexandria had been where the Egyptian teachings of the ancient tradition entered the Western world. It had scattered this wisdom until the Arabs took it up after the city was seized by them in AD 642. The early writers of the lives of the Islamic saints identified the prophet Idris with Hermes and Enoch. Idris-Hermes is sometimes compared to al-Khidr, who initiated Moses. There is a story from the first century AD, which was attributed to Apollonius, a philosopher and worker of miracles. He wrote a book in which he claimed to have found the tomb of Hermes, where he saw an old man seated on a throne, holding an emerald tablet on which was written a text. In front of him was a book explaining the secrets of the creation of beings and the knowledge of the causes of all things. The oldest known version of this story is from the sixth century and is in Arabic. The heritage left by the Egyptians and Hermes Trismegistrus is found in many religions, races and civilisations, and suggests that Egypt is indeed the mother of all traditions. It proves also that this esoteric detective story transcends time, race, nationhood and religions to point out something that we have known all along: *that we are all one.*

The Egyptian Link Between the Crown Chakra and the Heart Chakra

I first saw a dove at the crown chakra at Llyn-y-Tarw. At first it was a puzzle to find the connection between the dove and Egypt, which was found when it became known that the dove had an association with all goddesses. This includes Isis, and became true of Hathor also.

The realisation that the pit in Strata Florida was a place of initiation came after looking at photos of both it and the entrance to the initiation chamber at Kom Ombo, a temple in the Nile Valley. At Kom Ombo students of the initiates had to descend a flight of stairs and swim through an underground chamber where they were confronted by crocodiles. They then had to climb a flight of stairs on the other side. I just 'knew' that Strata Florida was modelled on this idea, thankfully without the crocodiles! I don't know how I knew this – I just *did*.

Strata Florida was a place of initiation through changing the energies of the heart chakra rather than swimming past crocodiles. I was told by the teachers in spirit that there was a connection with Egypt and when I asked for verification that this was indeed an initiation chamber, I was simply told to try it and see for myself. I have written what happened when we did, so I will leave that part of the story for now. A friend pointed out the significance of the placing of this pit within the abbey. It was in the position of the throne in Westminster Abbey at the time of the crowning of the king or queen. This surely indicates it is a place of initiation to a higher awareness.

There was found to be a connection with Hathor at both the crown and heart chakras. The temple at Kom Ombo was called 'Gold Town' by the Egyptians and was unique in being dedicated to two triads. This was because it was dedicated to the mystery schools of the right and left eyes of Horus. It has two gateways, two halls and two sanctuaries.

The northern part belonged to Isis's son, Horus. Hathor is usually recognised as the consort of Horus. Her name means 'Mansion of Horus', indicating her position as a sky goddess and supporter of Horus the sky god, whose right eye was the sun (masculine) and whose left eye was the moon (feminine).

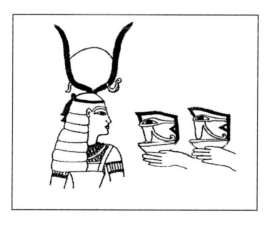

Hathor with two left eyes of Horus

But this was not the order at the temple at Kom Ombo. Here Hathor was the consort of the crocodile god Sebek, to whom the southern part of the temple was dedicated. Crocodiles were very common in this region, although Sebek's popularity throughout the whole country suggests that crocodiles were widespread. Indeed the Greeks called the city built around his temple 'Crocodilopolis'. Sebek's and Hathor's child was the moon god Khonsu. He is often depicted wearing the crescent moon with the disc of the full moon cradled within it. He was known as the god of healing. Hathor was the principal deity worshipped at the two cities which the Greeks called Aphroditopolis, since she was identified with Aphrodite, their goddess of love. Here is a link with the feminine energy of the planet Venus; the goddess of love is, through Venus, linked to the planetary alignment and the chakra system. Venus was shining over the Scilly Isles when we visited in 2002.

Hathor is a cow goddess of very ancient origin. She was shown on the column capitals of her shrines as a woman with the ears of a cow and a crown formed of cow's horns supporting the sun's disc. This same crown was later adopted by Isis, which means the two goddesses are often confused. One of Hathor's titles was 'Chieftainess of the West'. She was seen as guardian of the tree which offered shade and refreshment to the deceased as they journeyed from this world to the next. This tree was an important emblem of this goddess. The kingdom of the dead was called 'Land of the Western Ones' because the entry to the underworld was thought to be on the western horizon, where the sun sets. This idea of the west as the land of the dead plays an important role in Welsh stories, and was a part of the Druidic tradition. As 'Mistress of Heaven', Hathor was seen as the 'Celestial Cow' whose four legs were supports of the vault of heaven and whose star-spangled belly was the sky itself. She was the mother goddess who was particularly associated with the king.

At the Temple of Deir el Bahri in Luxor, Hathor is shown as the heavenly cow suckling the pharaoh. She was the daughter of the sun god and the goddess who protected women in pregnancy and childbirth. She was the goddess of love, the Egyptian equivalent of Aphrodite and Venus. She is the ancient cow goddess associated with the lake known as the Lake of the Bull. She is also the protector of women and feminine energy.

The Egyptian mystery schools were named after the eyes of Horus, the Right Eye teaching the mysteries associated with the masculine energies and the Left Eye teaching about the feminine energies. Students were taught for twelve years in each. The Druids studied for twenty (moon) years before they became initiates. There is a connecting link between these two peoples. When in the school of the Left Eye the students of the mystery schools explored the feminine pathway of emotions, sexual energy, birth, death and rebirth, and everything that was not of a strictly logical nature. They considered it vital that the emotion of fear should be overcome, and this was the reason for the crocodile initiation. Fear keeps mankind in chains. The Druids also believed this, and used this awareness in their initiations. It is something which modern mankind needs to address.

The goddess of the midnight sky, Hathor, had many titles, and was honoured in many ways with many annual festivals. The most important of these was the 'festival of the beautiful embrace' when her statue was taken on the Nile to Edfu to visit the statue of her consort Horus.

The 'Lady of Turquoise' was one of Hathor's lesser-known titles. The Egyptians often used blue and turquoise stones in their beautiful jewellery. Apparently, Australian Aborigine people have said that the Egyptians' planetary task was to work with crystals, so their special qualities were known to them. Turquoise brings the blue of Father Sky down to the Earth, mixing the energies of the heavens with the Mother Earth consciousness, symbolising the return of the wisdom of the heavens to the Earth plane. It is a stone of water, wind, fire and earth energies, bringing with it the marriage of Earth and sky. It reunites the dualism of light and dark, male and female, body and spirit – healing the queen and reuniting her with the king. Turquoise is a master healer; it strengthens and aligns all chakras, meridians and subtle bodies. It works with the throat chakra in particular and is good for communication. As well as bringing energies to a higher level, it can also be used for grounding and protection. Hathor was the goddess of love and this stone is said to stimulate romantic love. It was also used in ancient times for the healing of the eyes and for cataracts. Hathor was said to have healed Horus's eye after one of his fights with Seth, and, as pointed out, her son was the god of healing.

Hathor, an Egyptian goddess with cow's ears

Her festivals were a time of celebration, of joy, beauty, dancing and music. The people celebrated her with dance, grace and beauty. Her sacred dancers were for both private funerals and for pharaonic state rites. They were performed to evoke spiritual and cosmic principles to honour the divine. The *ka* was nourished by beauty expressed through sacred sound, gesture and movement, and as expressions of the divine they had a secret power. The goddess could bestow through her priestesses the blessings of life and happiness on her people.

'Pythagoras was likewise of the opinion that music, if properly used, greatly contributed to health.'[15] Iamblicus, his biographer, stated that Pythagoras studied at the Temple of Heliopolis for twenty-two years. The Egyptians believed that both sound and movement had healing effects at emotional, mental and spiritual levels. The experts of this type of healing were the priestesses of Hathor who held important positions throughout their temples.

The sacred dance, the Paneurhythm, originated in Hathor's temples. Hathor was the Lady of Dance and the Queen of Happiness. She was known as the Mistress of the Western Desert, Lady of the West (the Land of the Dead), where she gave a banquet for the departed and offered them flowers and a beaded necklace. She was also Mistress of the Sycamore, the tree dedicated to her, and she was thought of as a living tree in a land where trees were rare. She was a goddess of the Old Kingdom, a very ancient presence, seen originally as a wild cow of the marshy delta, and shown with stars on the end of her horns, ears and forehead. In later times she was depicted as a woman with a cow's head, or as a woman with cow's ears. She was Mistress of the Sky, Queen of the Stars, Ruler over Sirius, the Great One who makes the Nile flood, the Eye of Ra, Queen of the Gods and Lady of the Sacred Land.

Perhaps the importance of her cult is shown in the belief of the pharaoh that he was her eldest son, and it was only through her divine milk that the young prince may become a true king. Most importantly, though, for this story, she was the feminine aspect of the bull, and a vision of her appeared before me as I stood on the place where the statue appeared in the photo by the lake. The Egyptian star-watchers would have found that, circa 7300 BC, the stars of Orion rose, after becoming invisible for two months, just before sunrise at the spring equinox. But by 6700 BC at latitude twenty-five degrees north, all of Orion's stars had ceased to rise at the equinox, whereas further north this would have happened centuries earlier. So after this date the herald of the new year's sun would have been Aldebran, the eye of the bull in the constellation of Taurus. Does this not serve to emphasise

---

[15] See Hilary Wilson, *Understanding Hieroglyphs*, 1999 for more information on Hathor.

the importance of the bull in the lives of the ancients, and also the importance of the feminine aspects of the cow goddess?

Egypt – The Mother of all Traditions

The link with Egypt is a strong and continuous line. It flows from my first encounter with Merlin, the sighting of Hathor, and the discovery of the initiation pit at Strata Florida with its connection to the Temple of Kom Ombo. There then followed a link with Joseph, Egypt and the sacred bull. The tradition was continued by the Druids and priests of Ancient Britain, with their twenty years of initiation into spiritual practices.

There is a traceable link from the desert monk Saint Anthony of Egypt to Saint David, Saint Antwn of Llansteffan, and Saint Declan of Ardmore in Ireland, leading to the understanding that Celtic Christianity was totally different from that presented by the Roman Catholic Church. The ancient secret knowledge was forced underground, hidden, secret, but kept alive by those Celtic Christian priests and saints, the bardic tradition of singers, poets and storytellers in *The Mabinogion*, and many other books. It was passed on by the Knights of Saint John, the Freemasons and the Rosicrucians, until it was time for the stories to be told.

All of this may have begun in Egypt with a priest named Hermes Trismegistrus, and some mysterious texts attributed to him. Egyptian esotericism was taught in its mystery schools, which acted as both universities and monasteries, and were the guardians of its wisdom.

The great sages of Ancient Greece obtained their knowledge from their Egyptian teachers, and were initiated into Egyptian mysteries. Some Druids were initiates at these temples as well. Thales brought back Egyptian geometry to Greece, and Plato, who was there for three years, brought back stories of Atlantis. Pythagoras, after spending twenty-two years in Heliopolis, settled in Croton, Italy, where he continued to teach as he had done in Egypt. While in Egypt they learned science, astronomy, medicine, philosophy, magic and esoteric science, as they gradually appropriated their hosts' heroes and gods. The god Hermes was provided with winged sandals and before long, Thoth and

Hermes were thought to be one and the same.

Accelerated assimilation of Egyptian culture began in 333 BC, with the conquest of Egypt by Alexander. The city of Alexandria became the crossroads of Egyptian, Jewish, Greek and Christian cultures, and was the intellectual centre of the eastern Mediterranean. Its great library gathered all known knowledge of the world in its 50,000 volumes.

In 30 BC Alexandria became the capital of the Roman province of Egypt, so that Rome rapidly adopted Egypt and its cults. Hermes became Mercury, the messenger of the gods.

In the third century AD, Egypt began to fade away before the advance of Christianity. It was then that the Egyptians abandoned hieroglyphs and adopted the Coptic script, and at the same time adapted the secret knowledge of the pharaohs to Christianity. In AD 387, Theophilus of Alexandria destroyed the Egyptian temples, but they continued to be used up to the sixth century.

Solar Plexus Chakra, Tregaron Bog

Tregaron Bog

Tregaron Bog and the River Teifi
(Photo by Robert Wingfield)

What would the world be once bereft
of wet and of wildness?
Let them be left,
O Let them be left,
wildness and wet;
Long live the weeds and the wilderness yet.

Gerard Manley Hopkins
1844–1889

The Welsh name for Tregaron Bog is Cors Caron (Bog of Saint Caron). Bogs are semi-swampy habitats that harbour a rich diversity of plant and insect life, thus containing the fresh new energy of potential, alive with an abundance of elemental energies. There is a special connection with the Earth Mother, with the capacity for creating new life and for nurturing. Thus bogs contain wisdom, fresh energy and new beginnings, all in a wide-open space, teaching us to live with an open mind and heart.

As a solar plexus chakra, Tregaron Bog is the place for digesting energies and re-energising the land, like a giant stomach, moving, breathing, and very much alive. The bog is home to the red kite, buzzard, sparrowhawk, peregrine falcon and a vast number of other birds, animals and plants. The ground is a curious red colour, resembling somewhat the soil of Herefordshire, with trees and grasses and flowers growing in it.

The Town of Tregaron

As a solar plexus chakra, Tregaron is the centre of the chakra system but I was unprepared for the extraordinary sense of 'centre' which I felt on this visit. It almost felt as if Tregaron was the pivot of the world! It is very much connected to the heart chakra, and you should visit Tregaron Bog first in order to balance your energy before going on to Strata Florida. On a physical level it is a focus for Welsh culture and language. Some Welsh gold can be found here (which seems very appropriate). In her gold centre and art gallery in Tregaron, Rhiannon designs and makes beautiful gold and silver jewellery using Celtic art, history and culture as her inspiration. It is the chakra most associated with the Celtic horse goddess Rhiannon, and twice a year it becomes the meeting place for Europe's international trotting races.

One of its most famous sons was the Welsh Robin Hood, Twm Sion Cati, who was pardoned by Queen Elizabeth I in 1559, and went on to become the steward of the lordship of Caron in 1601. He was in fact a respectable gentleman, landlord and antiquary, well known for his talent as a herald or genealogist. Tregaron is Welsh to the very core of its being.

Saint Caron's Bog

This is one of the finest examples of the rare raised bogs of Europe, and is watched over by the Nature Conservancy Council. Covering a staggering 822 hectares, it was created at the end of the Ice Age. A lake was formed and over the last 10,000 years the peat that has accumulated has formed a raised dome to a level of ten metres above the original level of the water. It is possible that a moraine-dammed lake from the last Ice Age could have covered the whole valley and reached as far as Strata Florida. I was told in meditation that the land that the Strata Florida had been built on had been an island in the past. The River Teifi flows through the bog, and the energy is calming and peaceful, with an ancient, timeless feeling. It made my solar plexus chakra wobble, an uncomfortable feeling, but very fitting.

There is evidence that people did live in this area in pre-Celtic times, i.e. before c. 500 BC. Between 2600 and 2500 BC, the Bronze Age people lived here and farmed this land, leaving burial cairns at Carn Ffur and Castell Rhyfel. The weather became wetter and colder between 850 and 650 BC, and Tregaron Bog grew considerably, so that when the weather improved again around 400 BC, trees were cut down around the bog to allow animals to graze. The Celts ploughed the fields and established their hill forts. The church stands on a hillock that was supposed to cover the grave of Saint Caron. Before this, it is believed to have been the site of a Druidic circle. It has an aura of peace here. There is a holy well, Ffynnon Garon, which local people visited on Saint Caron's Day (16 March). No one seems to know who Saint Caron was; he might have been one of the priest-kings of old.

The Celtic people revered rivers, lakes, pools, springs and wells. They believed they were portals to the other world, and were sacred to the goddess Brighid. If votive offerings were made to her, it was believed that she could grant wishes and heal the sick. After their arrival in Britain the Romans began to venerate her, building well-shrines and throwing coins into the water. When the country was Christianised, the wells were adopted as Catholic healing shrines and the early Christian churches were built near them. These wells were, in fact, simply natural springs with a stone wall built around them to protect them. We still throw coins into wells today.

MEDITATION ON THE ENERGIES OF TREGARON BOG

'Where there is a bog, there is a tremendous transference of energy. The whole of the past and present life of this area is held in this cup or basin.

'This has been protected by the inhabitants for thousands of your years. We would put forward the idea that it is a sacred place, a crucible of the planet's energies. It is a centre of power, but more importantly, it is a centre for release, the release of previous energies held in the land of Britain. This energy

is an upthrust of power into the cosmos. This is why it is protected by a golden dragon of elemental energies. This form is very much an Earth form. It protects the land, and it has had help from the people over the centuries. Celtic people's awareness of dragons was exactly this – an awareness of the Earth's elemental protection. Dragons do exist in the etheric realms. This particular elemental is very wise. They are not always so. This is the reason for its golden colour. It also links with, and protects, the heart chakra of the land of Wales. It is very ancient and was set up as a guardian a very long time ago. It will respond to a sense of respect and reverence. Acknowledge its presence, let it know that you are aware of it. Its mission is about to be fulfilled when the Golden Age comes into being. It will not be needed any more but its service to the planet will always be remembered on the ether.'

The golden dragon of Tregaron Bog

SO WHAT EXACTLY IS A DRAGON?

While standing on the bridge called Pont Einon on the A485 where the River Teifi exits the bog, it is possible to see the whole of the valley before you. The river can be seen making its lazy way through, like a shining path. There is a sense of enormous primordial energy, as if the elemental energy of this place were so strong that it had risen into the air and was hovering over this huge bog with its wings outstretched to protect it. Its essence is benign.

I tried to allow this energy to come through in visual form, as a shape and colour. Gradually, in my awareness, it formed into a golden dragon. It also seemed to be protecting Strata Florida, which is further up the valley. Gold is the colour of wisdom and yellow is the colour of the solar plexus chakra, the sun centre. It would seem that shamans and people who are aware of the spirit of the land became aware of an Earth guardian spirit, and this guardian could be in dragon form. We know that Merlin could see them and so could the Celts.

It is a traditional idea that these dragons guard treasure, but in this case the treasure is the land itself. On a visit to Carmarthen we stopped at the bog to bring in the Fountain Meditation that we use for sacred sites. I saw the dragon and sent him love and light. To my amazement he turned his head sharply, exclaiming, 'Who said that?' I was so surprised that I did not mention what I had seen until we reached Carmarthen.

It is interesting to realise that the people of Tregaron refused to sell the peat commercially, but they did use it for themselves. The children attending the Methodist school were required to bring a clod of peat on Mondays to keep the room warm.[1]

---

[1] J L Davies, D P Kirby, W J Lewis and E Jones, *Tregaron, A Journey Through Time*, Curiad Caron

The Druid Path of Peace and the Link with the United Nations

The statue of Henry Richard in Tregaron

In the centre of this little market town is a statue to its most famous son, Henry Richard, who was born in Tregaron in 1820. He became well known for his belief in peace through negotiation, and was instrumental in founding the League of Nations.

The ideas behind this organisation later evolved into the United Nations. His work was supported by David Davies, also from Mid Wales, who was born in 1818 at Llandinam, near Newtown. He was the founding financier for the University of Wales at Aberystwyth. His son, also named David Davies, began a tireless campaign for peace when he founded the world's first chair of international politics at the university. This was known as the Woodrow Wilson Chair, which laid particular emphasis on the promotion of peace and was designed to increase the under-standing of the League of Nations. The UN is subject to the same human frailties as governments and each one of us, but its inspiration and vision, its hope for the future, is surely a part of the higher spiritual self of us all.

When touching the extraordinary energy of this place, it seems entirely appropriate that the establishing of a centre for peace and cooperation between nations should begin here. It is here that the energy of the Druids with their special emphasis on peace is very strong, strong enough to influence the living.

A MEDITATION TO SEND THE LIGHT TO THE UNITED NATIONS

There is a meditation room in the headquarters of the United Nations building in New York. It is here that all may find a place for quiet communication with the highest spiritual power, irre-spective of their beliefs. In the middle of the room is a block of iron – like an altar – which is lit from above by a shaft of light, symbolising the light from on high that gives light and enlight-enment to our world. It is to this room that we may all travel, in thought and mind, to join with all those who are, with thought and prayer, providing a channel for that light to reach down and guide the affairs of those who are seeking to help mankind.

THE MEDITATION

After relaxing the body, centre the mind. Enter the meditation room in thought and stand for a moment in silence. Imagine it as the central point of the councils of the world.

Visualise the room, with its symbolic altar in the middle and the shaft of light streaming steadily from on high. See this light reaching out to illuminate the minds of each single member of the assembly, each one working in a place of responsibility. Hold this thought; see the light kindling in them forces of goodwill and light. Send your goodwill and light, asking that wisdom and compassion may illuminate them in their work. Visualise light radiating out from this place, reaching every country, person, place of conflict, crisis, suffering and need.

See the differences resolving, the suffering lightening, the needs being met, the conflict dying away – hold this in mind.

Say aloud the invocation, or one of your own if you prefer:

May the forces of light bring illumination to mankind,
May the spirit of peace be spread abroad.
May the law of harmony prevail.
May the men of goodwill everywhere meet in a spirit of cooperation.
So let it be, and let us do our part. Amen.

When we meditate in this way, we create a powerful form in the world of thought which we then earth in the material world through our affirmation and offering of ourselves in the service needed to bring it to fruition.

Michael Eastcott, 'The Silent Faith'
in Dr Ian Pearce, *The Gate of Healing*,
Jersey, Spearman, 1983

The Druid Path of Peace

The Druids had great power and privilege, greater than any hierarchy since. For this, they had to make personal sacrifices and carried great responsibilities. They were not allowed to carry weapons, even for their own protection. They carried only their staffs, which were their badges of office. Sometimes these were topped by various symbols, e.g. a ram's horn.

It is sad that only one sentence of their philosophy has been preserved, but this sentence is very revealing. 'To be pious against the gods, not to do injury to anyone, and to practise bravery.'[2] So great was their aura of peace and the light of their spirit, that their

---

[2] J Pokorny, 'The Origin of Druidism', in J Matthews, *The Druid Source Book*, pp.60–73

presence on the field of battle caused the warriors to sheathe their swords, so that their differences could be settled by the Druids through arbitration. Their dedication to peace was such that every assembly began with the words '*A oes Heddwch?*' (Is there peace?) The meeting could only continue if the answer was '*Heddwch!*' (Peace!) If the answer was not peace, then they could not continue. This ceremony has its modern parallel in the Chairing of the Bard at the National Eisteddfod of Wales. A sheathed sword is held up before the audience and the question is asked, '*A oes heddwch?*' The audience shout back, '*Heddwch!*' This must be asked and replied to three times before the bard can be chaired.

This has always been a ceremony that has a deep significance for me, although I didn't understand why in the past. I now know that it was something which vibrated on the spirit within myself with an ancient recognition. It would seem that all Druidical ceremonies should begin with the question 'Is there peace?'

> *And did those feet in ancient time,*
> *walk upon England's mountains green?*

In William Blake's address to the Jews (a section of the poem, 'Jerusalem'), he informed them that all their priestly traditions had come from the Druids, and that heavenly Jerusalem would descend to Earth in England (and Wales, and Scotland and Ireland, I might add!). His authority for this was the eighteenth-century Druid revivalist William Stukely, who wrote *Abury* in 1743.

This peace ceremony can be seen on Sky TV, on S4C, every summer at the National Eisteddfod, and it was Lord Rhys who convened the first ever National Eisteddfod. It was the custom of Welsh princes to send their sons away to be taught by the Druids, and this custom was continued long after the Druids had gone. They were sent to centres of spirituality and culture. This made sure that the Welsh princes were not just rulers, but also spiritual people, with a great interest in poetry, music, stories and dance. This is what the eisteddfodau are all about.

What the Druids Did for Us[3]

It is becoming increasingly apparent as more discoveries are being made that the Celtic people were among the most highly educated and cultured people of classical times. So much so that Rome sought to learn some of their skills, such as enamelling and glass-making. One of their skills was making long, straight highways that were wrongly attributed to the Roman invaders. Before the invasion, Britain prospered from international trade. The Celts were well known for their metal-working skills, their intricate gold jewellery and their iron agricultural machinery and chariots. Contrary to popular belief, the mines were not Roman but Celtic, which were exploited thousands of years before the arrival of the Romans. These mines produced copper, iron, lead, silver and gold. The agricultural system was so advanced that Britain exported corn to the rest of Western Europe. There were sheep and cattle in abundance, so much so that British wool and cloth were exported to Rome, Greece and Judaic areas. Archaeological excavations of Masada have revealed evidence of Celtic cloth. This is relevant to this story because it provides evidence of a link in trade between the Celts and the Jews. Celtic society was highly civilised. The Celts were well known for their racial tolerance, together with their hospitality (hospitality is a strong ethic in Wales today).

They were deeply religious and were ruled over by a Druid culture. In Britain at that time there were forty Celtic tribes, which were subject to a system of oral law. This system, known as Brehon Laws, is considered to be comparable to those of any other great civilisation.

The ancient initiates, such as the Druids, guided their peoples as priest-kings, mediating between man and the gods to the benefit of all. The early Hebrew prophets and the Essenes have a great deal in common with the beliefs and practices of the Druids, which suggests a possible common racial origin.

Druid society held that peace, liberty and the rights of the individual were protected by law and their religion. The Druids

---

[3] To understand why Master Jesus was attracted to the Druid tradition and was believed to have come to Britain, please see *Jesus, the Master Builder*, by Gordon Strachan, p.51.

presided over the spiritual and political lives of the Celtic people and were their law-givers and judges. They themselves were supervised by the arch-druid, the supreme authority. The knowledge of the sophisticated Druids included philosophy, mathematics, sacred geometry, medicine, surgery, healing, law-giving, poetry, oratory and astronomy. All of this was taught to their students, of whom I was one.

Julius Caesar said of the Druids in Gaul, 'Of the two classes mentioned, one consists of Druids, the other of knights. The former are concerned with divine worship…'

'The cardinal doctrine which they seek to teach is that souls do not die, but after death pass from one life to another; and this belief, because the fear of death is thereby cast aside, they hold to be the greatest incentive to valour.'[4] The Romans were afraid of the warriors' military skills and their courage in battle.

When I first met Merlin at the crown chakra, he told me that I had been a pupil of his in the 'old time'. I was told that I was one of their pupils by the Druid at the third eye chakra, and I am aware of a past life as a Druid on Anglesey. I have no recollection of their teaching but I did have a vision of myself as a Druid, wearing white, and carrying a trident. The trident puzzled me, but I now believe it is the Celtic symbol of Brighid, the triple goddess. In retrospect, I must have known about the Welsh chakras and the crystalline grid in a former life. I also had a past-life experience at Castell Henllys at the Bronze Age village there.

Although this is a thirteen-chakra system, all but one of the seven chakras below the crown are in Wales. The Druids understood very well that just as their bodies had seven chakras so did the body of the Earth itself. Wherever these powerful points occurred on the landscape, they planted sacred groves of oak where they taught their novices. The pathway to illumination began at the base chakra in Bryher and led step by step, always under the instruction of an initiate, to the crown chakra at Llyn-y-Tarw. The Druids of this system also revered the Eternal Feminine, which took the form of their goddess Brighid who was served by her priestesses, the Daughters of the Moon. They were given this title not because they

---

[4] Gaius Julius Caesar, *The Gallic War*, translated by H J Edwards, Loeb, 1917, VI,13–14

worshipped the moon, but in order to show that they were the priestesses of the feminine energy. This goddess gave her name to Britannia and to Britain, and her symbol was the trident because she was the triple goddess. All along this chakra line there were groves and temples dedicated to Brighid and the divine feminine. There was one on Bryher, one at Strata Florida and one at Llyn-y-Tarw. These were visited by Mary, the mother of Jesus, when she came to this country at a later date, when she also followed the pathway of the divine feminine.

The Druids were Greek Pythagoreans. They used the Greek alphabet and mathematics and there was a relationship between them and the Greek world. They spoke Greek, as did some educated Jews, so this may be the language in which they communicated with the Jewish refugees from the Holy Land. Pythagoras believed that the universe could be explained through numbers. He also believed in the immortality of the soul. Clement of Alexandria claimed that Pythagoras learnt his philosophy from the barbarians, among whom were classed the Druids. He wrote:

> Thus philosophy, a science of the highest utility flourished in antiquity among the barbarians, shedding its light over the nations. And afterwards it came to Greece. First in its ranks were the prophets of the Egyptians; and the Chaldeans among the Assyrians; and the Druids among the Gauls; and the Shamans among the Bactrians; and the philosophers of the Celts; and the Magi of the Persians...[5]

This testified to a universal wisdom that pre-dated Pythagoras. It also underlines one of the reasons why members of the Holy Family came to Britain, because they would be living among a people dominated by the highest and purest of ideals, and speaking a language in which they could make themselves understood. Caesar said of the Druid religion that it 'forbids them to commit their teachings to writing', which obviously makes the understanding of their culture almost impossible. None of Pythagoras's works survived either. Caesar also said, 'Besides this, they have many discussions as touching the stars and their movements, the size of the

---

[5] *The Stromata, Or Miscellanies*, www.earlychristianwritings.com/clement.html

universe and the Earth, the order of nature, the strength and powers of the immortal gods, and hand down their law to the young men.'[6] To sum up the Druidical training, it was about natural philosophy and natural science and its relationship to mankind.

How far back in history all of this takes us is unclear, but there was a continuity of culture flowing between the Neolithic and Bronze Ages and the Celts, because the stone circles and mega-liths pre-date the Celtic civilisation by at least 1,000 years. None of these alignments could have been built without the ancestors' considerable knowledge of maths and astrology. The latest research tells us that Britain once had a national network of megalithic observatories at different locations for varying astrological purposes. Most of these prehistoric sites, from Skara Brae in Orkney down to the coast of Brittany, were constructed using a standard measurement, the megalithic yard, equal to 82.96656 cm. Newgrange in Ireland is 1,000 years older than the Great Pyramid in Egypt, and was built using this measurement.[7]

The Druidic Law

There were three types of people who had the right to public maintenance; they were the old, babies and foreigners who could not speak the British language. (A nation should be judged by how it treats its old, its young and its poor.)

There were three groups of people who could not carry weapons. They were judges, priests and bards. Because they were bound to God and keeping to His peace, they were never to carry arms.

Every British citizen was required to have legally attended the worship of God, the courts of law and to fight for their country should the need arise.

Every British citizen had the right to five acres of land, and the protection of the law (men at twenty-one years of age and women on their marriage).

All British citizens had the right to have access to, and use of, the forest, the right of hunting and any unworked mine.

There were three tests of civil liberty: equal rights, equal taxes

---

[6] Caesar, op. cit.
[7] See Robin Heath and John Mitchell, *The Measure of Albion*

and the freedom to come and go at will.

When tribes needed to unite as nations the Celts considered that sameness of laws, rights and language were indispensable. These laws were known as the Brehon Laws.

This then, is our inheritance: freedom, justice and equal rights. This is something of which their inheritors, the present inhabitants of these islands, can be proud. We should never forget that their tradition of free speech stems from their practice of holding their meetings in the open air, 'in the face of the sun and the eye of the light'. As we learn more about our ancestors we will learn to respect them, which will lead us to respect our ancient heritage and in turn to respect ourselves. We are the inheritors of this enlightened spiritual tradition.

Blessing of the Druidic Circle

This is the blessing used by the Gorsedd at the National Eisteddfod, and is a very ancient Welsh prayer.

> *Grant, O God, Thy Protection,*
> *And in protection, strength,*
> *And in strength, understanding,*
> *And in understanding, perception of justice,*
> *And in perception of justice, the love of it,*
> *And in the love of it, the love of all Life,*
> *And in all Life, to love God,*
> *God, and all goodness.*

> Dyro, Dduw, dy nawdd;
> Ac yn nawdd, nerth;
> Ac yn nerth, deall;
> Ac yn neall, gwybod;
> Ac yn wybod, gwybod y cyfiawn;
> Ac yng ngwybod y cyfiawn, ei garu;
> Ac o garu, caru bob hanfod;
> Ac ym mhob hanfod, caru Duw;
> Duw, a phob daioni.

Welsh translation by Bethan Lloyd

Perception of justice translates from Welsh as 'knowing the holy order of things'. The word for Druid in the Welsh language is *derwydd*, which comes from the word *derwen*, meaning oak tree. Roughly translated it means 'man of the oak tree'. Welsh is claimed to be Europe's oldest living language.

The Welsh alphabet is not the same as the English one. There is no letter 'v'; instead, there is a letter 'f' which is pronounced like the English 'v'. (Thus Avalon should be spelt Afalon – *afal* is the Welsh word for apple and Avalon is sometimes described as the Isle of Apples.)

For the sound 'f', 'ff' is used, as in the Christian name Ffion.

There is no 'k'; 'c' is used instead.

There is no 'q'.

There is no 'x'; the sound is spelt 'sc', thus box is *bosc*.

The use of the circumflex makes vowels long, e.g. Môna (as in the Christian name Mona); without it, it is pronounced Mon as in Monmouth.

Connections to the Sacral Chakra

A Message from the Daughters of the Moon at the Landscape Temple of the Zodiac at Pumpsaint

'We are here with you today for a purpose, and that purpose is the discovery of the past, the past of the sacred Pathway of the Beloved. You see, there are many, many ways in which discoveries can be made, and you have followed many already.'

I asked if some were in *The Mabinogion*.

'You may follow clues in this work; it is a part of the psyche of people the world over, but these ancient stories are really about the discovery of self.'

I asked whether I would be given some help with the clues.

'We will give you more clues when you are there.'

I found myself on top of a hill. The grass was very green and there was a golden circle on the grass in front of me. I knew that I must step into this circle, which represented the Landscape Temple, Pumpsaint.

'Star children, that was what they were. Children of the Pleiades. Priestesses were taking care of the temple and they are still there. They are waiting for your visit. They have waited a long time to be recognised.

'You carry with you the link with other star children, other priestesses. We are Taurean: we are the beginning, we are a part of a gigantic wheel (zodiac). The wheel has come full turning. We are there and we await a visitor from the present. This is about wheels within wheels. This is our main sanctuary, our main temple. There was a zodiac outreaching from this centre of our sanctuary that linked us with the stars and our starry guiding lights. We are overjoyed that contact has been made. This is about coming full circle into the present.'

I asked them what they did.

'We harmonised – we facilitated communication. We helped people to live in peace and prosperity with the energies which you have forgotten but you are beginning to remember. This memory, the memory of us, is within the Earth's memory and as the Earth reawakens to it, we can begin to function on the etheric levels as we once did on the physical Earth.'

The memory they describe here is contained in the crystal structure of the Earth.

'*Starlight, moonlight, balance and harmony.*
Energies lifting, energies soaring.
Light transforming, spirits rising
Life transforming.
Earth is rising,
Planet is birthing.
All is well.'

The Welsh Temple of the Zodiac

This is south-east of the town of Lampeter, between the rivers Teifi and Towi. The hills fall into a basin sloping towards the south, and here, in very ancient times, a temple of the zodiac was built. Its centre is one-tenth of a mile south-west of Ffarmers. Just below Ffarmers are two interesting place names opposite each other. One is Bryn-Brân (hill of Brân) and Ffaldybrenin (fold of the king).

In the very centre of the circle, there is an area bounded by the River Twrch in the east and now surrounded by the main road to Lampeter and the roads converging on Ffarmers. One road crosses the side of the hill that was the sacred mound of the sanctuary. In the water-sodden meadow that lies between the hill and the river, there is an embankment shaped like a horseshoe with the opening facing west. This mound and meadow are the site of the outer sanctuary used for general worship. Immediately to the south is another similar hill, the site of the inner sanctuary used for worship by initiates. Farm buildings now cover this site, but it has a sense of peace.

Travelling north along Sarn Helen, there is a field to the left of the road where there is a partly excavated mound known locally as Carreg-y-Bwci (*bwci* means bogeyman or ghost). It is an old burial mound with a large stone fifteen feet long lying on top. This stone remains there because it has a bad reputation. One farmer had thoughts of breaking it up for boundary stones. 'No sooner had I got out my tools than there was a violent thunderstorm, the worst I had ever known. I ran for my life, but it followed me all the way home. Three men have been killed there by lightning.'[1] Around it are a number of stones in no definite order, but a few suggest the outline of a circle. On a crest of the hill, a parallel line of stones was found eighteen feet apart, only the tips being visible. This looks like an avenue of stones leading to the mound, although one end seems to be blocked by some of them falling. This mound or circle is in direct line with the inner and outer sanctuaries.

In 1947 the historian Lewis Edwards suggested that each sign

---

[1] Lewis Edwards, 'The Pumpsaint Temple of the Stars', 1947

of the zodiac may have had its own temple. Cairns and tumuli situated on the other signs may prove to be burial places which were once stone circles, chosen for important burials because of the sacredness of the sites. The land to the north of the temple centring on Llandewi-Brefi is known as the Sanctuary of Saint David. The church of Llan-y-Crwys is dedicated to this saint, and means the Church of the Crosses (*crwys* being the plural of *croes* – cross). Tradition has it that this church has been named after the Stone of the Three Crosses, which once stood on the boundary between Cardiganshire and Carmarthenshire. In Welsh, this could be interpreted as the Stone of the Three-armed Cross, a possible description of a tau T-shaped cross.

There was once a wattle-and-daub church close to Hirfaen, with a stone paving which led from the standing stone at Hirfaen to this church. In this churchyard, there was a long oblong stone with square edges, with three small incised crosses within circles, one at the centre and the others on each side.

This description is based on a drawing of the stone. The church was Saint David's, the original Llan-y-Crwys. Later, this was rebuilt at a more convenient site near Ffarmers. This stone was moved and is now believed to be in Golden Grove. Wherever its whereabouts, it deserves great care and consideration. When it was moved, the workmen were disturbed by its characteristics. They said it was an 'echo stone'. There is another stone that was used as a footbridge over the stream below the farm of Allt Dewi (Hill of David). It is most probable that this stone came from the sign of the ram at Allt Dewi. Another story said it came from Llandewi Brefi, again linking with Saint David. There is a 'Field of the Cross' below Pumpsaint, so there were once three crosses. *Pump* is Welsh for five. There were five saints, who rested here on a pilgrimage to Saint David's. In 1966 Mrs Williams of Pant-y-Maen, an active old lady of eighty-five, said that the correct name of the Hirfaen Stone was 'Hirfaen Gundun Gwyn', who slew the seneschal of Arthur the Great.

According to Lewis Edwards, the headmaster of Ffarmers School said that Cwndwn Gwyn is the name of the farm nearby, and whose original name was Coed tir Mynach (Wood of the Monk's Land). In the tale of Culhwch and Olwen from *The*

Mabinogion, we read, 'Gwyddawg killed Garanwyn son of Cei'[2] (there is no 'K' in the Welsh language; 'Cei' is pronounced 'Kay'). 'Garanwyn' could sound a bit like 'Gundun gwyn' 1,500 years later. Could this stone be named after the son of Cei, which would prove a link with Arthur?

Culhwch has a 'Jason and the Golden Fleece' role, with a list of seemingly impossible tasks, all of which he is to perform in the process of winning the daughter of his opponent. He has a staggering number of thirty-five such tasks. Only two are described in detail: the rescue of Mabon and the hunting of Twrch Trwyth. This was a dangerous and wild boar who had destroyed a fifth of Ireland. He was once a king, but because of his sins God turned him into a pig. It was Arthur and his men who took the razor and the comb from between the ears of Twrch Trwyth and gave them to Culhwch, so that he could win the hand of Olwen. The name of the river flowing through the sanctuary is Afon Twrch. Can this be the connection between the sanctuary, *The Mabinogion* and King Arthur? Twrch is a unique name for a Welsh river, because it means 'boar'. Lewis Edwards thought that King Arthur would have worshipped at the temple.

'The Knights of the Round Table were members of an esoteric community and King Arthur is intimately connected with the Temple, and it is here that they would have worshipped.'[3] The Round Table, with its seats for twelve knights, is the physical manifestation of the zodiac. As above, so below.

Have we found the Court of Brân the Blessed?

Just west of Ffarmers is a village called Faldybrenin (*brenin* means king). So this is the 'Fold of the King', where he would have stabled his horses and his animals. On an 1888 map, there is a field called Ddol y Brenin ('Meadow of the King'), and in Llanycrwys there is a Llwyn Cwrt ('Grove of the Court'). This would suggest that the court of the king was at Llanycrwys, which is already established as an important place. There is also a 'King's Park'. This king must have been an extraordinary person for his

---

[2] J Gantz (trans.), *The Mabinogion*, Penguin, 1976
[3] Lewis Edwards, op. cit.

fame to survive for so long after he had departed this life. This is where he held land, had his court and stabled his animals, and his court would have hunted in his park. Who could he be, and would we ever know?

Opposite the village on the other side of the stream is a hill named Bryn-Brân. This could be a clue, so I dowsed.

'Is the king Arthur?'

'No.'

'Is the king Brân?'

'Yes.'

'Did Brân live here?'

'No.'

This was strange. The king was Brân but he didn't live at his court. Why was this? Through dowsing with further questions, we realised that the person who was the king at that time was not called Brân. His exploits were such that the stories about him eventually entered *The Mabinogion* where he answered to the name of Brân Bendigaid ab Llŷr (Brân the Blessed, son of Llŷr), king of all Britain, whose head was buried at the White Hill in London. Just across the fields from Llyn Cwrt is a farm called Wern-fendigaid (this is on the old map) and means 'the alder trees of the Blessed One'.

In a seventeenth-century Welsh antiquarian journal, there is a fragment of an englyn[4] which was once part of a larger medieval poem. It was about the battle of Achren, and there was a man in that battle, who, unless his name were known, could not be overcome. Gwydian ap Don guessed the name of the man:

> *Sure-footed is my steed impelled by the spur;*
> *The high sprigs of alder are on thy shield;*
> *Brân thou art called, of the glittering branches.*
> *Sure-footed is my steed in the day of battle:*
> *The high sprigs of alder are in thy hand;*
> *Brân thou art by the branch thou bearest,*
> *Amaethon the Good has prevailed.*

Translated by Elen Sentier,
'Battle of the Trees', 1999

---

[4] Englyn: a type of poem

He was found out through the alder tree. In the ogham tree alphabet, alder and Brân are both written with three horizontal strokes. Since it is known that Brân is closely associated with the alder tree, and is also known as Blessed Brân, Wern Bendigaid must refer to the 'alder trees of the Blessed Brân'.

Further study of the map revealed a Cwm Brân (valley) and an Afon Brân (river) flowing through this valley, while to the south-east is the well-known town of CwmBrân. Brân was king of Britain, which, in the story of 'Branwen, Daughter of Llŷr' is known as the 'Land of the Mighty'. This story tells of the battle between the Irish and the Welsh, of the magic cauldron that brings dead men back to life, and of Brân being wounded in the foot with a poisoned spear (The Fisher King, in Chrétian's 'Story of the Grail (Percival)'). The wounded Brân asked his followers to cut off his head. 'Take my head, and carry it to the White Hill in London, and bury it there with the face turned towards France. You will be a long time on the road; you will spend seven years feasting at Harddlech [Harlech] with the Birds of Rhiannon singing to you, and the head will be as good a companion as ever it was. After, you will spend eight years at Gwales in Pemvro [Pembroke]…'[5] They buried the head in the White Hill, 'for while the head was concealed no plague came across the sea to this island'.

This is how the legend came about that as long as there were ravens at the Tower of London, it would not fall to its enemies. The ravens are Brân's birds; they are also known in association with Merlin. The word *Brân* means a raven, rook or crow in Welsh. The raven offers initiation, protection, healing and the gift of prophecy. The initiation marks the death of one thing which leads to the birth of another; in this way it offers rebirth and the deepest form of healing. The healing which it offers is a resolution of the conflict of opposites, understanding that there is light in darkness and darkness in light. It is associated with the goddess, and the 'raven knowledge' of the Druids was a gift of the goddess given to the Druid seers, so that they could see into the future and the past through the veils that divide the worlds. It is a bird of prophecy and divination that

---

[5] J Gantz, *The Mabinogion*, op. cit.

are facets of the healer's art. It has been recognised as an oracle for thousands of years. There is also a tradition that Arthur became a raven after his death, and country people respected the raven for this reason. The fortunes of the Tower ravens reached their lowest point after the Second World War when there was only one left. Tradition says that Winston Churchill arranged that young ravens from Wales and Scotland should be brought to the Tower, and in October 2003 two new ravens, Branwen and Brân took up residence. There are now nine birds.

The raven appears in some of the earliest human art in the Lascaux caves. Its gift for locating land was used by Noah in the Book of Genesis, and ancient mariners carried caged ravens as a prototype compass.

In ancient Rome, it was the most important bird for soothsayers. The Vikings held the raven to be sacred and Thor was said to be kept in touch with all of human affairs through his two ravens, Munin (memory) and Hugin (thought). They are entwined in the mythologies of all native peoples encircling the North Pole and are on the flag of the Yukon Territory in Canada. It is the world's largest songbird and the collective noun for a flock is an 'unkindness of ravens'. One of the largest flocks in the world is at Newborough Warren on the south-western tip of Anglesey. This is where the new ravens at the Tower came from, and there is an official Keeper of the Ravens at the Tower of London.

Is it possible that Brân's talking head is a crystal skull which is buried somewhere beneath the Tower of London? It could be the Celtic crystal skull and would account for the cult of the head in Celtic mythology.

The story does make it clear that Brân (or his head) was in South Wales for part of his time, and Lewis Edwards says that there is a shape of a bird with some resemblance to the raven family formed by some woods at Allt tan-y-Coed and Allt Olmarch. This is above Llangybi to the west of the main road. I do believe that *The Mabinogion* characters started life as real people, whose exploits were a talking point from this time onwards.

It is said of Brân's companions that they 'buried the head in the White Hill, and that burial was one of the Three Happy

Concealments, and one of Three Unhappy Disclosures when it was disclosed. For while the head was concealed no plague came across the sea to the island'.[6]

One of the Welsh triads explains the three goodly concealments and the three ill-fated disclosures:

> First the head of Bendigaid Brân ab Llŷr which Owain the son of Maxen Wledig buried under the White Tower in London, and while it was so placed, no invasion could be made upon this island; the second was the bones of Gwrthefyr the Blessed, which were buried in the chief harbour of the island, and while they remained hidden, all invasions were ineffectual; the third was the dragons buried by King Lludd at Dinas Emrys in Snowdon.
>
> And the three closures were made under the blessing of God and his attributes, and evil befell from the time of their disclosure. Gwrtheyrn Gwrtheneu [Vortigern] disclosed the dragons to revenge the disclosure of the Cymry against him, and he invited the Saxons in the guise of men of defence to fight against the Cymry; and after this he disclosed the bones of Gwrthefyr the Blessed, through love of Ronwen, the daughter of the Saxon Hengist. And Arthur disclosed the head of Bendigaid Brân ab Llŷr, because he chose not to hold the Island except by his own strength. And after the three disclosures came the chief invasions upon the race of the Cymry [Welsh nation].[7]

It is known that the crown jewels, the symbols of Britain's sovereignty, are housed at the Tower, and are used as sacred instruments to bind the monarch to the land and the people. But these symbols are not exclusive to the monarchy. They belong to each one of us and are symbols of the power of the light within us all, held by the monarch until we are able to realise our own individual sovereignty of the light.

---

[6] J Gantz, op. cit.
[7] 'Bran and the Tower of London', www.thornr.demon.co.uk/bran/tower.html

The symbolic meaning of the crown jewels

The golden crown represents the crown chakra and the golden crown of light which we will all wear one day when we have raised our vibrations to a higher level. The sceptre represents the caduceus. The orb stands for Planet Earth which we all hold in our hands, and the equidistant emerald cross and the emerald jewel are the symbols for our planet.

The Mabinogion's Story of the Two Dragons

This has its origins in *The Mabinogion*, in a tale called 'Lludd and Llevelys'. It concerns Lludd, king of all Britain, who 'rebuilt the walls of London and surrounded the city with innumerable towers... Though he had many strongholds... he loved London best; he spent most of the year there, and so it was called Caer Lludd, and later Caer Llundein, though after the foreigners came it was called Lundein'. It is true that 3,000 years ago the population of London spoke Brittonic, from which Welsh evolved.

After some time three plagues came to Britain. The second of these plagues concerns the dragons:

A scream ... was heard every May Eve over every hearth in the island; it pierced the hearts of the people and terrified them so that men lost their colour and strength, women suffered miscarriages, children lost their senses, and animals and trees and soil and water all became barren.

King Llud consulted his brother Llevelys, who was the king of France. He told him that the scream was caused by a dragon. A foreign dragon was fighting with it and struggling to overcome it, and therefore Lludd's dragon was screaming. He said that Lludd should measure the length and breadth of Britain, and when he found the exact centre, he should have a pit dug, and place a vat full of the best mead that could be made, and place a silk sheet over the vat, and guard it himself. This is what would happen, he said. 'You will see the dragons fighting ... and when they have wearied ... they will sink onto the sheet in the form of two little pigs; they will drag the sheet to the bottom of the vat, and there they will drink all the mead and fall asleep. When that happens you must wrap the sheet round them and lock them in a stone chest, and bury them in the Earth within the strongest place you know of in the island. As long as they are within that strong place no plague will come to Britain.'

Lludd did as he was told and it was exactly as Llevelys had said. He buried the chest in Eryri (Snowdon), after which the place was called Dinas Emreis. This is the end of *The Mabinogion*'s version that does not mention Merlin. Later, when Vortigern tried to build a stronghold at Dinas Emrys, the walls fell down every night. His Druids mistakenly told him that a child without a father must be sacrificed on this spot, so that he could build his fortress. Merlin was that child, but he was not sacrificed because he told them to dig and they would find two dragons, one red and one white, fighting each other. The dragons were found and Merlin was saved, and he told Vortigern that he would not be able to build there.

The Grail Story has its Origin in the Welsh *Mabinogion*

'*Mabinogi*' simply means a tale or a story.[8] The stories are taken from Peniarth 6 manuscript dating from 1225, and the White Book of Rhydderch, c. 1325, but have been in oral form for a great deal longer than that, when they were told by the bards and storytellers. Its origins have been lost in time.

In these tales, King Arthur is first mentioned in Celtic prose; Bedwyr becomes Bedivere, Cei becomes Kay, Owein (Uwayne) Gwenhwyvar (Guinevere) and Brân turns up as Brân or Bron, the Fisher King. Peredur becomes Percival, Gwalchmai becomes Gavain and Medrawd is Mordred. The story 'Peredur Son of Evrawg' is mirrored in Chétian de Troyes' 'Percival', which says that Percival was a Welshman.

In the Grail story, there is a sympathetic relationship between the ailing king and a wasteland. Both Brân and Peredur's uncles were rendered sterile and their lands were similarly afflicted as a result of this.

Brân is wounded in the foot with a poisoned spear; both Britain and Ireland fall to waste. In Peredur, the lameness of the hero's Fisher King uncle is the cause of strife and battle in the land. Peredur himself seems rather naive, possibly because of his sheltered upbringing, and does as others tell him. It is because he blindly obeys his uncle that he fails to ask a question of the Fisher King. He is also very fond of the ladies and keeps falling in love with them; a ladies' man, in fact. As the stories tell of Arthur, they would have gone back to Arthur's time, c. AD 500, but as is natural for folk tales, they would have been updated as each century passed, rather like a language has to be updated to find new words for new discoveries (like television and the Internet). Historical clues are not clues at all and the only conclusion we can come to is that there aren't any clues at all concerning the dates.

'Oh, no man knows/Through what wild centuries/roves back *The Mabinogion*', to rewrite Walter de la Mare.

---

[8] In the Welsh dictionary, the definition of 'Mabinogi' is 'a youthful tale'.

This quest for the Grail began in Wales. It is fitting that what has become a Grail journey, touching on the story of Percival and the real Grail, should end with the discovery that Peredur is Percival, the knight of the Grail legend, whose story is written in *The Mabinogion*.

A Grail journey is a journey on many different levels, and if I could pick one out it would be the level of truth. Truth is the first casualty of war and manipulation, and it is the first casualty of time itself. It would seem that it is beholden to each of us to peer back through its mists as far as possible, so that we can understand what brought us here, who we are, and how we can set about our next journey, that of our future. I once asked my teachers if truth was relative. 'It is relative only in relationship to the individual concerned,' was the reply. So it is possible for us to discover truth; it is simply a matter of remaining open enough. This is far from easy, but the guidance is always there. We only have to ask.

I believe that the idea of a Grail journey originates from the fall of Atlantis, and a deep memory of something wonderful that we have lost. Each ensuing age has its own version of what exactly this loss is. In our age, it seems to be an awareness that it is the truth we have lost, whether by design, accident or simply forgetfulness, or a combination of all three. We have lost the true knowledge of past ages, and this is what we are trying to find. The Age of Aquarius is the Age of Truth. There is also a memory of a soul purpose – the reason we are here. This Grail journey may begin to provide some answers to these quests.

The Prophecy of Merlin Becomes Reality

When I began to visit these sacred places, much of my time was spent following clues which were given to research their past history, most of it obscure. But this story was never about the past. It is the story of the sacred energies and the people whose lives helped to preserve them, so that we, in the present, can now identify and re-energise them, to enable all of us to secure the future of this sacred isle. Some of these people of the past are ourselves in the present, lighting the pathway, and we will be here in the future in the Golden Age of Aquarius.

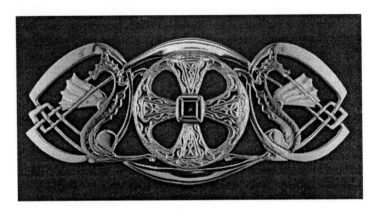

The Canterbury jewel

This is really what this story is about, and it is encapsulated in the prophecy of Merlin concerning the red dragon of Wales and the white dragon of England. This beautiful Canterbury jewel which was designed and made by Rhiannon of Tregaron, shows the red dragon made of red gold, and the white one made of white gold, united by the silver cross of Canterbury. It was worn as a clasp which joined Dr Rowan Williams's golden cloak at his enthronement. Merlin's prophecy of the red dragon eventually overcoming the white was not mentioned by Huw Edwards in his commentary at the cathedral. It was probably considered too confrontational, but it is not. This is about overcoming confrontation with love; the merging of the red and the white to give pink, the colour of unconditional love, and the unification of the two nations through the silver cross of Canterbury. Dr Williams is the first Welshman to become Archbishop of Canterbury for at least 1,000 years. He presides over 70 million Anglicans worldwide. Dr Williams spent three years as Archbishop of the Church in Wales before his appointment, where he was known for his wise leadership and warmth and humour. He is a poet in the ancient tradition of the bards, and was honoured for this when he was made a member of the Gorsedd. It was noticed that the enthronement was very similar to the Chairing of the Bard at the National Eisteddfod. The enthronement of the archbishop would appear to be a ceremony which has its origins with the Druids. I have 'seen' Druids carrying staffs with rams' horns which looked very like the bishop's crozier. This is not surprising; a lot more was borrowed from the ancients than just their knowledge of sacred sites.

People have had mixed feelings as to the value of the Welsh Assembly, but there can be no doubt that it has served as a focus for the nation. There is a flowering of creative talent which is exported to the rest of the world, which seems disproportionate to the small size of the country. The discoveries which I have been led to make and the guided wisdom which has been received leave me, at least, in no doubt that this is one of the threads of the tapestry which goes back through the ages to the Druids, bards and ovates. The country is, as I was given to understand in my first contact with Merlin at Llyn-y-Tarw, still under his protection.

Sacred Groves and Sacred Trees

The Welsh word for sanctuary is *lle sanctaidd* – sacred place. The Celts were well known for their veneration of trees, and they worshipped in sacred oak groves like the one that was once at Strata Florida and Chester Cathedral. The holy man's wand or staff is universal, whether it belonged to a Druid or a bishop. It was believed to have contained a resident tree spirit or dryad, who could detach itself from the tree and live in the staff, and work with the holy man or woman. They were called by the ancients 'the hooded ones' or 'the many-eyed ones'. Wood containing a dryad is known as 'livewood' and one of these was a little wooden peg that held the Druids' robes together, later known as the English or Albion knot. Sacred groves were used as places of worship in ancient times. They were always situated on a spring, a ley-cross or geodetic power node. They were used by the tribe or village for meetings, ceremonial and religious purposes, passing laws and making judgements.

Our present tradition of free speech comes from the ancient Druidic practice of holding all meetings in the open 'in the face of the sun and the eye of the light'. This is a tradition that we need to safeguard by holding it in the light always. The place name Llwyn Cwrt means 'grove of the court', and refers to the Court of Brân

Bendigaid. He would have held court in a grove of sacred trees, of which only the name remains to remind us. Parliament Hill (the Llandin), in North London, was an ancient Gorsedd, or meeting hill, from ancient Cymric times. Its spring has since been diverted.

Many villages had their own sacred trees. Even today many old villages have their special tree on the village green. The maypole was once a living tree brought to the village with its dryad. The dryad was called on to help the village and ensure a good harvest, its spirit represented by a mummer dressed as the Green Man. The ancients believed that a person's knowledge could be passed on at death and that the tree spirits were keepers of this knowledge. People were buried under sacred trees in the belief that their knowledge and wisdom would be joined with the dryad and would remain accessible to the tribe. This is the ancient meaning behind the reference to the 'family tree'. The tradition of planting yews in graveyards probably stems from this belief, and explains why the poet Dafydd ap Gwilym is supposed to be buried under the yew in the churchyard next to the abbey of Strata Florida. The older churches were built on sacred sites of the old religion containing yews. There are some wonderful yew trees in the churchyard of Pennant Melangell (referred to later in this story). Important meetings between kings and the Druids as tribal leaders, were held beneath sacred trees. This was because the ancients believed that the tree dryad would watch and record everything that went on, relaying the information to the cosmic memory banks, the Akashic records. I believe that the source of this story, 'the Pathway of the Beloved', comes from these records.

It is entirely appropriate that the story of the sacral chakra should begin with Merlin's oak. Returning home on my last journey for the Welsh line, I lost my dowsing crystal. I was told that I should get a wooden one. So now my means of dowsing is through a piece of Welsh holly which contains a dryad. When I consulted the dryad it confirmed that there are far more elementals and 'little people' living in a mature oak than in any other tree. This is one of the reasons why the Druids revered the oak so much. It is a very serious matter, then as now, to cut down a mature oak. Permission should be asked of the tree dryad and of the 'little people'.

DEE'S STORY OF THE DEATH OF AN OAK

I had been having trouble sleeping for some time, waking often and feeling uncomfortable. I have occasionally felt that I had 'things' walking or crawling all over my body. Eventually we asked a dowser who is an expert in distant house dowsing to have a look at the house. She replied that a tree was demolished on the site of the house and that the nature spirits and devas were still locked into that space. All the discomfort seemed to have been their way of attracting attention to their plight. I tuned into them and found them very angry. I apologised about the tree, but told them that the tree was taken down long before we came here. I really wanted to help and offered to take them to another tree, to a stone circle, or wherever they would like to be. They were adamant that they wanted their tree. They were giving me a sensation rather like pins and needles all over my body and I became aware that it was their sharp pointed teeth that were creating this sensation. I really didn't know what I could do to help them, when suddenly something said to me, 'You're a Druid – fix it!' I still was not certain what I could do or whom I could ask for help.

I thought first of Merlin, but found it difficult to ask him about this, as he always seems rather stern to me, so eventually I asked the universe to help me to help these little nature spirits. A little while later as I sat quietly, I suddenly became aware of a tree growing out of the ground. I watched its branches unfolding and becoming quite quickly a mature oak tree. The nature spirits went very happily to this tree and I watched them climbing and playing joyfully. I thought this was quite wonderful and sent up my thanks to the universe for their help. The following day Megan rang me and I told her what had happened. When I got to the part about feeling that I couldn't trouble Merlin, the phone suddenly went dead. I rang Megan back and she told me that this often happens to the phone when Merlin is mentioned. She also told me that it had been confirmed to her that my thought reached Merlin and it was he who manifested the tree in the etheric for the nature spirits, so naturally I sent a big thank you to Merlin for this wonderful help. After this, because I was very tired, I went to bed and had the best night's sleep that I have had for a long time. Long may it continue.[9]

---

[9] By kind permission of the author, Dee

All of this had a far too familiar ring. The name of our house is Trederwen. '*Derwen*' means oak and Trederwen means 'Place of the Oak Tree'. Our house was built on a Druidical sacred place, with the sun rising on the summer solstice, over the hill directly in front of my bedroom window.

It seems that a mature oak was cut down on the site of our property. This happened eleven years before we moved in, and was nothing to do with us. However, the Druid guardian blamed whoever lived in our house, so it was up to us to make peace with him.

We asked a friend to come and perform an Earth-healing ceremony and dedicate a young oak tree and a flower bed to heal the site. We already had a mature oak on the property that is about 150 years old. I was also told to dedicate a crystal and bury it among the roots of this mature oak. After a series of ceremonies of blessings for both the site and the nature spirits, we are now on good terms with the Druid and he is helping us with our work. We have discovered nine more young oak trees growing on our land.

> *As we walk the ancient sacred places of our land,*
> *May we also remember the fairy folk who guard them.*
> *May we always act towards them with courtesy.*
> *So that what is done in our world will not disturb theirs.*

A CONNECTION WITH CARN INGLI

After their visit to Saint Anthony's Well where she had collected some water, Dee 'knew' that they were meant to climb Carn Ingli. She did not know why, but we did know that Carn Ingli has its own chakra system. This is her account:

Following my visit to Saint Anthony's Well and the collection of the reactivated water, I found myself needing to climb Carn Ingli, which is a mountain on the west side of the Preseli Mountains in the Pembrokeshire National Park. After a wet and windy holiday, the day we went to Carn Ingli dawned bright and clear. As we climbed, I felt that we needed to keep to a path that I was told I would find to the left of the main route. This we did, and after a while we stopped in a particular place where we were enveloped in a wonderful sense of peace and great stillness. In this place

John was healed of something that had been troubling him. A little further on, I was again stopped by the amount of energy coming through my feet and legs. I kept finding a path to the left of the main one; it really was incredible. When we came to a rocky part of the hill, I was told that the path I had taken was the old way, the feminine way. We carried on climbing to the next rocky outcrop and sat there in the sunshine feeling the presence of the hill. I suddenly became aware that this was the heart chakra of the hill, and that we had climbed through the base chakra (John's healing), the sacral (energy), and the solar plexus (rocky outcrop). I was told that walking up the hill integrated the energies, not just of the hill, but our own energies also. I knew that we had no need to walk further because our energies needed to be centred in our hearts.

After lunch, we started out to find the well. I knew that I had to bring the water from Saint Anthony's Well to the well at Carn Cwm. We had no real idea where the well was, but our pathway took us there. It was a beautiful place but it was difficult to see where the water was. Then we found a damp patch and peering between the rocks, I found a lovely little pool. We said a prayer and put some water into the well, saying, 'This water comes from the crystal, arise and awaken!' When I came out, there were two buzzards overhead and I found myself saying, 'This is for Merlin, and for all the Celtic and Druidic people everywhere, for their time is now.' As I sat meditating, I was told that the Preselis and Cwm Carn had a direct relationship to a place in Ireland that I would visit in the future.

THE IRISH CONNECTION

In July 2002, we went to visit our daughter, Jo, who lives in Cork. I had taken with me the activated water from Llansteffan, not knowing what I had to do with it. I had to rely on my intuition. Whilst driving to Cork from the ferry terminal at Rosslare, I was drawn by a signpost to Ardmore, but thought no more about it. Whilst talking to Jo about places to visit, she suggested we might be interested in a rock at Cashel. I suddenly found myself asking if there was an Irish Saint called Declan, but she did not know. After doing some research on this, we found that there is a pathway of pilgrimage which runs between Ardmore and Cashel. This felt right and fitted in with what I had felt on my journey to Cork. I had a definite feeling of awareness of a church, and when we arrived in Ardmore we found the Church of Saint Paul, which meant nothing to me, but continuing further we discovered the ruined Church or Cathedral of Saint Declan. Within the church the energies were very beautiful and it felt timeless. There were also two very interesting ogham stones, which I found out had been brought there later. On the outside of the church were biblical pictures and in the adjoining cemetery, there was a 100-foot-high Irish round tower. I felt drawn to the left and on the far side of the cemetery, we found Saint Declan's oratory. This was his original church, and looking through the bars which guarded it, I was aware of a figure sitting in the corner. In the centre of this small enclosure was a pit where Saint Declan had been buried. People came to take soil from his grave, for it was reputed to have healing properties. This pit is now open and all the remains removed.

I felt myself again being pulled to the left and we set off towards the headland where we found a signpost directing us to Saint Declan's Well and hermitage. It was here that I found what I had been looking for. We said prayers and drew water from the well and then added the water from Llansteffan and dedicated it. I felt a wonderful sense of connection, and the Hermitage, although a ruin, has a wonderful atmosphere.

At this point, we were getting very anxious because this had made us late for our ferry home. We need not have worried, for when we got there we found that it had been delayed for an hour and a quarter. This was exactly the length of time we had spent at Ardmore. After we had left Ireland, I stood on the deck and could see the Irish hills on the horizon. I was filled with emotion and found myself promising that I would be back. The connection between Llansteffan, Carn Cwm and Ardmore had been made and the energies would now flow out and return, just as I was going to.[10]

There are two sacred energy lines flowing from Strata Florida to Ireland. One of them flows near Cork to Old Kinsale Head, where it goes into the sea. It was at this point that Jo saw the whales swimming past on their migration. In our meditation joining the Scillies and Llansteffan, we had taken whale essence and linked with them so that they might join us in our work for the crystalline grid.

---

[10] By kind permission of the author, Dee

Saint Declan of Ardmore

Where a fifth-century Irish saint lived at Ardmore Declan, five miles east of Yougal harbour, there stands one of the most remarkable groups of ancient ecclesiastic remains in all Ireland, all that is left of Saint Declan's city of Ardmore. There is a beautiful and perfect round tower, a ruined church known as the cathedral, and a second church beside a holy well. The water from the well is diverted into a shallow basin, in which pilgrims can wash their hands and feet. There is a primitive oratory and a couple of ogham stones.

Declan was descended from the race of Eoghan Mac Fiacha Suighde, whose kings held the country of Decies, in which Ardmore was built. At the age of seven, he was sent to study with a holy man named Dioma, after the Celtic custom. He later went to Rome where he was made a bishop by Pope Hilary.

When he returned to Ireland, he was greatly honoured both for his lineage and his spirituality. 'Gentleness and charity manifested themselves in Declan to such an extent that his disciples preferred to live under his immediate control and under his jurisdiction as subjects than to be in authority in another monastery.'[11]

This must have been a hard act for Saint Patrick to follow. Being warned by an angel that Patrick intended to curse Declan's people and country, Declan set out with all haste possible to meet Patrick, and was received with all honour. Patrick said, 'On account of your prayer not only shall I not curse them but I shall give them a blessing.' This is in accordance with the Celtic custom, which required members of royalty or their religious agents to pronounce formal curses on wrongdoers or enemies, like Queen Macha cursing the men of Ulster, which made them feel the pains of childbirth when their province was attacked. When Saint Patrick went to Ireland, he was responsible for burning around 145 sacred books, which were all that were left of the Druidic manuscripts.

Following the Egyptian custom, these Celtic saints used bells to drive away any mischievous or evil spirits ('The curious do say

---

[11] 'The Life of Saint Declan of Ardmore', www.ccel.org/d/declan/life/declan.html

that the ringing of bells exceedingly disturbs spirits.'[12]). Solemn oaths were sworn on bells, and they could empower curses and exorcisms, hence the bell, book and candle familiar in exorcism. The sound of a bell helped the soul depart in peace and in safety, and this is the origin of the 'passing bell' tolled at funerals. Both Saint Declan and Saint Patrick possessed bells. Declan was reputed to have been given his as a wondrous gift from God. The only remaining one belonged to Saint Patrick and is in the National Museum in Dublin.

---

[12] John Aubrey, *Miscellanies Upon Various Subjects*, Project Gutenberg etext, 2003

The Sacral Chakra in Carmarthen Bay

Carmarthen, Caerfyrddin – City of Merlin

The fort or town of Merlin (Myrddin) was mentioned by Geoffrey of Monmouth in *Historia Regum Britanniae*, in which it is claimed to be the birthplace of Merlin. Until quite recently, one of the town's main landmarks was the wizened remains of Merlin's oak, a gnarled stump held up by iron hoops and concrete. It had died back in the 1800s, when a local trader allegedly poisoned it. It was linked to one of Merlin's most famous prophecies:

> When Merlin's tree shall tumble down
> Then will fall Carmarthen town.[1]

There was another prophecy which read:

> Carmarthen, thou shalt have a cold morning,
> Earth shall swallow thee, water take thy place.[2]

By 1978, what was left of the tree was declared a traffic hazard and was carted off to the Civic Hall, where part of it can still be seen today. Then in 1987, the worst floods struck Carmarthen in living memory. Was this anything to do with Merlin, they wondered?

Welsh place names, as well as being poetically beautiful, are also a source of valuable information for my research, as many of them go back to the year 'dot'. In isolation, they don't mean a great deal, but looked at as a part of a story that has just been revealed, place names can give verification. The Abbey of Strata Florida lies at the end of the village of Pontrhydfendigaid. This means the 'Bridge over the ford of the Blessed Ones'. So who were the 'Blessed Ones'? One or two of the monks might have been, but perhaps not blessed enough to have an ancient ford named after them. Instead, the epithet refers to Mary, the mother of Jesus, and Joseph of Arimathea. Both of them came to Strata Florida on their journey through Wales after they had landed in Carmarthen Bay.

---

[1] *Guide Book for Carmarthen Town*
[2] *Ibid.*

Joseph is intimately associated with the Nanteos Cup, the Welsh Grail, which is associated with this abbey, and there is much further evidence of Mary in this story of the discovery of the chakra line. Folk memory and place names are very much interrelated, and are often associated with an object like the Welsh Grail. It may never be known whether it is the Cup of the Last Supper, but what really matters is the fact that there is this folk memory in this part of Wales. It is simply, like the place names, a tangible form of this memory, leading us back into the dim and distant past, a remembering of a time when Wales saw and recognised some very important visitors to this sacred land. We should remember also that a Grail journey is a journey of discovery within ourselves, which is the reason why we sometimes feel the need to set off on a pilgrimage.

A little to the north of Carmarthen are two villages with intriguing names. There is Salem, and the much better known Bethlehem, where the children send their cards to have them stamped for Christmas.

Mary visited the landscape Temple of the Zodiac just north of these villages, which was a temple dedicated by priestesses to the service of the feminine energy, which explains why Joseph did not go with her that time. It was here that I found a farm called Wern-fendigaid, which means 'The Alder Trees of the Blessed One', and another clue to follow. Mary and Joseph then travelled north to Strata Florida, where the ford over the River Teifi was named after them.

Due east of Carmarthen is the town of Llandeilo, where Dinefwr Castle was built by Rhodri Mawr, who united Wales in the ninth century. It became the seat of the kingdom of Deheubarth, where the Lord Rhys made it his stronghold against the Normans in the twelfth century. There are soaring views from its battlements almost to Carmarthen, and beyond is Garn Coch, the largest Iron Age fort in Wales.

The Sacral Chakra

This is under the water in Carmarthen Bay, and must belong to a period of time before the land sank. This occurred around

7000 BC when the British Isles separated from mainland Europe. When dowsing on the map, the area above the water was Llansteffan, on the inlet leading to the town of Carmarthen. There is a church, a castle and a holy well dedicated to Saint Anthony. He was a third-century hermit of the Coptic tradition who gave up his wealth and possessions to live alone in the Egyptian desert. He was joined by others who were attracted by his solitude and life of prayer, which resulted in the first community of monastic living. The Coptic stories say that he was fed by a raven who brought him half a loaf of bread every day. On the occasion when he met Saint Paul (another hermit) the raven brought a whole loaf to feed them both. They also tell that Saint Anthony was tempted by noisy, foul-smelling beasts. These Coptic stories are almost unknown in the Western Church, so once again there is a link with Egypt through this chakra system.

The influence of the Coptic desert tradition on the Celtic Church has been documented, and the Church on the Celtic fringes of Britain followed a monastic structure. The abbots had more influence than bishops, and the saints and heroes were monks and hermits. The desert structure pioneered by Saint Anthony of groups of hermits centred around a holy man or leader suited the Celts who lived in loose communities themselves. Indeed, they were influenced to such an extent that the Christian settlements of Wales, Scotland, Ireland, Cornwall and Brittany had more in common with the Coptic Church of Egypt than with the Roman Church, with its emphasis on power and control. These differences were one of the reasons for the downfall of the Celtic Church at the synod of Whitby in AD 644. This tradition probably arrived via Gaul and Saint Martin of Tours. He was converted in AD 351 and formed a large monastery at Liguge, which became the model for early Celtic communities.

He was the maternal great-uncle of Saint Patrick, who was trained in the island of Lerins, off the coast of Gaul, which contained a community of Egyptian monks.

The monks searched for an isolated area in which to live and called the place 'dyserth', which means a wilderness, or deserted place. There is a dyserth near Prestatyn, and one in Radnorshire in Mid Wales. Monasticism is to live alone in a lonely place.

Sometimes these places were islands, like Bardsey and Puffin Island.

The Holy Well of Saint Anthony at Llansteffan

It was a wonderful Easter Saturday when we parked our car by the church and set off up the lane towards the well. We came to a wood and took the middle path, which went along the edge of the cliff. On the side of the path, the star-like celandines reflected the golden rays of the sun. There were blue periwinkles and banks of tiny violets. Everyone we met smiled and wished us a good day, and there was such good energy. The birds sang in the trees overhead and down on the estuary the wading birds were searching the mudflats to the sound of calling sandpipers. At the end of the path was a large pink house where the path turned sharply to the right. About thirty yards along on the left was a door in the wall with a notice over it, which said 'Fynnon Sant Antwn' (Well of Saint Anthony).

As the door opens, some steep steps can be seen leading down into a tiny courtyard with the well in the corner. It was low and very difficult to get into to reach the water. There is a notice on the wall, which tells that Sant Antwn was a local saint who was the namesake of Saint Anthony of Egypt. He used to baptise people at this well. With difficulty, we collected some water and put some on our crown and third eye chakras. The beautiful energy seemed to have spread over the whole area of the estuary and Llansteffan; it was peaceful and spiritually uplifting. Feeling spiritually 'tuned', I dowsed whether Joseph of Arimathea had come to this bay. The answer was 'Yes'.

I also asked if he had been taken to the ancient church near Red Roses. Again the answer was 'Yes'.

I asked if Mary had been there but again failed to pick up her energy and was told 'No'.

On the way back we called in to see the Church of Llansteffan. The village is named after a sixth-century missionary, Ystyffan ap Mawan ap Cyngen ap Cadell Deyrnllwg (but I am sure they just called him Steff!).

The window in the church of Llansteffan

There is considerable evidence of Bronze Age people living in this area, with a fortress, standing stones and cromlechs still to be seen. The church would have been a '*clas*', that is, a simple wooden building with a strong wooden fence around it. Legend associates Saint Ystyffan with Saint Teilo, and the only other Llansteffan, in Radnorshire, also has a Saint Teilo Church nearby.

In the twelfth century the Normans took possession of the castle and lands and the church became known as Saint Stephen's. Circa 1170 it was granted to the Knights Hospitallers of Saint

John. The east window is one of the most unusual and beautiful windows in any church. It was made by an artist who lived in the village, John Petts, and was given in the memory of a local lady, Doris Baker. It comprises over 800 pieces of painted and fired glass that took more than eight months to complete.

The trinity emblem of interlaced circles is at the top of the window, and from it flows rich patterns of varied forms in ribbons, symbolising the abundance and diversity of God's gifts. Each unit of this pattern is a visual metaphor in flowers, fruits, leaves, stars and symbols. The rose is the symbol of victory and triumphant love, the daisy is for the innocence of the Christ Child, the butterfly for Resurrection, and the harebell for the Word of God. Holly is for the crown of thorns, the oak leaf for strength, the scallop as the pilgrim's badge and there is the Chinese yin-yang symbol. There are several medieval signs for the cross, the trinity and the anchor (for faith). There are the ancient symbols for the seasons. There is a cog for modern industry and a cotton reel for the stitch-craft of the ages. The plain white circles represent the wafer, the Host for Communion, and are cut out of undulating Venetian glass to catch the light. Two narrow streams of red and selenium glass are for the blood of the cross, and the flames of the spirit. This is truly a window not to be missed.[3]

> *Earth, crammed with heaven,*
> *And every common bush afire with God:*
> *But only he who sees, takes off his shoes…*

Elizabeth Barrett Browning

There is an evocative carving of the Madonna and Child made in lime wood by John Taulbut RWA.

I had lost the Mary energy, but here, in this church dedicated to Saint Ystyffan, was a beautiful depiction of her and her child. Had I found her again? Dowsing the question, 'Was this church once dedicated to Mary?', the answer was, 'Yes.' Dowsing again, 'Did Mary come to this sacred site?' 'Yes.' The roses in the place

---

[3] The Church of Saint Ystyffan, Flower Festival Programme, 1996

names had been telling the truth. Looking closely at the window again, I noticed the predominance of roses, the ones with five petals. It may even explain the pink window, so unusual in churches as to be unique – a rosy pink window? This is not to suggest for one moment that there was a conscious awareness of this energy, but such an energy will still be emanating at this spot to influence those who are 'open', and artists are intuitives.

The visit on the following day to Fynnon Ddrain was disappointing because we could not find the well, though obviously there was one once because it is called Thorn Well. Previously I had dowsed that Joseph had been here when he came to Carmarthen, which is why it has the name of Joseph's Thorn. A stream running through the village was dowsed and the pendulum was swinging strongly when asked if this was water from this well. Holy wells were just springs, so it is possible. This village is in the hills behind Carmarthen.

I believe that Joseph of Arimathea and Mary, Jesus's mother, reached land on the sands near what is now Llansteffan in Carmarthen Bay. I had previously 'seen' their ship in my

meditation, entering the bay. Also in meditation, I had been told by the Druid who was a star master that Mary had stayed in a house of rest for travellers. I believe this house of rest was at Llansteffan.

(Left) Plaque at Saint Anthony's Well

The First Visit to Saint Anthony's Well

Our friends Dee and John were the first to visit this well and this is what happened to them:

> A beautiful quiet place, full of energy. I found the energy coming up through my feet – coming up and over the top of my head and pulling me towards the well, whether I was facing it or had my back to it. I felt a great need to have water from the well to place on my forehead at the level of the third eye chakra. My husband felt the same way and had been asked to 'take some water from the spring and place it on the child's head'. Having anointed my forehead, I felt a very warm glow behind my third eye and a band of energy going around my head. Something said, 'Welcome back, beloved.' We stayed there for quite a while.
>
> Sitting on the beach later, I realised that this was the beginning of the healing of my third eye, and I understood why I was beginning to learn Welsh. A Druid appeared before me who told me that I would come again and visit all the chakras, because to release the energy, words must be spoken – words of power, in Welsh. When this happened, the energy released would revitalise Wales. The Druid said that I needed to remember and that he would be with me until I did. I had a feeling that this had something to do with Atlantean energies and that the chakra was situated in a south-west line from Llansteffan through Worms Head on the Gower Peninsula.
>
> On a walk along the coastal path the following day, I was confronted by a different Druid, with long flowing white hair and beard, who stared hard at me – through me – then stamped his staff three times on the ground. I think that he was saying something but I couldn't hear what, and then he raised both arms to the sky. Since then, I have been aware of him sitting in a circle of people, talking. On another occasion he was very irritated, saying that he had been awakened but that no one was ready. As I was going to sleep I was aware of him again, just staring at me.[4]

A MEDITATION ON THE SACRAL CHAKRA

After Dee's experience with the Druid of Carmarthen Bay, we felt that we should try to contact him, so we sat in meditation. One of

---

[4] With kind permission of the author, Dee

the Druids was a little fierce, and we thought he could be Merlin. At first, I saw a man in a black robe with a hood, similar to a monk. I thought he was a monk until he told me he was a Druid.

'I am a form of the Druid relationship with the stars. Druids studied many things, and they had Druid masters for different subjects. I am one of those.'

'Is this to do with a merkaba?'

'Yes, a gateway to the universe.'

'Would you like us to go to the crystal?'

'No, that will not be necessary. It can be activated from a distance. All things are possible when you walk in the light.'

'How?'

'You will be told when you are ready. Thank you for making this connection with us.'

'Did Joseph come here?'

'Yes.'

I 'saw' a small wooden ship sailing into Carmarthen Bay. I felt that I was watching the arrival of Joseph of Arimathea. The crystal, whose deterioration was causing its Druid guardians some anxiety, was a beacon that could be seen or felt from a great distance away. It guided ships into the bay as a lighthouse would do, but I feel its influence would have reached much further, perhaps even to the Holy Land itself. It marks the beginning of the Pathway of the Beloved in Wales. I then saw our candle contained in a huge infinity sign.

THE SECOND MEDITATION

There was an angel very close to our candle. Next, there followed a long-stemmed red rose.

'What was Joseph doing there?'

'He was following the Pathway of the Beloved.'

'What was that?'

'It was a river of light and each chakra is a station of light. There are energies which will give light and enlightenment there.'

'Is the water in the bay polluted?'

'Yes.'

'How can we clear it?'

I saw red roses and was told to ask Dee. It was understood that sound must be used – singing? Because the roses were red, we thought it should be keyed to C, and John suggested a tuning fork in C.

'We are talking Atlantis,' I was told. I then saw lots of threads coming together, like pathways joining. I think John saw something similar, but at the crown chakra. We have decided to perform a ceremony that will be on the ether to clear the crystal, using roses, candles and a tuning fork.

The Ceremony of Red Roses

This ceremony was performed on the ether because we were not able to physically reach the sacral chakra in Carmarthen Bay, and we knew that we were needed to help to activate and clear this chakra.

There were four of us, two men and two women. We sat around a stand which was holding a large glass bowl filled with spring water. In this bowl was a newly cleansed, large amethyst crystal. Floating in the water were five golden rose candles and twelve red roses.

We asked for help from the spirits of the light, the Druids and the Merlin energy. I became aware of a circle of Druids standing around us. Then I seemed to find myself up in the cosmos with Merlin; he was wearing a cloak of stars, and as he strode around, the stars fell off and joined the other stars in the sky. It was beautiful! Then I realised that I was not supposed to be there. I was meant to be down on the Earth with the meditation. So when I got back to the room, I found that the crystal in the bowl had turned into a heart that was radiating light. I saw the iron bars imprisoning the crystal break open. John took a tuning fork in the key of C, and passed it three times round the bowl, ending with placing it in the water. We then joined hands, and I saw the Druids moving around in a circle. Faster and faster they went until they were just a whirl of light, so that I was feeling giddy, but I knew they would slow down and waited for them to stop. As they did so, they brought their staffs down hard on the ground in unison. This was the act of grounding the energy, and I could feel the grounding. This was when the ceremony ended and they thanked us. Dee said that the crystal had begun to transmit energy very gently. We know that we have more of this work to do.

The following day I realised that there was sacred geometry being used here. There were four of us, the number for the Earth, who formed a square, the symbol for the Earth. The circle of Druids placed the square within this circle, the symbol of matter contained within spirit. When we joined hands we, too, formed a circle. I felt there were twelve Druids, and we had twelve roses (I was not able to count the Druids or the stars), but at one point I saw a circle of stars which I felt were twelve in number. None of this was consciously planned by us, but arrived at through guidance.

Red Roses

Looking at the map of Carmarthen Bay, the words 'Red Roses' jumped out at me. I was shown a red rose twice in the meditation. Did this mean a visit to this village? Dowsing on the map confirmed 'Yes', but also that we were not asking the right questions. What were the right questions? On the map there was a tumulus.

'Is this significant?'
'Yes.'
'Is this to do with Joseph?'
'Yes.'

However, when reading a book, *The Marian Conspiracy*,[5] I found that the rose is the symbol of Mary, mother of Jesus, and this is the meaning of the rosary – rose garden. Was this the connection? So we tried these questions:

'Is this to do with Mary?'
'Yes.'
'Was Mary buried here?'
'Yes.'
'Are her bones still here?'
'No.'

She was reaching the end of her life; she was ill and wanted to see the Holy Land for the last time, but it was not to be. She died

---

[5] Graham Phillips, 2001

on her journey home somewhere near Red Roses. Her body was placed in the tumulus, which was the most sacred place for the people of that area. The Druid in the black robe told me:

'There is a little house which is where Mary rested on her journey. This house was a religious house. In those days the religious houses were run by Druids with a hostelry for pilgrims and travellers. The monks continued with this custom many centuries later. Food, shelter and protection were given to all those who needed it. This tradition was so since the beginning of time.'

It would appear that the tradition of the hostelries of the Knights of Saint John and of the monasteries had their origins in the time of the Druids.

So it seems that a visit to Saint Anthony's Well must include a visit to Red Roses. This seems to follow the need for an awakening of the feminine energy for this chakra line. So far, it feels very masculine. Looking at the map there is a profusion of roses in this area. There is Rhosgoch and Rhosyn Coch (red roses), West Rose Farm, West Rose Hill, and Rose Down. Near Milford Haven there is a Rose Hill, Rose Cottage Farm and the better known Rosemarket. There is Rosebush in the Preseli Mountains. A whole bunch of roses!

That the hostelry tradition was established by the Druids was later proved by research. Saint Columbanus, born AD 543, was one of the most learned of all the Celtic saints, and was called the Prince of Druids, a title of great honour. As well as theology and literature, his monks also taught astronomy, maths, geometry and handicrafts. His monastic rule was considered harsh even in his day, but he went on to establish about one hundred monasteries in France, Germany, Switzerland, Austria and Italy. These rich and populous monasteries were on important trade routes and provided a network of hostels where Celtic wayfarers could stay on their pilgrimages. This meant that travelling was so much easier than we might imagine, and we do know that they travelled a great deal, mostly by sea, but when on land they used the ancient trackways which crisscrossed the land. Some of these trackways are still walkable, like the one known as the Monk's Trod which links Strata Florida and the coast with Mid Wales, and follows the Rhayader to Cwmystwyth road, through the throat chakra. The trackways are on high ground above the wooded valleys.

There are stopping places marked by isolated boulders, cairns, thorn trees, standing stones and crosses. These old routes show an intimate knowledge of the landscape, with moderate gradients and crossings at fords in the rivers. There were also holy roads to link sacred places, like the one linking the shrine of Saint David's with the holy island of Bardsey.

On a sacred circuit, pilgrims visited a related series of sanctified places, undergoing a wide variety of sacred experiences that caused a change of consciousness. These pilgrimages can be done singly, if preferred, but they are at their most powerful when performed collectively. A Grail journey is exactly that: when your inner journey parallels your outer physical journey. It brings enlightenment, it brings about healing, and a new sense of awareness on a higher level of vibration. It will bring changes within you, your life and your companions' lives. So don't rush through the chakras; take your time to adjust and assimilate the energies so that you can gain maximum benefit from this incredible journey of the soul.

A Visit to Red Roses

On a visit to Red Roses, dowsing had produced a message about Mary, mother of Jesus, being with Joseph and somewhere near the tumulus. Although we searched for the tumulus and knew where it was, we were unable to reach it due to the lack of a path and overgrown vegetation. It was at this point that the Mary energy seemed to get lost, which was sad. So we went back to the village and stopped there, wondering what to do next.

I felt drawn to cross the road and go down the B4314 in the direction of Pendine. Once over these crossroads we saw a notice about an ancient church that had been built on a Bronze Age site. This church is called Eglwys Cynin (the Church of Cynin), which is about halfway between Red Roses and Pendine. High on a hill, it has a circular wall around it, a sign of antiquity. It is built on Bronze Age earthworks in the form of three circular embankments which can still be seen at the car park. It must have been a sacred place for thousands of years. There is a timeless and peaceful energy. The church has a treasure from ancient times: a fifth-century inscribed memorial stone to Avitoria, the daughter of Saint Cynin. It has a Latin inscription 'AVITORIA FILIA CYNIGNI', and Irish ogham down the side.

The fifth-century memorial stone to Avitoria, the daughter of Saint Cynin

In this church is a window dedicated to Saint Cynin, the grandson of Brychan. Brychan was a saint, king and priest. A fourth-century pioneer of Christianity in south-west Wales, who came from Brycheiniog (Brecon). He was a warrior, a chieftain and a religious leader, 'one of the three saintly men of Britain'. He shares his window with Saint Teilo, Bishop of Llandaff, and a sixth-century contemporary of Saint David. Cynin is shown in two roles, as a bishop and as a warrior king. The words *Esgob* (bishop), *Abat* (abbot), *Brenin* (king), and *Sant* (Saint) indicate his status. His good memory was mentioned in the Welsh triads, which proves he was trained by Druids. The church is dedicated to the three Margarets: Saint Margaret, Queen of Scotland, Saint Margaret of Antioch and Margaret Marloes, from a local family. There is a claim that it may be the oldest church in Wales.

I dowsed, asking, 'Did Joseph of Arimathea come here?'

'Yes.'

'Did he bring the Grail Cup?'

'Yes.'

'Did Mary come here?'

'No.'

The Secret of the Crystal

The Australian Aborigines believe that they are descended from a race which came from the Pleiades, and they have many beautiful stories, including this one which concerns a crystal which we had contact with in Carmarthen Bay.

Long, long ago, when the Earth was still all one continent, seven brothers came from the stars, from a planet that had been destroyed in a cosmic catastrophe. Each of the brothers was given a special task to protect this planet. One of these brothers was their original ancestor, and he gave to them the job of setting up the ley lines and energy grids. The descendants of another brother were the Egyptians, who had to understand and care for the crystals. They placed some of these crystals on the four corners of the Earth at the north, south, east and west points. The whales and dolphins were given the task of carrying the cosmic crystal and magnetic energy through the oceans of this world, until the harmonic energy has taken over the whole surface of the Earth. The crystals will sing in harmony together as we move to the next vibration.

We became aware, when we were at Llansteffan, that we were being influenced by a crystal far out to sea, and we were made to understand that it was the Crystal of the West. *On no account was the presence of this crystal to be disclosed until we had been given permission to do so.* Merlin said it was sub rosa, and there was a warning that a grid of energy would only be disclosed to those who had acted responsibly (this permission has now been given). We were also made aware that the condition of this crystal was giving the Druid guardians cause for concern. When I 'saw' it in meditation, it was huge. It was mounted on a dais and there were three circular steps leading up to it. Bob said it was an amethyst. I was aware that it appeared to be contained within iron bars, both vertically and around it. Dee told me that what I had seen as bars was in fact an energy containment field, which had been put around it in Atlantis, and that feminine energy had been trapped in it. It was our task to find some way of clearing and releasing this energy. This was the message given to us one year later when this had been done.

The crystal was programmed with specific energies in the later days of Atlantis and anchored to the planet so that these energies would be available at a later time. See how you all gave freely of those energies, anchoring them to the planet knowing that there would be a great need for them in the future. You did not know why but you knew that it needed to be done, as you knew that you would be here again to release them. As the group met and grew, history began to repeat itself. There was a great need for understanding about the past. This was not always present and it has taken time for this to manifest itself in your remembering. This has been activated through a Druidic presence in you and through the ancient chakra system present in Wales. This is all you need to know because you are aware that the crystal of the West is now released, its energies discharged, and its movement to the fifth dimension is complete.

RELEASE OF THE CRYSTAL OF THE WEST

'When Megan talked to me about the Welsh chakra line she was being shown, and the sacral chakra in Carmarthen Bay, it produced within me a remembering of a crystal I had been aware of occasionally over a period of many years. I realised that this crystal needed to be released to aid the activation of not only this line but other lines too. In meditations we saw this crystal on its plinth within a circular structure at the bottom of the sea. We saw that the crystal was chained into this structure, and meditated for its release. These energies had been anchored to the Earth, to the planet, so that they would not be lost. This happened during the latter days of Atlantis because it was known that there would be a great need for them in future times, and that the people who anchored them would return to release them when the time was right. During the time of its release it infused the waters of Saint Anthony's Well in Llansteffan, and this water has been taken from there to the whole chakra line through to the crown chakra at Llyn-y-Tarw. The crystal has now been fully released and its energies have returned to the crystalline grid of the planet to enhance its function. The crystal has now returned to the fifth dimension.'

This is what Dee was told and we were also told that it is awaiting our reunion with it in the fifth dimension. I knew about a crystal about ten years ago when I first met her, and she told me that there was a huge crystal that she was meant to find. I remember thinking that it sounded exciting and hoped that I would be there at the time!

Joseph of Arimathea

Since the Roman Empire stretched from the Persian Gulf to the north of France, Britain was the only place where political and religious dissidents could live in safety.

Gildas, writing circa AD 545, claimed that some of Jesus's original disciples did exactly that. They came in the last year of Tiberius's reign – AD 37, only a few years after the crucifixion and some years before Saint Paul began his teachings. Most of the leading disciples are accounted for in Palestine, but Joseph and his followers were not. Nothing more was heard about Mary, the mother of Christ. Robert De Boron said that Joseph of Arimathea spent fifteen years with Our Lady, the Virgin Mary, who arrived in AD 37 and died circa AD 52, at around seventy-five years of age.[6]

It may surprise most people to find that there was an extensive trade between Britain and the Mediterranean countries from at least 500 BC, and tin, copper and lead were exported from Cornwall, Somerset and Wales. It was mentioned by Herodotus in c. 460 BC. This is why the Romans came here, and there were established trade routes known for centuries by the traders, of whom, it is believed, Joseph was one.

Anglesey has an enormous copper mine on Parys Mountain which was worked from pre-Roman times until the eighteenth century, and it was one of the three most important centres of industry and on a major trade route. This means that Wales would have been well known as a major trading country long before the Romans.

A manuscript in the Vatican Library dated AD 35 states that some of the friends and relatives of Jesus left Judea for other countries. It was no longer safe for them to stay in Judea. Some of them were put in a boat without oars or sails and set adrift at the mercy of the winds and tides, in the manner in which people punished undesirables in the ancient world. Joseph of Arimathea was one of them and they eventually washed up, safe and sound, at Marseilles. From here Joseph went to Britain where he spent the rest of his life preaching the Gospel. It was in Britain where

---

[6] Robert De Boron, c. 1200, *Joseph d'Arimathie*

he eventually died. 'Now hear how Joseph came to England, but at the time it was called Britain, then fifteen years with Our Lady, as I understand, Joseph waited upon her.' Robert De Boron, in his book *Joseph d'Arimathie*, written circa 1200, claims that the source for this quote was a book written by a group of Christian clerics.[7]

He was a man of wealth, which equates with power and influence. His name was Joseph de Marmore from Arimathea and he had lived at Marmorica in Egypt before moving to Arimathea. The title Decurion meant that he was a Roman minister for mines. He would have had his ear to the ground and would have been aware of any danger in time to make a hurried, but not unplanned, exit from Judea in one of his many ships.

John had been given the guardianship of Mary by Jesus from the cross, but became a fugitive and was exiled to the Island of Patmos. In the New Testament John wrote to Mary: 'The elder unto the elect lady and her children whom I love in the truth; and not I only, but also all they that have known the truth ... Grace be with you, mercy, peace, from God the Father, and from the Lord Jesus Christ, the Son of the Father, in truth and love... Having many things to write to you, I would not with paper and ink: but I trust to come unto you, and speak face to face, that our joy may be full.' (2 John 1:1, 3, 12, King James Version)

A Catholic priest named Polydore Vergil, born in Italy in 1470, who became Chamberlain to Pope Alexander VI, was asked to write a history of England for Henry VII. He said that it was partly through Joseph of Arimathea that Britain had been the first kingdom to receive the gospel. This antiquity of the British Church had been challenged by the ambassadors of Spain and France before the Roman Catholic Council of Pisa in AD 1417. The former Archbishop of Canterbury, Henry Chichele, and Thomas Chillendon, won the day, and the Council affirmed that the British Church (not the Church of England and not the Roman Catholic Church because it was pre-Catholic) was the first Christian Church. A Roman Catholic Council of Constance, also in AD 1424, confirmed the findings. Finally, at the Council of

---

[7] See Graham Phillips, *The Marian Conspiracy*, p.166 for further information.

Basle in 1434, it was laid down that the Churches of Spain and France had to accept the precedence of the British Church, which, it was affirmed, was founded by Joseph of Arimathea 'immediately after the Passion of Christ'. Gildas the Wise wrote between AD 515 and 547:

> These islands received the beams of light – that is, the holy precepts of Christ – the true Sun, as we know, at the latter part of the reign of Tiberius Caesar, in whose time this religion was propagated without impediment and death threated to those who interfered with its professors.[8]

So it would seem that Mother Mary, her children and Joseph of Arimathea, arrived in Carmarthen Bay, using the crystal as a navigation beacon to guide them.

Joseph was able to do this because he was a crystal master. His talent in this area was how he became the Roman minister for mines. They came as refugees, and, as all refugees, then and now, they were looking for safety and protection; but they wanted to begin to work with the crystals and the grid, connecting and focusing the Earth's energy in this sacred isle.

There is a tradition that Jesus had already visited Britain and set up his Church. Saint Augustine states in his letter to the Pope, that there existed a church constructed by the hands of Christ. We have no reason to disbelieve him, especially when we know this was not good news for the Roman Catholics.

There is another source of information from Taliesin, the Welsh bard, 'Christ, the Word from the beginning, was from the beginning our teacher, and we never lost his teaching.'

Then there is Gildas, who said, 'these islands received the holy precepts of Christ' towards the end of Tiberius's reign. Since Tiberius died in AD 37, this obviously means that he must have been referring to a time before Jesus would have begun his ministry, because this was the date when the family left the Holy Land for good after the crucifixion. It was after the crucifixion that the Gospels tell nothing of where Mary lived or died, and there is not a single reference to her burial. Logic dictates that this

---

[8] Gildas, 'De Excidio Britanniae', from J A Giles (trans.), *Six Old English Chronicles*, London, G Bell & Sons, 1891, Internet Medieval Sourcebook, Paul Halsall, 1999

is because they did not know. In 1950, Mary's physical ascension into Heaven – the Assumption – was made the Church's official doctrine by Pope Pius XII, so after this date Mary's mortal remains were not to be found anywhere on the Earth. Up until this doctrine, it was left to individual Catholics to make up their own minds.

A Local Story of Our Lady

On an 1891 map, the abbey church of Strata Florida was called Saint Mary's Abbey. This may not seem much in itself, but there was a notable pilgrimage in honour of Our Lady in Cardigan during the Middle Ages.

A legend tells of a statue of the Lady Mary which was found on the banks of the Teifi at Carmarthen. She had her son upon her lap and a lit candle or taper in her hand. Since it was not thought suitable to leave it where it was found, the people moved it into the parish church. But the statue simply returned to the place where it had been until they built a church (Saint Mary's Church) over its original spot, which is now the present church. The candle continued to burn for another eleven years, so the story says.[9]

'Cromwell ordered all principal images of Our Lady ... to be sent to London for destruction.'[10] This legend is concerned with time before the foundation of the priory and before Saint Mary's Church existed. It refers back to the dim and distant past, to folklore and tradition. It is a legendary account to explain why the church was built on this particular site. Why should this be necessary? What is the real story hidden by time? The dedication was evidently determined by an already existing devotion from way back in past ages, around AD 37 perhaps? But it is important to remember that the Welsh Grail Cup was known by the monks of Strata Florida as 'Saint Mary's dowry'.

In 1987 the parish priest was asked by the Welsh bishops to commission a plaque of Our Lady of Cardigan to be placed in the

---

[9] Rev. Silas M Harris, *History of Our Lady of Cardigan*, 1952,
www.cardigantaper.org/cardigan/history.htm
[10] *Ibid.*

courtyard of the Basilica of the Annunciation in Nazareth. Countries all over the world place copies of their national shrines there in testimony to the Catholic devotion to Mary. A vignette also features Strata Florida (Ystrad Fflur) because Cistercians are noted for their devotion to Mary, and it is one of the most sacred sites in Wales.

Tracing the route taken by Mary and Joseph to Strata Florida

To celebrate the summer solstice, we went to Saint Anthony's Well at Llansteffan. I had wanted to find this route for two years but had been unable to do so. Looking at the map I had noticed some biblical place names that were situated close to each other. They were Salem, Horeb, Capel Isaac and Bethlehem. Our first visit to Capel Isaac did not reveal any particular energies. We then went on to Salem. Here, I experienced a strong Jewish energy. We then proceeded to find Bethlehem, but ended up at Myddfai instead. There was a beautiful energy in this village that felt very light and uplifting. I knew there was something very special about it. Since ancient times the village of Myddfai had been famous throughout Wales for its physicians and healers, and it is important to realise that the village is not far from Bethlehem.

Nearby is a lake called Llyn y Fan Fach that gave birth to the legend of the physicians of Myddfai. A cowherd whose name was Gwyn fell in love with a beautiful fairy lady he saw standing in the lake. He offered her some of his bread, but she refused it saying it was too hard-baked, and dived beneath the lake. The next day, he tried some unbaked dough but she refused that, saying it was too moist. The third day he offered half-baked bread and this time she accepted it. She agreed to marry him but said she would leave him after he gave her three causeless blows. The white lady of the lake (whose name was Nelferch) brought a dowry of fairy cattle and sheep, and they lived happily for many years and had three sons. One day, they were going to a wedding and Nelferch decided to ride a horse there. Gwyn flicked her playfully with gloves to make her hurry; this was the first causeless blow. Sometime later they went to a christening; Nelferch wept because she could see that the child would have a life of suffering. Gwyn tapped her on the shoulder to perk her up and gave the second causeless blow. The baby later died and at the funeral, Nelferch was happy because the baby was now free of pain. Her shocked husband touched her again, just enough for her to point out that this was the third causeless blow. She returned with her dowry to the fairy world beneath the waters of the lake. Gwyn drowned himself in his despair. The sons were instructed by their mother on how to be healers, showing them the herbs in Pant y Meddygon (Physician's Dingle). They and their descendants were reckoned to be the best doctors in all of Wales.[11]

When the Holy Family came to Wales, their settlements were given Jewish names. One of their gifts to the local people would have been their ability to heal. When looking for clues as evidence of their stay, there would appear to be a link between Jewish place names and renowned healers. Some members of the Holy Family settled in the village of Myddfai and the gift of healing was handed down through their descendants. When Mary and Joseph left Salem, they set off to Strata Florida, guided and helped by the Druids and their people. They went up the valley where Talley Abbey now stands to Pumpsaint and Ffarmers, passing through the Landscape Temple of the Zodiac on the way. From Ffarmers, following the valley of the River Twrch on horseback, they took to the high ground, leaving the safety of the mountains only when they reached the sanctuary of Strata Florida.

For further information on Joseph of Arimathea in Britain (but not the Lady Mary) see *The Keys to Avalon* by Steve Blake and Scott Lloyd.

---

[11] W Jenkyn Thomas, 'The Lady of the Lake', *The Welsh Fairy Book*

Connections to the Base Chakra

The Celtic Goddess of the Daughters of the Moon

The Priestesses of the Moon were responsible for the shrine on Nornour, and the Temple of the Zodiac. They were the original keepers of Strata Florida and the sacred site at Llyn-y-Tarw. The goddess whom they served originated from Atlantis. She became a member of the Celtic pantheon, so what was her name? This was not revealed until Christmas 2003 when I was given an insight into Mary's route after she had been to Strata Florida.

Joseph of Arimathea and Mary came to Strata Florida, but I was not sure which route they took after that. In December 2003, a Bronze Age artefact made of gold was found in a mine just below the throat chakra and was declared a treasure trove. This meant that the Ystwyth Valley had been more important than previously realised, and prompted another look at the map. This time I noticed that there was a mountain to the south-east of Blaenycwm, which was 520 metres high and named Banc Cerrig-fendigaid. It translates roughly as 'the Blessed One's mound of stones'. Once again, who was this Blessed One?

I dowsed, 'Is it Joseph of Arimathea?'

'*No*'

'Is it Mary?'

'*Yes,*' came the very positive response.

'Did Mary come up this valley?'

'*Yes.*'

'Did Joseph come too?'

'*No.*'

'Was she going to Llansantffraid Cwmdeuddwr?'

'*Yes.*'

Here she stayed for a little while. Llansantffraid Cwmdeuddwr means 'the Church of Saint Brighid in the valley of the two rivers', Wye and Elan. The present church was built on the land held sacred to the Celtic goddess Brighid.

This was the spiritual and administrative centre for the entire area of Mid Wales. It was the spiritual centre for the feminine energy, and for Mary it was a very sacred place. Joseph was not allowed to visit feminine temples and he had his own work to do.

This is why they did not stay together all of the time, and the Druidic protection was such that he had no need to fear for Mary's safety. The Druids and the Celtic people understood the necessity of keeping their presence a secret. This presented no difficulty because they were a secretive race; they had a long tradition of secrecy. Not only was all knowledge oral but it was always in code, a double protection. However, they left clues in the Welsh language that was not written in books but was written on the very land itself.

Banc Cerrig-fendigaid, a sacred mountain to the Druids, and Llansantffraid Cwmdeuddwr are two of these descriptive clues and acknowledge that the Lady Mary passed by and visited these places. She was on a personal journey of discovery, visiting the sacred shrines dedicated to Brighid, who was the goddess of light, fire and healing. She was the original goddess of the eternal flame in Britain. Worshipped by the Druids for her perfection, she has sometimes been confused with Our Lady. Because she was the goddess of light, it is understandable why Mary visited her sacred places. Her feast day was 1 February, the Celtic feast of Imbolc, or at the closest new moon to this date, and her prime function was that of fire and illumination. The Daughters of the Moon officiated at her temples and shrines. They brought with them from Atlantis their awareness of the feminine Earth energy and their ceremonies of its celebration. When Dee first went through the initiation pit, she found herself being escorted to the altar by these priestesses.

When I first visited Llyn-y-Tarw, I took a photograph of something which was not there. It appeared to be a statue, the head of a female figure with a white dove on her shoulder. I wanted to know more, but no more was given to me. It now seems that this was a statue of the goddess Brighid or more realistically, it is a photograph of the etheric blueprint of the statue. The dove was the ancient symbol of the goddess energy and represented love, gentleness and compassion. The statue was made in Egypt and carved from Egyptian stone and white marble. The female Druids carried on this service to Brighid and were still honouring this Atlantean feminine energy when Mary arrived in Wales. These temples and shrines would have been the spiritual and teaching centres of the area. The Daughters of the Moon (priestesses of the light) were the keepers of the crystal knowledge of Atlantis, and the crystals are keepers of the knowledge of the Daughters of the Moon. They held the Atlantean knowledge of crystals and a map of the Earth's crystalline grid, which was handed on to the Druidical priestesses of the goddess Brighid. By Mary's time, much of this knowledge had been lost or forgotten, but there was an understanding of working with crystals which was still valuable to those who needed to work with the crystalline grid.

As I looked back over the messages that I had been given by spirit, I could see that they had given me clues. At the Welsh Temple of the Zodiac they had said: 'This memory, the memory of us, is within the Earth's memory and as the Earth reawakens to it we can begin to function on the etheric levels as we once did on the physical Earth.' They were talking about the memory contained in the crystalline grid. At Bryher they had said that Mary and Joseph came to Britain, not to teach Christianity or to establish churches (because this had already been done) but to 'lay down the necessary energy in the grid pattern to strengthen it for the time that they knew that the planet had need of it.'

It seems that the Atlanteans were responsible for the creation of the energy grid, and the Daughters of the Moon maintained it at its junctions to make sure of the energy flow. At Inishmurray, they had a roofed temple made of marble, which had marble pillars. This kind of temple seems to have gone into our collective memory because it seems very familiar to us, and maybe this was one of the ideas behind stone circles.

The thread for this tapestry began in Atlantis, was established by the Atlantean priestesses of the Daughters of the Moon, and led forwards to the female Druids at the temples of Brighid, who were visited by the Lady Mary. We already knew that Mary and Joseph of Arimathea knew about the Atlantean crystals, because they used them in Carmarthen Bay for navigation. They followed this pathway so that Mary could visit the temples of Brighid and learn from them the secrets of the Atlantean crystals. They would have only visited sacred places on this grid system and this explains why they took this particular route, because, we are told, 'that is why they came'.

Brighid was the goddess of light, Mary was the light, and crystals are fire and light in physical form. The importance of the crystalline grid has not been fully appreciated since the time of the priestesses of the moon. So it seems that if anyone wants to follow in the footsteps of the Lady Mary, they must follow the crystal pathways of our land. There are large quartz crystals in the graveyard at Strata Florida, one of which can be seen by the side of the ancient yew tree. There is so much quartz that the locals use it for topping their gateposts. It is well known that the ancestors wore it as pendants and used it for enhancing energies.

The Celts and the Welsh held men and women equal. It was the Greeks who practised the inequality of the sexes and sold the idea to the Romans who brought it with them when they arrived in Britain. This caused the energies of the island to become unbalanced. The original holders of the sacred flame at the temple of Strata Florida were the Daughters of the Moon, and their goddess was Brighid. It now seems that there are two pathways of similar but not identical energy. The Pathway of the Beloved of the thirteen chakras from Bryher to Whitby is overlaid by another pathway taken by Mary, mother of Jesus. She visited the Celtic temples dedicated to the goddess Brighid in a wonderful celebration and acknowledgement of the feminine energy of Mother Earth, when she travelled through Wales from the Scilly Isles on her way to Anglesey. Brighid was the threefold goddess of light, fire and healing, combining her attributes with those of her two sisters.

> A goddess whom the bards worshipped, for very great and noble was her perfection. Her sisters were Brighid, the woman of healing, and Brighid, the smith-woman.
>
> Bishop Cormac, ninth century
> in Nigel Pennick, *The Celtic Saints*, p.20

The Base Chakra,
The Island of Bryher in the Scilly Isles

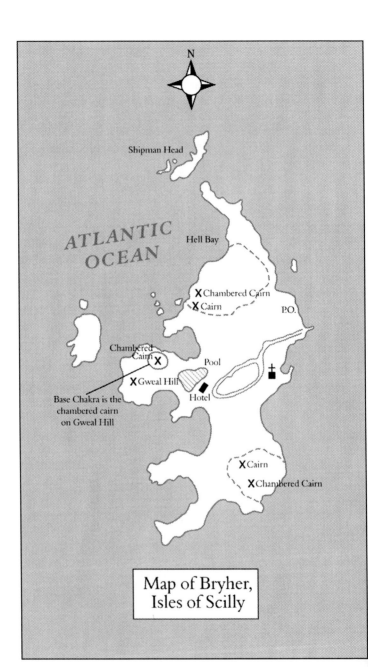

N

Shipman Head

ATLANTIC
OCEAN

Hell Bay

X Chambered Cairn
X Cairn

P.O.

Chambered
Cairn
X

Pool

✝

X Gweal Hill

Hotel

Base Chakra is the
chambered cairn
on Gweal Hill

X Cairn

X Chambered Cairn

Map of Bryher,
Isles of Scilly

The rosy moon and the sacred landscape of the Scillies showing the three peaks of Nornour, where there was a major shrine to the goddess. In earlier times, Bryher was a part of this island.

First Impressions of Bryher

A wild place – in this sense Bryher has a great deal in common with the mountain and the lake which form the crown chakra. The elements are very powerful and command the utmost respect. If the weather is bad, it is very, very bad and there is no alternative but to stay at home. Llyn-y-Tarw is high, about 1,600 feet, and the Scilly Isles have nothing between them and America but 3,000 miles of Atlantic Ocean. The elements of wind and water are in charge! The islands are twenty-eight miles west-south-west of Land's End. The 140 isles, islets and rocks were originally one landmass. At the end of the last Ice Age 10,000 years ago, the melt water caused the sea level to rise so much that by 3000 BC the islands had begun to separate. They called their island Ennor (The Land) and the Neolithic and Bronze Age peoples built their settlements and ritual monuments on it. By about AD 500 it had separated into three main islands, with Bryher joined to Tresco.

All of it may have been called Sillina after the goddess of the Isles. Sillina is a Celtic name, and may have given her name to the islands rather like Sabrina, the water goddess, gave her name to the River Severn. Since Minerva superseded the Celtic Brighid at the shrine at Bath, and the similarity between the names Sillina and Sulis (the goddess of Roman Bath) has led to suggestions that they were related, the original goddesses of fire and water must have been Brighid. A beacon fire was lit on Saint Martin's where later a Christian lighthouse chapel was built. Scilly was an important pagan centre in Romano-Celtic times, with a significant goddess shrine on Nornour dedicated to Sillina, perhaps linked to other temples on the mainland. Here were found hundreds of bronze brooches, nurturing goddesses and Venus figurines like the one shown on page 184, making them truly the isles of the goddess. Possibly the three prominent peaks or cairns of Nornour may have represented the triple aspects of the triple goddess Brighid. It was once a sacred holy place where the spirit of the goddess flowed through the hills to the sea.

Bryher is the smallest and wildest inhabited island. To the north are treacherous cliffs and windswept moorland, with flower fields and sandy bays to the south. Shipman Head stands as a bastion between the island and the sea. There were once burial tumuli on its summit but time and the ocean have taken their toll. Shipman Head Down has a unique system of prehistoric boulder walls running across the moorland, which are interlinked by over a hundred small cairns. These were boundary markers or had a ritual use in religious practices, and were aligned to the summer solstice. In 1756, a 'circle of Druid origin' was recorded on the highest point, but there is no trace of this now. Cist graves (stone burial chambers) and tumuli belonging to the Bronze Age can be seen on Gweal Hill, Samson Hill and Shipman Head Down. The archaeological evidence shows that the land was occupied by early settlers from c. 3000–2500 BC.

Bryher is one and a half miles long and half a mile wide. When it was joined to Tresco they were both called Saint Nicholas after the patron saint of travellers. In the sixteenth century the ever-encroaching sea finally divided it in two, forming Tresco (Place of the Elder Trees) and Bryher (Land of the Hills). It is unlikely that there was a church before 1742, when the Church of All Saints was built. The church stands on the seashore where the damp from the salt spray has caused the plaster to peel from the walls. It is believed that Christianity was brought here from the Mediterranean or Middle East, following the Coptic Celtic tradition of Saint Anthony and not the Roman version. This is because the ancient sites resemble the Christian oratories as found off the Irish coast, and may have been derived from there.

On the other hand it is much more likely that they are following the Celtic tradition from Brittany. It is suggested in the museum that the first Christians would have travelled up the Brittany coast.

In 1999, an Iron Age grave was found when the wheel of a tractor fell into it. It contained an Iron Age sword, thirty-four inches long in a bronze scabbard, probably dating from 250–125 BC. There was also a bronze mirror from the same period. Both graves with mirrors and those with swords are extremely rare, and this is the only known grave in north-west Europe to contain both. It throws into question the sex of the occupant. Was it a man's or a woman's grave? Did it contain people of both sexes, or was it the grave of a warrior queen? DNA sampling was tried but the bone was so decayed that the tests were inconclusive. The discovery has established that Bryher was a very important place in Iron Age times.

Unlike every other Scillonian island, Bryher has clung fiercely to its own identity. There are few cars, only one or two tractors and Land Rovers. Electricity arrived in 1986. There is no doctor, pub or school, and water shortage is acute in summer. The idea that the people should cling to the 'old ways' is exactly how you would expect it to be at the root chakra. Earthed and practical they may be, but sometimes very earthed people can become stuck, and be unwilling to move forward or in any direction.

There is no doubt, however, that the Scilly Isles were, and still are, a sacred landscape. When Scilly was one island, the fertile low-lying land was farmed, leaving the hilltop slopes for the cairns, graves, tumuli and chambered cairns of the ritual landscape which denoted the sacredness of the land. There are over 500 identified so far. These were where the living came to worship and connect with the ancestors and the Earth goddess. The Earth Mother was in this land. The outline of her body was formed by the land itself, which can still be seen today if we look through the eyes of our ancestors.

A clay goddess figurine from the shrine at Nornour

The bronze mirror from Bryher (250–125 BC)

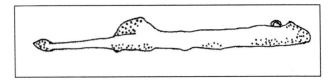

An Iron Age sword in a bronze scabbard, from Bryher

The Base Chakra

This is situated about a third of the way along the island towards the north end. There is a chambered cairn that dowses as a twelve-pointed star. When asked if it was a burial cairn the answer was, 'No, it was used for religious purposes only,' for ceremonies honouring the goddess. When water from Llyn-y-Tarw and the other holy wells was put into the pool, what we were doing when performing this act was to re-energise the water of this sacred place.

It just so happened that our friends who had been the first to visit Llansteffan were again going to be there at the same time as we would be on the Scillies. We had arranged to join in meditation from both sides of the sea at twelve o'clock on 21 May, linking the Scillies and Carmarthen Bay in a pathway of light.

As we did this I was aware of this energy pathway. We linked also with the whales and dolphins, the carriers of the crystal energy, because the sacral chakra is under the water in Carmarthen Bay and the Scillies are very small islands surrounded by ocean. While meditating at Carmarthen Bay, Dee was aware of a whale's tail at Worms Head, and also of a cloud whale. She says that she was aware of a Celtic equidistant cross, and of the whales crossing over the centre of this cross from one direction while the dolphins were crossing over from the other direction. This felt magical.

Water is the overwhelming link running through this system. We were forming a thought-energy pathway of crystal light.

2002 was the year of mirrors and the mirror image. Although Llyn-y-Tarw is 1,600 feet up in the Welsh mountains and the pool on Bryher is at sea level, the similarity between them is almost that of a mirror image. There are rushes around both lakes, boggy ground and rough, coarse grass. The terrain is very similar, and if someone mixed the photos of both places it would be hard to notice the difference. All of this is a celebration of the feminine energy, the water re-energising and healing the 'old Earth' and preparing it for the age to come. In the symbolism of the sword and the mirror – the coming together of the masculine and the feminine, the sun and the moon, darkness and light – it brings about a balance, a harmony of both within ourselves, that we may be healed, and go on to heal our Earth.

A week later we found ourselves at Llansteffan adding the water from Bryher to Saint Anthony's Well. This was accepted as a special gift for the chakra, because when walking along the cliff path I was aware of two Druids who escorted me, one on each side. There was a third who wore a grey robe and had a long grey beard. I think he was Merlin, although he did not look as I had seen him before. He was throwing his staff from one hand to another to generate energy and he thanked me for what we had done. Sitting on the seat by the path I thought of Bryher and sent some energy to the pool. There was a circle of priestesses standing around it. The energy link had been made from both directions.

Asking the whales and the dolphins to carry the crystalline energy

An Update on the Bryher Burial

After cleaning, the mirror was revealed as beautifully decorated, with an elaborate curved handle, and around the rim there is a border of incised chevrons. There is a circular decoration with spokes that could possibly represent the sun. There was also a brooch, a ring from the sword belt, a shield, a spiral ring and a tin object. We saw the mirror and the sword in the Museum of Saint Mary's. The tin object may have been a decorated bronze canister like the one from a female cart grave in Yorkshire. There have been about twenty other mirror burials in Britain. Although DNA sampling was not successful, it is now thought that the bones belonged to a high status person, either a priest or a priestess, and that the mirror was not used for personal reasons but for scrying or prophecy. The burial dates were from between the third and first century BC, and from the time when Bryher was part of one island, which included the shrine at Nornour.[1]

What we have been able to find out, through means not very different from those which the grave's occupant would have used, is that the grave contained the body of the high priestess. She was a priestess of the Daughters of the Moon, who looked after the shrine of the goddess. This shrine was an oracle where prophecy and scrying were done for the people. The same thing was done at the crown chakra by the priestesses there, who were also Daughters of the Moon. The sword was used for channelling the energies into the mirror, which would have taken on the properties of a crystal ball. For the Druids, the sword – never to be drawn – was a powerful symbol of protection, and of peace. It forms the shape of a cross. There is a strong connection between these islands and Atlantis. The daughters would have practised many Atlantean beliefs, and the crystal of the west was somewhere off this coast.

When Roma, a friend who accompanied me to the Scilly Isles, put water from the chakra line in the pool on Bryher, she was aware of two hooded figures standing on either side of her. They were priestesses who had come to support and acknowledge her. Later, when I had returned to the mainland at Llansteffan, I 'saw'

---

[1] Cheryl Straffon, *The Earth Mysteries Guide to Ancient Sites on the Isles of Scilly*

a circle of priestesses standing around the pool on the island and knew that the contact was complete. At Llyn-y-Tarw I 'saw' priestesses laying flowers before the statue, and was told, 'The Pleiades represent the feminine energy of this land. They are the Daughters of the Moon.' These daughters were the very same sect who worshipped and officiated at the shrine at Nornour (the mirror image again). The inspiration behind my painting, 'The Rosy Moon', was this feminine energy manifesting itself in these islands.

There was another artist who visited Bryher in 1961, who painted the female form in the shape of a flame. In his painting, entitled 'Rose moon' (1964), he combined the rose with the moon's sphere of light which replaced and enhanced the flame motif. The moon was partially eclipsed by pirouetting figures born from a living rose. The artist's name was B S Andrews. Clearly, the rose, the moon and the feminine energy are still there in a vibrational form for people to tune in to.

The sun setting on the island of Bryher, from Saint Mary's
(Photo by Roma Harding)

Connections to the Scilly Isles

When 'tuning in' to the energy of a place, there seems to be much information that can be accessed in several ways, but mostly through meditation and dowsing. Since seeing the red rose in meditation and realising that it stood for the Madonna, I 'saw' someone who looked similar to the statue of Mary which can be seen in Catholic churches. I 'saw' her in connection with Llansteffan and again on the island of Saint Mary's. Dowsing produced the information that Mary had been on Bryher and had visited the two sacred sites there. She had also bathed in the pool, but had not drunk the water, possibly because it was polluted with seawater.

It is necessary to try to understand how Joseph and Mary must have felt and what their priorities would have been, while trying to put it in the context of their time. This was AD 37, and they were political refugees. Joseph had been given a precious charge from his Master Jesus which was to safeguard Mary. He would have risked his own life but he would never have risked hers, and would have moved with extreme caution. As a travelling merchant, he would have known how to avoid the Romans and the main trade routes. Britain was the only place in the known world at that time where they could have sought sanctuary, ruled over as it was by a group of people whose spirituality was such that Joseph and Mary knew they would be understood, welcomed and protected. So they sailed up the coast of Brittany, helped by the Druids there, and stopped off at the Scilly Isles. They then sailed on to Carmarthen Bay, to seek sanctuary and protection from the Druids of Wales. They used the Crystal of the West in the bay to navigate their way to safety. A crystal is a candle that never goes out. A powerful crystal like this is like a lighthouse, which never fails and can be seen and felt from a great distance on the ether. It would have been easier than navigation by the stars, which cannot always be seen. This Atlantean crystal played its part in their escape. We know that their trust in the Druids was not betrayed, because they were never heard of again. But there was a powerful following of Mary in Wales. All of the churches beginning with 'Llanfair' mean 'Church of Mary'. Mary is 'Mair', which has mutated to 'fair'.

Other information that came through was that Bryher was dedicated to the Pleiades, and to Taurus (again there is a mirror image of the crown chakra). It also had a connection with Atlantis and the feminine energy. It has some connection to the bull which was understood to be the constellation of Taurus.

We first encountered the goddess at the crown chakra in the form of Hathor, the Egyptian goddess, and now we have met up with another goddess in the Scilly Isles – but who is she really? She is the embodiment of the feminine energy of the Earth. She is reminding us of the wisdom of the ancients who said that the Earth is a feminine body. She is our Earth Mother. It is not really important what name is given to this energy of the land, as long as we recognise the energy as the loving, nurturing, gentle energy of the beautiful Planet Earth. It is energy that gave us life.

There is this strong sense of the deep love that these people had for their land. They really did regard the land as their mother. It nurtured and fed them, sheltered them and provided them with all their needs, and in return they treated it with love and deep respect. The cycle of seasons, springtime and harvest, winter and summer guided their year, marked their calendar and was the reason for their very existence. This was the foundation of their lives and of their faith, the reason for the feminine religion of the Daughters of the Moon.

This line is on the feminine grid, so the priestesses held in their hands the protection and energising of the land. This is why it is so important now in the present time, when the masculine energies have unbalanced the Earth. Sacred places are light portals where light beings and angels can reach through to us. They are the gateways in the web of ley lines and the crystalline grid. It was, and still is, essential that these stargates are kept clean and pure. This was done by the priests, priestesses and Druids of old. Now is the time for all of us to take over these tasks.

'Yes, the priestesses of the moon were connected with Atlantis and were guided by the Pleiadeans. This whole pathway is connected with the Pleiadeans, all connections which have come up on this pathway are Pleiadean. This is where the feminine energy guidance for the Earth planet originates. This energy has been buried for around 2,000 years but now the time has come to uncover it and allow it to flow through and over and around this planet.

'This is why water is feminine. It is why Celtic rivers were feminine. The Pleiadeans are calling on you to reconsecrate and sanctify this energy pathway as the sacred way.

'This is what is meant by the Pathway of the Beloved. It is the path

The base chakra's guardian
(Photo by Annie Henry)

The base chakra is between the two boulders
(Photo by Annie Henry)

way of the feminine Earth, of the seven sisters of the Pleiades. You were right to bring flowers to our sacred sites. The only celebrations we allowed were the laying of flowers – all else was banned. Our pathway is the path of peace, gentleness and love.

'When Mary and Joseph came here, they knew this. That is why they came, to enter this energy and find the peace to continue their work uninterrupted by violence. They found the energy vibration to continue their work, not in the teaching so much as in the laying down of the necessary energy in the grid pattern, to strengthen it for the time when they knew that the planet had need of it. That time is now.'

The Base Chakra and the Guardian

The base chakra's wonderful guardian seems to be made up of two images: a powerful monster of the 'don't mess with me' type, combined with the image of a turtle sitting on top of him. These two energies flow into each other in a connection reminiscent of Celtic flowing energies. The monster's face is very masculine, while the turtle is the symbol of the Earth Mother, the goddess energy. The markings and sections on some turtles' shells total thirteen, the lunar cycle and the symbol of the primal mother. The sea turtle has often been described as carrying Mother Earth on her back. In energy medicine, described as 'healing from the Kingdoms of Nature', the sea turtle energy is used for helping those who are spaced out and ungrounded to get into their bodies and become fully grounded on the Earth.[1] A truly amazing connection with the base chakra and its grounding force!

In 2005, the giant leather-backed turtles began to visit Cardigan Bay in Wales, causing great excitement. They were signalling the return of the goddess and our awareness of her. In August of that year, a pod of 2,000 dolphins and sixteen whales were seen off the coast of Pembroke. So many had never been seen there before. When the people of Bryher cared for and nurtured Mother Earth, they knew she would do the same for them. We need to see this connection between all things, because we cannot separate ourselves from what we do to the Earth, any more than the turtle can separate itself from its shell.

---

[1] Sabina Pettitt, *Energy Medicine*, p.184

Connections with Brighid,
The Native Goddess of the Welsh Chakra Line

Snowdrops were known as Candlemas bells,
Mary's tapers, or purification flowers

At Last the Goddess Lifts Her Veil

As I have described, it gradually became apparent that this chakra
line on the crystalline grid was a feminine energy line, which was

responding to the energy of the Earth Mother. There were glimpses of this goddess energy in Hathor, Brighid and, finally, in Mother Mary. Like peeling back the layers of an onion, we began to go backwards in time. First there was the Lord Rhys and the building of the Cistercian monasteries: Strata Florida, Valle Crucis, Fountains Abbey and Rievaulx, which now seems like yesterday in comparison with what was to follow. The next layer was c. AD 37 with the Welsh Grail and the arrival of Joseph of Arimathea bringing with him Mary, the mother of Jesus, who visited the shrines of Brighid, the 'bright one', on this line. Another layer revealed the Druids, and their reverence for Brighid, in particular as the patron goddess of the muse and the fire of inspiration. Next, the Daughters of the Moon, Brighid's priestesses, revealed themselves to us as the original feminine guardians of the crystalline grid. They kept the shrines of the perpetual flame on Bryher in the Scillys and at the landscape temple of the Zodiac just south of Lampeter. They were the first keepers of the temple at Strata Florida and they kept her shrine at Llansantffraed Cwmdeuddwr and officiated at her shrine at the crown chakra.

It is safe to say that any temple which kept a perpetual flame was originally dedicated to her; she was the goddess of fire, light and water. The final layer revealed the exciting concept of Brighid as the Earth Mother goddess of the temples of Atlantis. This goddess was connected with both fire and water, with the streams, rivers, wells and lakes with which we have been privileged to become acquainted. This was where the pathway we were following backwards through time was leading. It was in Atlantis that they kept her temple of the perpetual flame.

This has been a Grail journey and there have been different versions in this story, but the origin of the Grail is to be found in Atlantis. The original chalice or drinking cup was given by an angel to the Atlantean royal family who were responsible for the element of water. It is from here that our stories of the Holy Grail are descended. This memory has remained in our psyche, surfacing again and again through the ages. The quest is the search for knowledge of things of the spirit and the ultimate overcoming of the baser self, so that the spirit may one day soar.

We are also searching for the knowledge of where this came from, where it all began, because some of us were there, some of us remember. It all began in Atlantis, and the connecting link through the elements of fire and water is this Atlantean goddess. She is the bridge. Because of this connection, her priestesses also kept the knowledge of crystals. This knowledge has surfaced once again within ourselves quite recently.

They were keepers of the knowledge of the crystalline grids. They were able to see the grid system at this time, and this is why they built their shrines and temples along the Welsh chakra line. This was the time when the feminine energy system ruled supreme and men were not allowed in the sacred precinct of Brighid's temples and shrines. The priestesses were aware that the pendulum had swung too far in their own direction and there would come a time when it would swing to the other extreme – to masculine dominance. The Druids knew this also, and the swing began with the coming of the Romans and their Church. There are stories of female saints who refused to bow to the dominance of powerful men: Saint Melangell who fled from Ireland to escape a forced marriage; Saint Bride, the Christianised version of Brighid, who disfigured herself to avoid matrimony; Saint Winifred of Holywell, who had her head cut off by a rejected suitor; and Saint Cecelia, to name but a few. Their stories illustrate the removal of the freedom of women, and their domination by masculine energy, led by the Church. This was bound to happen, as the pendulum swings wildly from one extreme to another before it is able to settle down to a more gentle and balanced movement, which will happen in the Aquarian Age when masculine and feminine energies come into harmony.

Brighid the Bright was a divine being, a goddess with exalted human and angelic qualities, who may be seen as a sister of the Archangel Michael, the Son of Light. In its early Gaelic form, her name was pronounced 'Bree-it' from which came the English word 'bright'. She was the great goddess of these islands and elsewhere before the coming of Christ, and was held in deep reverence in Ireland, Wales and the Scottish islands even after the advent of Christianity. For those who feel that the ideas of Christ and the Archangel Michael are completed when balanced by a feminine counterpart, let your prayers rise to Brighid. Use rose oil and petals in your ceremonies to celebrate her presence and feast day, and send out the light in her name.

Brighid was the one all-powerful goddess at a time when the goddess energy reigned supreme, and she was all things to all people, the goddess of fire and light and water. The Atlantean connection came via the western seaboard of Britain and it is possible to understand this through the following Irish tradition. As the temple goddess, she and her two sisters, also named Brighid, were daughters of the Irish god the Daghdha, an Earth and father god and one of the two greatest kings of the Tuatha Dé Danann (people of the goddess Danu). For the Druids he was the god of wisdom, the fertility deity and sorcerer, a primal father deity of enormous power. Brighid represented the sister aspect of the great goddess.

As the goddess of fire and light, the exalted one's primal function was that of fire and illumination, which inspired the poetry of the Druids. Celtic gods and goddesses frequently personified the qualities distinctive in Celtic society. Inspiration, poetic skill, heroic valour, artistic and creative ability and of course eloquence. They even had a god of eloquence. The eternal flame burnt in her temples, and she was fused with Minerva in Romano-Celtic temples. *Sulis* or *sul* is Gaelic for gap, orifice or eye, and Brighid's wells were thought to heal eyes. She was associated with both the sun and the moon, and when I had a vision of Brighid at the crown chakra, it was at night and there were stars in her hair. At first I thought she was the moon goddess, until I saw the trident in her hand and recognised it as her symbol (as in Britannia, another of her aspects). This makes sense when we realise that the feminine energy is represented by the moon, but this all-encompassing goddess represented both the sun and the moon, light and darkness held in balance.

She is the feminine counterpart of Govannon, the Welsh smith god who forged magical weapons in a secret castle on top of one of the highest mountains in Snowdonia, when a druidic priesthood, the Fferyll, lived in a city called Emrys. They were alchemists and metal-workers skilled in producing fire which represented an initiation into the higher powers of the mind. This smith god's Irish counterpart was Goibhniu, the divine smith and leader of the triad Trí Dée Dána, which means 'three gods of craftsmanship'. After their final battle, they were given the underground half of their realm, and the Daghdha gave each of the Tuatha Dé Danann an earthen barrow to live in. This was called a '*sidh*', which is connected with the Welsh '*caer*', as in Caer Sidi (a reference to the sacral chakra). Goibhniu was accompanied by the two other deities of the Trí Dée Dána, sometimes referred to as his brothers. One was Creidhne, the god of metalworking, and Luchtaine, the divine wheelwright. All three were active in the second battle of Magh Tuiredh, when they worked at lightning speed to make and repair the weapons of the Tuatha Dé Danann. It is easy to see a link with the ancient sister goddesses of skills and inspiration which were known throughout Indo-European tradition. It was claimed that the Celts originated in India and migrated across Europe. It would seem that the origin of Britannia's trident was not the one seen with Neptune, but the lotus-shaped holder of the sacred flame which links with the eastern religions.

Water is also the symbol of this goddess and she has proved to be the goddess of this line of water. The lakes and rivers and the sacred well at Llansteffan were sites of power and were dedicated to her. The water from the wells with their source deep beneath the Earth was thought to contain the energy of the night sun, and the way in which water catches and traps the sun's fire was believed to show the similarity between fire and water. Sparkling sunbeams dancing on its surface suggested the eye of the light, and led to the Celtic people's association of Brighid with eyes. At the crown chakra the dancing light we saw inside the tiny waves reminded us of this eye of the light. Any sacred well believed to heal eyes was originally dedicated to her. Saint Anthony's Well at the sacral chakra was once Brighid's, because when Dee visited it she was made to understand that she must place some well water on her third eye. Saint Non's Well, situated at Saint David's in Pembroke, has a reputation for healing eyes and must have been Brighid's well originally. Her priestesses also lived by the lake at the crown chakra, where they acted as oracles.

Brighid's distinctive cross was woven at Beltane from straw saved from the previous harvest. It resembles what is called the 'eye of God'. This is where corn-dollies came from. Her feast day was 1 February at Imbolc, and was Christianised as Candlemas Day on 2 February. There was a Welsh song: 'Candlemas Day, plant beans in the clay, put candles and candlesticks all away.'

At this time she was thought to take the form of a snake awakening from hibernation, which was a symbol of her connection with healing. This was also called the Feast of the Milk because lambs are born at this time, and snow at this time is known locally in Wales as the lambing snow. She herself has survived from Atlantis and is known as the goddess of survival, whether physically, emotionally or financially. She is the goddess of survival against all odds. One of her names was Bright Arrow, and her symbols are her cross, an arrow, water, an eye, a snake and the trident. The snowdrop is her flower.

As an Atlantean goddess she represents crystals, their knowledge and use. In her Mary aspect she is associated with lapis, the crystal for the third eye. When the early artists began to paint the Holy Family, they used ground-up pigment of lapis lazuli for her robes. They also used gold leaf, which must have made their depictions radiant.

Brighid's importance had to be recognised by the Roman Catholic Church; they simply could not get away with leaving her out, and so, as Saint Bride, she became acceptable as the midwife or foster-mother of Jesus. In the Hebrides, she was said to have delivered Him in the stable at Bethlehem, putting three drops of pure water on his brow. This is the Christian version of an ancient Celtic myth regarding the birth of the Celtic son of light and the blessing of three drops of wisdom on his brow. It is possible that she was given this association because she fostered the perfect Christ qualities in the hearts of men and women prior to his coming. It was the Master Jesus who, of all people, opened himself in complete surrender to the incoming Christ spirit.

The goddess is the divine feminine energy of the cosmos, whichever form she is perceived by us to take. I have been granted a vision of this energy in her original form in Atlantis. In her temple where a series of long steps led up to it, she appeared as swirling patterns of rainbow light, moving, changing, shimmering. A kaleidoscope of coloured light – that was all she was: light. Somewhere in this moving pattern of light was a beautiful shining feminine face. Her energy was the pure energy of love. This was the original Bright One.

To celebrate her, use candles of orange, yellow or red reflected in dishes of water. Burn rose oil and decorate her altar with her cross, an arrow, a snake or a picture of an eye.

The most important is water and the bright flame of a candle. The goddess's arrows of transformation will work for you if you sprinkle some of the water onto some coins, which you then give away, to show that you are willing to give away outworn ideas and energies.

An Invocation to Brighid

Goddess of light, we honour you,
Bright Flame, we give thanks to you.
Bless the goddess energy within us.
And help us to shine as brightly
As the star from whence we came.

THE CONNECTION BETWEEN THE GODDESS AND THE SAINT

The ancient gods and goddesses were revered and worshipped by the Irish people, and Brighid was one of the greatest. In Irish folklore she was associated with literature, poetry, healing, smithcraft, nurture, fertility, and fire – just as in Wales.

When Christianity came to Ireland it slowly took root, assimilating older beliefs and practices like the celebration of Imbolc, fire ceremonies and the use of sacred wells and candles. At this time of transition the historical Brigid (Saint Bride) was born circa AD 453 according to strong local tradition at Umeras, five miles north-west of the town of Kildare. Her father Dubthach, was a local chieftain whose descendants may now be called Duff or Duffy. Her mother was a bond-maid in Dubthach's household and is believed to have been a Christian.

Brigid the saint inherited much of the folklore associated with the goddess, and separating the two is now impossible. They are so interwoven that Saint Brigid stands at the rather uneasy meeting of these two worlds, belonging neither to Christianity nor to the ancient religion exclusively.

Brigid established her abbey and church in Kildare beside a great oak (the Gaelic name Cil Dara means cell or church of the oak) around AD 480 on the site now occupied by Saint Brigid's Cathedral. This was probably as an evolution of a previous sanctuary of Druidic priestesses of the goddess who were converted to Christianity. Of course, this would explain the perpetual flame kept burning at their fire temple and why it was out of bounds to males. This was also true of Brighid's Temple of the Zodiac and her sanctuaries of Strata Florida and Llansantffraed Cwmdeuddwr in Wales. She held a unique position in the early Irish Church, presiding over the church of Kildare and as the abbess of a double monastery for men and women. Her abbey was acclaimed as a centre of education, culture, worship and hospitality. There was a parallel with Saint Hild of Whitby, whose abbey was a centre for all of these in the Celtic tradition. Likewise both abbeys were burnt and destroyed by the Danes between AD 835 and 998. Later the monastery for men was taken over by the Augustinians, who also took over Whitby. After the Reformation, the bishops of Kildare were required to be either English or of English descent and education. In 1807 Daniel Delaney, Bishop of Kildare and Leighlin, restored the Ancient Order of Brigid at Tullow, County Carlow, bringing an oak sapling from Kildare which is now a mighty tree, and provides a link with the Druidic priestesses of old. Brigid's Fire was relit in 1993 by Mary Theresa Cullen, and since then the Brigidine Sisters of Kildare have kept it burning at Solas Bhride.[1]

She is remembered in Wales as Saint Ffraid in villages called Llansantffraid (church of Saint Ffraid or Fraed), of which there are six in Wales (my two children were born in one of them, proving a link with Brighid of which I was unaware at the time). A bay in Pembroke is known as Saint Bride's Bay. There are four Saint Brides, all of them in south and west Wales: Saint Bride's in Pembroke, Saint Bride's-Super-Ely, Saint Bride's Major, and Saint Bride's Wentlooge, so it can be said that she is remembered well in

---

[1] Rita Minehan, *Rekindling the Flame*. The Celtic Goddess Brighid's name is usually spelt this way. In Rita Minehan's booklet, Saint Bride is called Saint Brigid, spelt as shown.

Wales. The story goes that Bride wished to become a nun, but was threatened by her father with marriage, so she mutilated herself by popping her eyes out. When the danger was over she popped them back again, and wandered around with a group of nuns looking for a place to build her convent. She found it at Kildare, the holy place of the oak. She is said to have restored the sight of a blind companion, a healing linking her with the goddess.

Shrine of Saint Brigid at Kildare
(Photo by Charmane Bridges)

In Wales, medieval travellers would say the prayer 'Saint Bride, bless our journey' before setting out. That Brighid's mantle fell on Mary can be easily seen in Welsh customs. On the Gwyl Fair y Canhwyllau (the Festival of Mary of the Candles) on the second day of February, the people sang a wassail song which includes the words:

Gwyl fair hefyd sydd wyl hyfryd
Mair yn gwmwys aeth i'r Eglwys.
A gwyryfon o'r cwmpason
Ai canhwlle i gyd yn ole.

(The Festival of Mary is a delightful festival,
Mary went to church
with virgins from the locality,
their candles all alight.)

On this day candles were blessed and distributed to the people, who afterwards carried them, lighted, in solemn procession. After the Reformation, this blessing was discontinued but the symbol of lighted candles was too strong to be put aside. In Kidwelly in Carmarthenshire in 1915, people still lit candles on this day and put them in every window of the house. This custom was probably widespread and it is a custom which we could all revive: opening the front door to let in new energy, and opening the back door to let out the old.

In Ireland at Candlemas, the people made special Saint Bride's crosses out of rushes which had to be pulled and not cut, and must be woven from left to right. They were then set in place over the door as a sacred protection until being replaced the following Candlemas.

Saint Bride is welcomed back into the house by rekindling the hearth fire after it has been put out and the house is spring-cleaned. The fire was very central to their lives; it kept them warm and cooked their food. They kept it alight by banking it up at night, and this would have been the only time it was extinguished. We can light candles in our own homes at this time and join in this age-old ceremony of celebration of the return of the light.

As this final piece of the puzzle falls into place and the connection between the Celtic goddess and the Lady Mary has been traced, it is easy to see why Mary visited Brighid's shrines and temples on her journey through Wales. Mary was heading for Anglesey, and it was on Holy Island that she made her base.

where she remained, protected by the Druids. Mary was not a goddess, she was a real person. She needed safety above all else. She needed to continue her learning process among the Druid branches of the University of the Ageless Wisdoms as her son had done before her. This was so that she could help Mother Earth and her human family.

A MESSAGE FROM MARY, THE MOTHER OF JESUS, RECEIVED ON ANGLESEY, 12 MAY 2004

'I am Mary. I have been here for a long time waiting for the right moment, the moment when this centre of light would be opened for the peace of the world. This is a very spiritual centre for the entire planet. It is a beacon of light at the head of Wales and the Celtic people. It is a shining light that has been ignited and now pulsates through the planet above and below ground. There had to be a moment when the time was right and this was it.

'The crystals are linked. In the last week there was an ignition and a movement from this place around the world. It was like an explosion of extra power through the crystalline grid. You are right to understand that this is what I did when I came here. I laid energy down in this grid. I worked on the lines set in place by the Pleiadeans. My link with them is a strong one although I was not from this star system. Continue your work, you will be guided.'

So it becomes clear that the Irish goddess Brighid, both the goddess and the saint, links the pagan Celtic and medieval Christian traditions. She acts as the bridge between the Celtic and Christian cultures. As a warrior-maiden, she is nationally venerated as a symbol and authority of justice in Britain, and is personified as Britannia, the Roman personification of Britain still on our coinage today. She was known as Mistress of the Mantle, and Minerva had her mantle exhibited at the Acropolis, another link with Brighid. In the Russian Orthodox Church, the Mantle of Mary was venerated as the 'Mantle of the Very Holy Mother of God', Brighid's mantle literally falling on Mary. As the goddess of the perpetual fire, the role of fire-keeper was an honoured title and usually fell to the women. There were many such sisterhoods in Britain, the native vestal priestesses who were scattered about the land as guardians of sacred wells, hills, caves and trees; many of these are still waiting to be rediscovered by ourselves. This helps to explain how this story of the Grail journey through Wales came into being. In Celtic tradition, the woman of the fairy hills and the seer-poets were the mystical sisterhoods and brother-hoods who preserved the poetic function of the goddess Brighid with their prophetic storytelling and fire-keeping.

The Goddess has the Last Word

Between 500 BC and AD 500 the qualities and images of the goddess were assimilated into public consciousness, which, by the Middle Ages, were borrowed to adorn Mary, the Mother of Jesus. Many of the cults of the goddess involved the ritual guardianship of sacred fires, but these fires were now to be extinguished. Around AD 380, Christianity became the state Roman religion, and devotees to the Blessed Virgin Mary replaced the cult of the goddess. At the Council of Ephesus in 431, where only a few years before the goddess had ceased to be worshipped, Mary was formally declared to be the Mother of God, or God-bearer. The goddess cycle had begun again. Within the Church itself there is no evidence for the goddess survival in the shape of the Mary cult until the fifth century. If the church eventually turned its Virgin into a new Isis, it was because the need for a goddess was overwhelming.

There was an old Church tradition that Mother Mary as-cended bodily into heaven. Members of the Church were divided between this belief and those who thought that her mortal remains had been interred according to the local customs where she had died. However, in 1950 the Assumption was declared dogma by Pope Pius XII. From this date Mary's bodily ascension into heaven became official. So this was the moment when she finally became the goddess.

I am Brighid

I am Brighid, the fiery one,
My name means Bright Flame,
I am the dawn,
I am the moment when the dark night turns to day.

I am the moment when the light illuminates the sky,
I am the bringer of springtime out of winter,
I am the beginning.
As the wheel turns so do I.
I am the dawn at springtime.
I am the gift of life.
I am the protectress of all women.
I am the joy of new beginnings.
I am the goddess of the Light.

Further Information On Brighid

This is Brighid's promise on her day: 'Every second day will be fine from my day onwards, as well as half of my own day.' The Feast of Imbolc is the second of the great quarterly feasts of the Celtic calendar and marks the mid-point of the half of the sacred year. Modern Irish explains the name as 'in the belly' – winter pregnant with summer – but an alternative form in old Celtic is 'ewe's milk'. Another version of the meaning of Brighid's name comes from the stem – *brig*, meaning 'height', 'summit' or 'top', as applied to hills and mountains. Brigantia would mean 'She who raises herself on high – who is exalted'. However, from the modern Celtic languages, it seems the term '*briga*' originally meant force and power, meaning invigorating essence, as well as 'hill'. Also in the Brythonic languages '*bri*' means fame, respect and value. Thus '*briga*' means both raised up and also something that imparts strength – an upwelling of force. This fire or force is an energy which wells up and imparts strength and meaning.

As such, Brighid is the universal muse, maybe even the same as the *awen* invoked in the Welsh Bardic traditions. '*Awen*' means literally 'flowing spirit' and was known to the Druids as divine inspiration or blessing. Brighid is accompanied by a white cow (her link with Hathor) and her flower is said to be both the snowdrop and the dandelion – the latter being a flower with many medicinal properties and which contains a milky juice, linking it to cow's milk. At one time this might have been coltsfoot, which flowers much earlier – nearer the time of Imbolc. Her messenger bird is the oystercatcher, which shares its sacred status with all other beings that are naturally black, white and red. The snake – our native adder – is her divinatory animal, linking her to the mythology of the serpent goddesses.

Brighid was portrayed ceremonially as a doll or statue, or a female who took on her role. At Imbolc, hands, feet and head were washed as purification by water (compare the Welsh – *ymolchi*, washing). Traditionally Imbolc marked the point after which it was no longer necessary to carry a candle when going out to early morning work. Another talisman in addition to the four-armed cross was 'Brighid's mantle'. This was a length of cloth or ribbon left at the window on the night of the feast to absorb the power of the goddess. It would be worn for healing or protection, often taking seven years to reach full potency. Often the eldest daughter of the house would go outside, gather a bunch of rushes, then on the threshold call out: 'Be on your knees and open your eyes and let blessed Brid in' (any female or even a man could do this).

The other members of the household would say, 'Thrice welcome, noble lady.' The rushes were then placed on a central table and the Brighid substitute would bless the house. After this, the entire household would make crosses, called *crosoga*, later to be blessed by a priest, and hung over the doors to protect against want. A loaf of bread shaped like the cross was placed over the rushes and eaten in a ritual atmosphere, and in Wales they would make a cake-like bread with fruits called *bara brith* (currant bread).

Still in vogue in parts of Ireland, notably County Kerry, is a straw doll wearing child's clothes. It was carried from house to house by young men and women who begged hospitality and in return sang songs and recited blessings and prayers. The female who took the part of Brighid was expected to have outstanding moral qualities and be, if possible, a mirror of Brighid. Some wore visor-like masks to emulate the spirit of the land. A bed was prepared for the doll and during the night Brighid was thought to rise and strike the hearth-fire with her wand. If the mark was evident in the ashes in the morning, this was a very good omen.

On the Isle of Man the head of the house would stand at the door and sing:

> '*Brede, Brede, come to my house,*
> *Come to my house tonight,*
> *Open the door for Brede.*'

Besides the effigy of the goddess, the people carried 'Brighid's belt' – a large hoop of braided straw decorated with four woven crosses, which marked the quarters of its circumference. At each house visited, the inhabitants would be invited to pass through the '*crios*' or hoop in order to obtain supernatural blessings, especially blessings of physical health. The bearers would recite the verse:

> '*My girdle is Brid's girdle,*
> *The girdle with the four crosses.*
> *Rise up woman of the house,*
> *And go out three times.*
> *May whoever goes through my girdle be seven times better*
> *a year from today.*'

Men would pass through the *crios* sideways, beginning with the right foot, while women would bring it down over their heads and step out of it. For maximum effect the ritual had to be repeated three times. Clearly the hoop is a representation of the birth canal – the canal of the land goddess who is the symbol of fertility and the source of all physical benefits. The ceremony is meant to be a rejuvenation – a rebirth from the womb of the goddess.

This ritual only survived on the condition that Church-approved prayers to the saint were included. A final ritual object was a *crosoga*. Strips of peeled rush stems were pasted onto a disc-shaped board representing the sun, a half-disc representing the moon, with four seven-rayed stars and a ladder with three rungs.

In Scottish tradition, the snake was invoked at Imbolc:

> '*On Brede's morn the serpent will come out of the hole.*
> *I will not harm the serpent,*
> *Nor will the serpent harm me.*'

Sometimes an actual snake was used as an oracle, but in Ireland, famous for its lack of snakes, it was a hedgehog that was consulted about the weather. This ceremony is continued in America with a rodent taking the place of the hedgehog as Groundhog Day.

Because the snake was her divinatory animal and she was sometimes said to take the form of a snake, it is clear that Brighid was a snake goddess.

> When the Celts migrated from India they brought with them the cult of the nāga serpent deity. Members of this priesthood were known as the Shining Ones and were said to have come from a submerged land, maybe Lemuria or Atlantis. The Tuatha Dé Danann were said to have come to Ireland from the Far East, and the serpent cult was called the Naaseni. The serpent-worshipping Naaz, Naas or Naasini also worshipped Sophia, the goddess of wisdom or light of the serpent (the Wise One). These were Christian Gnostic sects. The Naasenes and Essenes were connected with the Ophites who were part of the Egyptian Therepeutae at Karnak and Qumran, who worshipped the snake as the sovereign beast, the divine emblem of the pharaohs. The original name for the Druids was 'adders' (*gwiber* in Welsh), and they were in touch with many religious sects across the known world. The Celtic neck jewellery, the torc, represented the snake.[2]

A few miles from Kildare there is a town called Naas, linking it with the Naasenes. The true message of this religion was the kundalini enlightenment achieved through the raising of the twin serpent energy of the male Pingala and the female Ida through the spine and out through the crown of the head in the form of three plumes of light like a fountain. This was a part of the Druidic experience and the true meaning of the symbol of the Prince of Wales's feathers. This is why they travelled from one land chakra to another along the Welsh chakra line in order to enhance this ability.

In Ireland there was a problem for these people – there were no snakes, and a hedgehog hardly fits the bill. When Saint Patrick supposedly banished snakes from Ireland, it was a euphemism for banishing the snake goddess Brighid and her followers. The Gnostic enlightenment experience associated with the snake cult

---

[2] Philip Gardiner, Gary Osborn, *The Serpent Grail*.

was something which the Church wished to suppress, so it began to demonise the snake and the dragon. This was so that people would be forced to rely on Christian priests.

The colours associated with Brighid, mentioned earlier – red, white and black – are the colours of the serpent deities. In Celtic culture, gods and goddesses of sacred wells and healing were linked to serpent guardians who were believed to live in the wells to protect them.

There is a story by Gerald of Wales that Naas in Kildare was the very place from which the stones of Stonehenge came. His story says that Stonehenge was known as the Giant's Dance because a race of giants had taken stones from Africa to Ireland where they built a monument on Mount Kildare. The king of Britain, Ambrosius Aurelianus, asked Merlin to bring these stones to Stonehenge, which Merlin was believed to have done. Merlin carries with him the caduceus staff (the entwined snakes). Have we come full circle like the Celtic symbol of the dragon swallowing its own tail? The battling dragons reflect the contrasting energies of human awareness that must be balanced before the person can reach the kundalini enlightenment.

The Search for the Goddess's Historical Connections in London and the Rest of Britain

There was a wayside holy well dedicated to Brighid by the side of the River Fleet in London, where a small stone church dedicated to Saint Bride was built near to present-day Fleet Street. This church showed a remarkable similarity to the church of Saint Bride of the same date in Kildare. It was followed by a second church that may have been built by the Dancs. The late twelfth-century Norman church built on this site was one of the four city churches to ring the curfew. King John held his parliament there in 1210.

Circa 1500, Caxton's apprentice brought the printing press to Fleet Street which made it a Mecca for poets, writers and journalists. Again the spirit of place is influencing the people and happenings, because the Druids honoured Brighid as patron goddess of the muse, inspiration and poetry. They also valued the truth very highly, and journalists are meant to safeguard this.

Saint Bride's became the church serving the journalists.

Henry VIII built a royal palace on the banks of the Fleet River and named it Bridewell. It is the scene of Holbein's painting, 'The Ambassadors', painted in 1553. It was here that preliminary conferences took place with the papal legate on the king's proposed divorce from Catherine of Aragon. It was probably the last place where the queen saw her husband. It is not a coincidence that these conferences took place at the former shrine of the goddess Brighid, which would loosen the hold of the Roman Catholic Church on the British people. This was the goddess energy which they had banned, and it has been proved to me over and over again that the energy from the past remains to influence the future. It makes no difference whether people are aware of the history or energy of a place or not.

In 1553, Edward VI gave the palace to the city for the reception of homeless children and vagrants, and for the punishment of petty offenders and disorderly women. This building was destroyed in the Great Fire and so was the church. Sir Christopher Wren designed the new one which cost £11,430 5s 11d and took five years to build. The spire was added in 1703 and consists of four octagonal arcades of diminishing size, capped by an obelisk and a ball and vane. Mr Rich, a pastry cook who lived in Fleet Street until his death in 1811, became famous for his wedding cakes modelled on the spire. Wren's church was damaged in the blitz and was rededicated in the presence of Her Majesty the Queen 282 years to the day after the opening of his original church.

A Countrywide List of Place Names Connected to Brighid via Saint Bride

ENGLAND

Bridekirk, Cumbria. Bridestones, Cheshire. Brightwell, Berks. Brightwell, East Suffolk. In Oxfordshire, Brightwell Baldwin, Brightwell Upperton and Brightwell-cum-Sotwell. Bideford, Devon. Bridestowe (Holy Place of Saint Bride) and Brides Valley, Devon. Bridestowe and Sourton Common, Devon. Bridport, Dorset. Bridstow, Hereford (church dedicated to Saint Bridget).

London

Bride Lane, Bridewell Place, Saint Bride Street, Saint Bride's Passage. These are all around the Fleet Street and Ludgate Circus area, EC4.

Bride Street, N7. There is a church marked here. The church and street are about half a mile east of what is now Pentonville Prison. Running in front of the prison is a long road called Roman Way which cuts off Pentonville from Bride Street. Bridewell, Windsor, a small area of streets in the Clewer Green district, backing onto the Windsor Safari Park. Like the North Thames Saint Brides, and Bridewell Place in Wapping, this is a tiny cul-de-sac.

Saint Bride's Close, a tiny cul-de-sac off Saint Katherine's Road, Erith, Thamesmead, Greater London. It is in the Belvedere area south of the River Thames, very near a huge marshy area, much of it now reclaimed. South of this is a place named Abbey Wood, and some open land with the remains of Lesney Abbey on it. Bridewell Place, E1: Wapping Docks area on the north side of the Thames. Again a tiny cul-de-sac between Wapping High Street and Wapping Lane.

This causes me to wonder whether such very short streets were built over wells or some old religious structures. Here is an interesting one: Saint Bride's Avenue, Edgware, North London, is flanked by Saint David's Drive and Merlin Crescent. They are near a place called Cannons Park.

Nearby roads have Welsh names: Tenby Road, Haverford Way and Prescelly Place.

SCOTLAND

Brideswell, Aberdeen. Brydekirk, Dunfermline. Hebrides means 'The Island of Bride' (he-brides).

ISLE OF MAN

Bride.

SCILLY ISLES

Bryher (the base chakra).

WALES

Wales has already been listed, but Bridell, Pembroke, was not mentioned. Saint Bride's Major (Saint Bride's Church), Glamorgan.

IRELAND

Brideswell, Roscommon. River Bride in Cork with a Bridebridge. River Bride in Waterford, and in Ireland they recognise the femininity of rivers. The most important of all is the shrine to Saint Bride at Kildare, where the nuns tend the reignited perpetual flame dedicated to the saint. It is very likely that most of the wayside and holy wells were sacred to Brighid originally. The word 'bride' has given us our 'bride', as in wedding, because, as the goddess of fertility, she was the goddess of pairing.

Painting Brighid – a Personal Experience of the Goddess

Since the discovery of the crown chakra in 2000, there have been tantalising glimpses of Brighid. In 2004 the goddess finally revealed herself as a majestic Atlantean spiritual being. This was the inspiration which brought my painting into being. This was the goddess of the ancients, the people who built Stonehenge long before the Druids, but whom they held in great reverence. She has so many aspects that it was impossible to choose which one to paint, but it seems to me that her power and majesty are the least known and understood.

She was the great goddess, the Exalted One, the one goddess known to all the people of these islands, though with different names and different aspects. She was not mentioned in *The Mabinogion* because she was just too 'big' for these stories. As a people the British know almost nothing of our inheritance from the ancient ones who lived before us, and this inheritance begins and ends with Brighid.

Springs and wells all over Britain were dedicated to her, and she must have been the original guardian spirit of travellers, because people would have travelled from one water source to another, whether on foot or on horseback. She was so important even the Roman Church could not ignore her. It seems that Candlemas (Festival of Light), Groundhog Day and even First Footing in Scotland can all be attributed to her customs at Beltane. It is this energy which she wished to bring through in this painting. The latest information on Stonehenge is that it was not just a solar temple but a lunar one as well. Seeing this goddess by moonlight with stars in her hair, I realised that she wished to be seen in her lunar aspect as well as those of fire and light.

The lunar calendar was the one they used for planting and ceremonies. The Druids understood that the sun made plants grow but with the sun's energy alone, leaves, blossoms, seeds and fruit would grow unchecked; they knew that the moon energies were also needed to bring plants into being. Druid science was moon science; the rays of the moon work on the soil, wind, weather, plants, animals and our bodies. They understood this but we have forgotten. Now is the time to remember that the Daughters of the Moon taught this science. Everything flowed from one thing to another; there were no 'experts' to compart-mentalise everything in boxes because nothing was separate from another. This was known by all. Brighid presided over all of this and was honoured through the priestess at her shrines and temples.

We need to take a reasoning approach to our ancestors. They were completely at one with the natural world and knew inti-mately the spirits that governed that world, for their survival depended upon that knowledge. They did not worship any of these spirits; they simply respected and honoured them every day of their lives, as we need to do. Druids did not 'worship' the oak, which implies that they thought it was a god. They were not stupid. They honoured it, and their ceremonies came into being in order to honour it. They noticed its connections and honoured them too. They celebrated all natural things in their proper seasons.

If I have been able to uncover the secrets of this chakra line it is simply because I, too, have a deep sense of honouring, which has grown stronger as the revelations grew in number. In the very beginning, before even the lake was visited, and we noticed the bull's head etched on the standing stone, I was told that it had revealed itself in response to my deep respect for its ancient lineage. This is all we need to take to these sacred places – respect.

The Goddess Tradition is a Christian Tradition Linked to Judaism

Judaism has been presented as being a predominantly masculine spiritual stream, so that it has been argued that Christianity had to balance this masculine Judaic side by bringing in the cult of Mary. But this is not true. According to sources left behind by the Essenes, including *The Secret Book of James* discovered at Nag Hammadi, one of its cardinal teachings was that of the feminine aspect of God, namely Sophia, Wisdom or the Holy Spirit. Jesus was said to have spoken of 'my Mother, the Holy Spirit',[3] and to become a 'child of the Holy Spirit'[4] was a pathway which formed a strong relationship to this feminine side of God. This tradition was especially associated with Jesus's brother, James, whom the Druids believed was the true leader of the Christian Church. In 1945 at Nag Hammadi, several secret gospels were found. In the Gospel of Thomas, the Master Jesus is quoted as saying, 'Wherever you arrive, go to James who is righteous, because of whom even Heaven and Earth came into existence.'[5]

On the other side of this question, the origins of the devotion to Mary is obscure, but it received great impetus when Constantine became the first Christian emperor in the fourth century AD. The only route for ordinary people to appeal to him was through his mother and so the cult of the mother of God and the saints grew up in obvious parallelism to his court. This did not soften Christianity's hard masculine emphasis; it in fact led to its involvement in power politics, and pulling strings. James's traditions are much truer to Christian origins, where there was an understanding of the feminine aspect of God. In the Book of Proverbs, this power is shown as a feminine being sharing God's innermost thoughts.

---

[3] Alan Jacobs, *The Gnostic Gospels*, London, Watkins Publishing, 2005
[4] Ibid.
[5] Ibid.

By me kings reign,
and rulers make laws that are just;
By me princes govern,
and all nobles who rule on earth.
I love those who love me
and those who seek me find me
The Lord brought me forth at the beginning of his work,
before his deeds of old;
I was fashioned from eternity,
from the beginning, before the world began.
When there were no oceans I was given birth,
when there were no springs abounding with water;
Before the mountains were set in place,
before the hills, I was given birth,
Before he made the earth or its fields
or any of the dust of the world.
I was there when he set the heavens in place,
when he marked out the horizon on the face of the deep.

Proverbs 8:15–17, 22–27

It can be seen from this beautiful psalm that the tradition of Sophia (explained below) went back to the very beginning, even before the creation. Since it is known that the Druids and the early Celtic saints believed in James's version of Christianity, it can now be seen that the Synod of Whitby was about far more than the dates of Easter and wearing the tonsure. It was about the leadership of James and the true understanding of the Holy Spirit. The feminine spirituality is not missing from the Jewish and Christian tradition but occupies an almost hidden place in the esoteric.

It is not hidden by the Russian Orthodox Church, however. For them, the Holy Spirit is recognised as feminine energy and is named as Sophia, the goddess of wisdom. In the figure of Sophia there can be seen the connection to the myths and cosmic rites which were practised in the ancient world. These brought the people into balance and harmony with nature and the divine through an initiation process of rebirth that was present in

Judaism and Christianity. In these faiths these esoteric teachings acquired a new and significant life-force. This hidden teaching needs to be rediscovered, because it is through this feminine channel that our true relationship to nature and the divine can be recognised. The triangle is the ancient symbol of the trinity, holding in balance the masculine and feminine energies of God, the divine cosmic spirit, together creating the Son, born of light. God the Father, God the Mother (Holy Spirit) and God the Son. The goddess tradition is very ancient, very real and very relevant to all our lives, and always has been.

Bryn Crugog: The Third Eye at Last

Looking south over Mid Wales from Aran Fawddwy
(Photo by Ian Henderson)

At last, we are able to visit the third eye

The farmer phoned to tell us that we had a window of opportunity, a week when the bull was off the mountain and there were no cattle there. We made the most of it. Remembering that *crug* is Welsh for a cairn or pile of stones, this is what we expected to find, but it turned out to be a natural rock formation, an outcrop which formed a raised platform which dropped away steeply at one end; a natural stage, in fact. There was some exposed rock that formed a chair that could be sat on. The rock outcrop contained a lot of quartz, which proved to be significant. The truly amazing discovery was that the view of the sky was 360 degrees from this platform. Just imagine, from here could be seen every star system in the sky at all times; every point of the sunrise and sunset, moonrise and moonset. It was astounding. It is a natural planetarium. The only other time I had this experience was on Snowdon.

We introduced ourselves, asked permission to enter the sacred site and said some prayers for peace and healing. As I walked back down the hillside I could 'see' a Druid who appeared to have a halo of circulating stars around his head. His hair was white and he wore a midnight-blue robe. It did not seem surprising to meet him, and later in meditation, he spoke to me and gave me some information about the Druids' usage of Bryn Crugog. This was his message:

'Welcome, welcome, welcome. We have waited a long time for your

visit. Yes, this is the position from which we studied the stars. It makes perfect sense, you see. From here, we can see the sky for 360 degrees. This was a chakra station of the stars. Many, many priests and Druids went through our hands at this place, where we taught them everything we knew about the star maps of the heavens. Yes, of course we knew about precession. We knew so much more than you do today. It will take some time for modern mankind to catch up with our knowledge, but we are very pleased with you because you are trying to do this. You are most welcome at our holy sites and we would so like you to visit more sites and enhance your knowledge. Our studies of the stars were the most important thing we did and this study was reserved for our brightest and most spiritual pupils only. You were one of them. Silver stars were worn on their garments; this is how they were recognised. You have forgotten this knowledge but this is no matter. You are not required to understand the stars at this moment in time. Go in peace, my child.'

With that, he put his hands together in prayer mode and bowed. This greeting had an Eastern look, and is one more link with the East. I feel that this was the traditional Druidic greeting. The next question is, how did they know more than we do today? We found out more on our next visit.

Cosmic and Celtic connections

We revisited the spot on 21 September with two of our friends who had worked with us at Carmarthen Bay with the crystal. That morning, I had felt very strongly that I should take some music by James Twyman, 'May Peace Prevail on Earth', but did not know why exactly. When we went through the gate, Dee felt that she must walk to the top although she did not feel very well at the time. She found some energy on the very edge of the platform which could be felt as heat through our feet. Bob and Dee both felt that there would have been a standing stone or obelisk of some kind on this spot. Bob drew a picture of it when we got home and Dee agreed that it looked as he had shown it: a tall stone which came to a point and looked like a hooded human figure. It was decided to empty the water from all the chakras over this energy, and we scattered rose petals at this spot as well. Then there were prayers and a peace meditation, and the energy at the end of this ceremony was truly beautiful.

It was then that I felt it was time to play the music, and as the chanting began I understood why it had seemed so important. Turning to look at the track we had climbed, I could feel the people of ancient time coming up this track singing and chanting joyously. I felt some nausea and a solar plexus 'wobble' which I had come to recognise as a former life experience clicking in. Dee agreed with this vision and added that they would have processed from their village at Llyn-y-Tarw, and climbed the hillside in spiral formation, which is why she had felt that she, too, must walk up the track. They would have done this twice a year at the time of the solstice.

Once again we had the experience of sighting a red admiral butterfly at our ceremony, at a place where no such butterfly should have been. There must be something really special about this particular insect. A fairy messenger, perhaps? When we got to the gate, a warplane roared over the spot on which we had been standing and we hoped that it was a positive sign that it had kept away during our ceremony. At the side of the gate was a heap of stones which the farmer had left there from his land-clearance activities. Among them was a huge boulder of white quartz and a smaller pillar-shaped piece of quartz, making an important contribution to our story, as you will see.

As you give, so you receive: it does seem that when we give to the Earth, the Earth gives in return, and this is true for us all. While passing the boggy field at the very top of the mountain, we sighted a small flock of lapwings. This was a wonderful gift because they are an endangered species, although they used to be plentiful in this part of the world. The RSPB is trying to raise awareness of these exquisite birds.

The following day, Dee phoned to tell me that the priests and Druids had used moldavite on Bryn Crugog. This crystal is known to work best with quartz as it concentrates the energy to give greater clarification. Dowsing gave answers to the following questions:

'Did the priests wear moldavite?'

'Yes.'

'Was it from Czechoslovakia?'

'Yes.'

'Was this crystal connected to the Egyptians?'

'Yes.'

Since 2002 was the International Year of the Mountains, this discovery of the Druids' use of Bryn Crugog is an important Welsh contribution to this celebration.

Did the Celtic Druids adopt the 'natural philosophy' which Julius Caesar said they did, from the direct descendants of the original builders? They inherited the remnants of a much, much older megalithic science which had a highly accurate knowledge of lunar and stellar astronomy, demonstrating an understanding of complex geometry. Had this knowledge been used to construct megalithic monuments? Caesar said of the Druids in Gaul and Prydein (Britain), 'They dispute largely concerning the stars and their motion.'

In the twentieth century, a book entitled *The White Goddess* by the poet Robert Graves was published. In this book he made an analysis of a poem by Taliesin (a sixth-century Welsh poet). He made great efforts to decipher the hidden meaning encoded in the poems. As well as singing the praises of their lord, prince or king, they entertained, together with the bards and minstrels, with storytelling that contained the ancient wisdom of the Cymric peoples.

Robert Graves found astronomical data encoded in 'Hanes

Taliesin' which at least some of their listeners would have understood. Could poems such as this be part of the ancient astronomical knowledge passed down through countless generations in simple, yet encoded, story form?

When Robert Graves began his analysis of ancient Welsh poems, he found they often took the form of riddles composed according to very strict rules. Taliesin wrote many coded astrological references into 'Hanes Taliesin'. He was writing of the 'revolving castle' of Caer Sidi, and the Cauldron of Ceridwen. Caer Sidi means the 'circle of Sidi' and Cadair Idris means the 'chair of Idris'. There is a 'revolving castle' in which the 'Cauldron of Ceridwen' is to be found. The ancient skywatcher viewing the stars from Bryn Crugog, Cadair Idris or Caer Sidi, could have described the apparently revolving belt of stars over their heads as a revolving castle or a magic cauldron. Of course, they do not 'revolve'. It is one of nature's optical illusions that the rising and setting of various celestial bodies are only apparent. The ancient peoples around the world were very much aware of this. Back in the time of the open-air universities of the Druids, the teachers had the 'live sky' to illustrate that. At particular seasons certain constellations were opposite the sun, whilst other constellations formed the individual 'houses' or 'castles' in which the sun was regarded as being imprisoned. Observers at Bryn Crugog would have had a wonderful location to view all this, and it would have been within easy reach of the village at Llyn-y-Tarw. Standing on the summit, it is possible to 'feel' the energy of the ancient star-watchers. This ever-changing backdrop of star groups was viewed as directly affecting the Earth, and changes were observed at the various seasons. As Caer Sidi or Sidin was 'the Elysian fortress where the Cauldron of Ceridwen was housed', and Caer Sidi was the ancient Welsh term for the stars of the zodiac, is the Cauldron of Ceridwen in the skies? If it is, there is a physical earthly counterpart, 'as above, so below'. In 1947, as we have seen, a local historian, Lewis Edwards, believed that it did, and that a Welsh Temple of the Zodiac was located in northern Carmarthenshire, centred on the village of Pumpsaint.

For further information, see the following website:

http://www.morien-institute.org.uk/caersidi.html

Moldavite – the Only Extra-terrestrial Gemstone

This beautiful green stone, which is a form of glass and when cut looks like an emerald, is said to be from the Pleiades. It was sent through the ether to land on our planet and activate its crystalline structure, in which it manifests perfection. It helps those who are aligned with the Pleiadean energies and the energies of our sun. Because it works with the sun, its sympathetic metal is gold.[1]

So now we have a greater understanding of this sacred pathway, and why we have been asked to work with it by the Pleiadeans at this time. We must continue to work with the feminine Earth energies and the crystalline grid. Because it works with the sun rather than the moon, it would seem to be balancing the feminine, manifesting perfection (balance) in our world, remembering that the divine cosmic spirit is neither masculine nor feminine, but a balance, a harmony, of both. Perhaps this will bring our planet a little closer to the cosmic spirit.

'Moldavite is a tektite, which is made of molten glass and probably formed in an interplanetary collision. This green variety fell on Czechoslovakia 14 million years ago. It has been used by humans for at least 25,000 years. It was used in Atlantis and Egypt. It has been suggested that the missing cap stone of the pyramid was made of this green stone,'[2] and we now know that it was used by our ancestors which helps to explain how they knew so much more than we do, as the Druid had said.

There is a link between this stone and the Grail legend. In some traditions, the Grail originated as a jewel, an emerald that fell from the sky. Once again in this story, we have mention of the Grail and Percival (see chapter on the heart chakra). This time it is not a wooden cup but a stone of the purest kind, which could give immortality to those who looked at it.

> It was an emerald in the crown of Lucifer, which fell with him from heaven and from which a cup was later carved. Much later, it was believed to be a bowl made of emerald and called the Saint Graal.[3]

---

[1] Robert Simmons and Kathy Warner, *Moldavite: Starborn Stone of Transformation*, 1988
[2] Ibid.
[3] Ibid.

The Story of the Grail Journey

There is a very sick and wounded king who lives in a castle in a wasted and barren countryside. He waits for a knight with a pure heart (Percival), who must ask the right question of the king. If he does so, both the king and his land will be restored to health. The knight will then become the guardian of the Grail, a cup containing some kind of precious and magical liquid.

It seems that the story has a deliberate mistake to take us in the wrong direction. It is not the king who is wounded, but the queen. She is the embodiment of the feminine energy, the Earth goddess, the very Earth itself. This is what we need to heal through the crystalline grid. It is by healing ourselves, bringing ourselves into balance between our masculine and feminine sides, that we will no longer be divided against the self, and our kingdom on Earth will be restored. The moldavite activates the crystalline structure to manifest perfection – this perfection is within ourselves. Lifting the Earth's vibration is up to each one of us.

As for the question we have to ask, that is between ourselves and our divine self, and is different for us all. But I believe the question we must ask ourselves is this: 'Am I willing to give up everything in order to follow in the service of the light? Am I ready to go wherever I am required to go, to do whatever I am required to do in order to fulfil my soul's task?'

If the answer is 'Yes', the queen will be healed and the Earth will be restored. In present-day awareness, waking the goddess energy to make us whole human beings is what the Grail story is all about. The male symbol (the king) was appropriate in times past, when the male energy was the driving force in consciousness. The symbolic queen shows the process of our human pathways to the higher consciousness relevant to our time.

Rising from a marshy piece of ground on the side of Bryn Crugog is a red spring. It looks very much like the Red Spring or Blood Spring at Chalice Well in Glastonbury, known for its connection to the Earth Mother and for its healing abilities. The alchemical combinations of red and white waters represent the male and female potencies behind all creation, and hold the power to rejuvenate our bodies and spirits, and the body of the Earth itself. So, flowing down from the hillside of Bryn Crugog is a spring which must be mixed with the waters of the other chakras on this system. As the red waters mix with the white waters, their combined healing powers will rejuvenate the Earth and heal and restore the wounded queen. If you would like to take some of this water to do this, you will be performing a service for our planet.

The Grail Legend of the Damsels of the Wells

The native British goddess of the land is the guardian of the Grail. In Celtic tradition, cups and cauldrons of rebirth are manifestations of the goddess's power. Misuse of the Earth creates a wasteland, but in Christian tradition the Grail became associated with the cup of the Last Supper, and the two traditions became interwoven in the Arthurian way of wisdom: the Grail quest.[4]

One of the Grail legends concerns the damsels of the wells who, at a time before King Arthur, would emerge from the wells and offer water from their golden cups, and so minister to travellers. However, King Amangons raped one of the damsels and his men followed his example by raping the others, so that no well-maidens would come forward as before. The men also stole their golden cups and used them for themselves, and from this time the land was laid waste and desolate, and no one could find the court of the rich fishermen or the earthly paradise. At this time also, the voices of the wells were lost and these represented the voice of the goddess of the land.

After Arthur had set up the Round Table, this story came to the ears of his knights and they swore that they would not rest until they had avenged the damsels, and erased the sin of Amangons from the Earth. But despite their good intentions, they could neither hear the voices nor find the damsels. They set off in quest of the evil knights and eventually came upon a mysterious group of knights and maidens wandering in the forest. They captured one of them and listened to their story. The mysterious company were descendants of the damsels of the wells and King

---

[4] Nigel Pennick, *The Celtic Saints*, p.41

Amangons and his men. They were fated to wander the Earth until the Court of Joy was found, where the Grail would be found also. The knights then realised that it was useless to seek vengeance because to kill the kin of Amangons was to kill the children of the damsels also, so they decided to go on a quest to the court of the rich fishermen. One knight managed to win through to that hallowed place and asked the Grail question correctly, whereupon the wasteland was restored to its former fruitfulness.

The damsels of the wells are the voices of water. The voice of water is the voice of the Earth, and the people on Earth have lost the ability to listen to this voice. The descendants of the damsels and Amangons can only wander over the Earth and tell this story until others are prepared to act. Because of their mixed ancestry, they are powerless to bring the Grail to manifestation and heal the wasteland, because they are only the messengers.

Our own story tells of how we began to listen to the damsels of the wells, and in turn to the voices of the wells, the voice of water and the voice of the Earth goddess. As the line has been walked, the voices of the damsels of the wells have been listened to, and heard. Blessings have been asked for the water, prayers said and the waters mixed, one with another, so that the whole system has been energised. In this way the land will once more be reawakened and rejuvenated, and wherever there is water, this can be done by everyone.

The Element of Water: How to Bring about a Spiritual Change in Your Environment

A MESSAGE FROM THE GUARDIANS

'Start with the river. The river made the valley. Make an offering to the river of flowers and in a sense, get it on your side. Bless the river. This has not been done since ancient times.

'All water is sacred, the sacred gift of life is given through water. Honour the water. Recognise the power it has to give life to all on Earth. Make a joyful connection with water and the spirit of the river. There are deep, deep connections to be found (or accessed) from doing this ceremony. Deep within the Earth there is a consciousness, an energy, which can be released

for the nourishing of the physical world, for the whole planet in fact. All that is required is the will and the understanding. This is an ancient knowledge. We are going back to the Druids and when the Earth was young. It is a beautiful ceremony to take part in. It is awakening an energy that goes back to the dawn of time in the planet's awareness. Love is at the root of this ceremony as it is at the centre of all things. When you go for the second time, the spirit of the river will recognise and welcome you. A special blessing given with love is all that is needed. It is a good thing to do this twice in quick succession. May we suggest three times? At the third time, there will be an awakening of spiritual and planetary energies that are needed at this moment. This is the right time for this ceremony. The Earth is groaning with the effort of changing and lifting vibrations. To help the Earth, a physical ceremony would be appreciated. Thank you.'

Merlin's Prophecy: A Grid Network is Revealed

After finally arriving at the third eye chakra that linked all chakras up to the crown, I was inspired to 'look' for the one above the crown, which, although I was aware of it, I had never felt prompted to do before. All I did know was the line continued to Whitby in a north-easterly direction. So, armed with a road atlas and a pendulum, I began to move the pendulum in this direction, asking to be shown the chakras above the crown, not knowing where or how many of them there were. Starting at Llyn-y-Tarw, it moved along the lower land to the east of the Berwyns and began to swing at Valle Crucis Abbey, just above Llangollen, number eight. It then continued to Chester where there is a cathedral, number nine. It disappeared through Manchester and surfaced again on the other side of the Pennines at Fountains Abbey, number ten, then on to Ripon Cathedral, number eleven, Rievaulx Abbey, number twelve, finally reaching number thirteen at Whitby. This made a total of thirteen chakras, which follow the Egyptian chakra numbered system.

On this line, there are five abbeys, four of which are Cistercian, and two cathedrals. The Pleiadeans had said that the Cistercians followed in the steps of the master. This was not all. Guidance led me to follow the line of the axis using the heart chakra as its centre.

This went towards Dublin and ended at Knocknarea. Continuing its south-east direction, it went through Bath, Stonehenge and Winchester, and continued through to Tel el-Amarna, Dendera and Kom Ombo in Egypt. Altogether eight lines were plotted, including one that went to Southern Ireland (where we had already been as a part of this story). The whole formed an eight-petalled flower that I was told was 'the sphere of influence'. So it was that we once more set off on a continuation of our journey, beginning at Valle Crucis Abbey. When I saw its eight-petalled rose window, I was stunned! It seemed that the Cistercians were aware that it is the eighth station above the crown and the eighth note of the octave, bringing in a higher vibration and a new note. The letter 'C' at this point also stands for 'completion' in the sense of an octave. Merlin had told Roma in a meditation in December 2001, 'There is an Earth grid or network of energy that will be revealed, a) in stages, and b) to individuals who can be trusted to act responsibly.' I am privileged to be able to reveal this network to you.

FINDING THE CHAKRAS ABOVE THE CROWN

I have numbered the chakras according to the dimensional portals after the crown.

4. Valle Crucis Abbey, fourth-dimensional chakra/portal, corresponds to the chakra just above your crown. Connected to the ascended masters and angels.

5. Chester Cathedral, fifth-dimensional chakra/portal, corresponds to the chakra one foot above your head. Connected to the Pleiades and Pleiadean emissaries of light.

6. Fountains Abbey, sixth-dimensional chakra/portal, corresponds to the chakra two to three feet above your head. Connection to Sirius and the Sirian archangelic league of the light and your higher self.

7. Ripon Cathedral, seventh-dimensional chakra/portal, corresponds to the chakra about ten feet above your head. Connected to Andromeda and the Andromedan intergalactic beings of light.

8. Rievaulx Abbey, eighth-dimensional chakra/portal, corresponds to the chakra about fifteen feet above your head. Connected to Orion and the brotherhood of light.

9. Whitby Abbey, ninth-dimensional chakra/portal, corresponds to the chakra thirty feet above your head. Connected to your Christed overself of the light and the divine cosmic spirit, the great central sun and *all that is*.

There are six chakras in all. There are four abbeys and two cathedrals, proving that the ancients certainly knew about this line and the infinity symbol of energy. It also means that it is very special indeed.

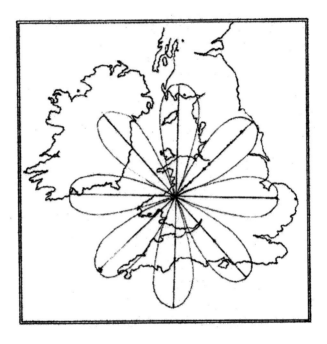

The sphere of influence of the grid system:
the eight-petalled flower

PLACE NAMES FROM SOUTH-WEST TO NORTH-EAST

1 Bryher, Isles of Scilly	6 Bryn Crugog	11 Ripon Cathedral
2 Llansteffan	7 Llyn-y-Tarw	12 Rievaulx Abbey
3 Tregaron Bog	8 Valle Crucis Abbey	13 Whitby Abbey
4 Strata Florida Abbey	9 Chester Cathedral	
5 Blaenycwm	10 Fountains Abbey	

Merlin's Way

As I walked this pathway, I began to have flashbacks to former lives. Then I was 'told' that I had spent several former lives as a Druid and it all began to make sense. This was not a new discovery so much as a rediscovery. It was much more than just the experience of former lives, it was the recognition of genetic coding of the DNA. Of course, whatever is in our genetic material has to be in our energy field also, as an etheric memory. How could it be otherwise? As friends joined us, they too felt themselves awakening to their ancient memories, and those of you who have been reading this story and found that it strikes an inner chord, will know that it is working for you, too.

The Druids knew and used this chakra system in order to raise their consciousness from the root to the crown and beyond. No wonder it took twenty years. The novices would have spent a year or two (as long as it took) at each chakra under the guidance of an initiate who had already gone through the system themselves. At three of the chakras, I met three of these Druids. It was a supremely difficult course and the unsuitable would have been weeded out along the way. As they worked their way up the line, they would have been under instruction all the time, constantly assessed as to their progress and ability – just as if they were at an Egyptian mystery school. They spent time at each chakra for their physical bodies to adjust, balance and strengthen. They would have dealt with the physical, mental, emotional and spiritual challenges at each point. How fortunate they seem to have been compared with us and our struggle in the present day, and it is necessary to be aware of this and be prepared to take our time.

The story of Merlin mirrors this system as if he were saying to us, 'This is the way I went; follow in my footsteps if you can.' He was born in Carmarthen, the sacral chakra, and travelled through Wales until he reached the crown and beyond it. His stories say that he went to North Wales. He was travelling in the direction of this chakra system, his physical journey illuminating his journey of spiritual enlightenment and showing us 'the way' whenever we had the wit to follow. This chakra system could be called 'Merlin's Way'. His story was left in myth and legend as a blueprint for us. Some of these Druids, but not many, eventually reached their goal, having activated the ability to create their light-bodies and reach immortality as Merlin did. This is what they meant when they told me, 'This is our land and we are its people. This land has never changed from being our land. We are always here in the etheric realms. We are the guardians and protectors of the light.'

The arch-druid himself, Merlin, as planetary guardian, allowed a small part of his spirit to incarnate several times in Earth's history, guiding, teaching and experiencing life on Earth. Walk the Pathway of the Beloved and you will be walking in his footsteps.

Valle Crucis

The Way to Valle Crucis

Once we knew where the line went from Llyn-y-Tarw, it was possible to stand by the lake and, on a clear day when the Berwyns could be seen, our eyes could follow where the line went ahead of us. It was also possible to see Bryn Crugog from here, and so for the first time we could get a sense of the line in the landscape, and also something of the magnificence and majesty of it. It was truly awe-inspiring. As it passes through the

lower valleys to the east of the Berwyns, a mountain came to light called Mynydd Tarw (Bull Mountain). This cannot be a coincidence; it has to be connected with the line. I was told that the mountain had been sacred to the Druids and once again we linked with the Taurean Age. Next to it are two narrow valleys with single-track roads and passing places. From Llanrhaeadr-ym-Mochnant, Wales's highest and one of its most beautiful waterfalls, 240 feet high, can be visited. In an adjoining valley is Pennant Melangell, and

(Above) Valle Crucis Abbey

the church and shrine of this saint. It is not surprising that this is a unique and special area, and the fascinating story of Saint Melangell will be included, because I feel that she was touched by the magic of the line as we all will be.

The Story of Saint Melangell[1]

Melangell was an Irish princess who was fleeing from a forced marriage. She came to live in an isolated valley in the Berwyns. One day, Brochwel, a prince of Powys, had left his court at Pengwern (Shrewsbury), and was hunting from his summer palace at Meifod. His hounds raised a hare that took refuge under the skirts of a young woman. The huntsmen urged the hounds to kill the hare but they seemed rooted to the ground. There is a legend that a miraculous thorn hedge sprang up around the princess. She told him that she had dedicated her life to God, and had fled to Wales where she had lived as a hermit in that valley for fifteen years. Brochwel was so impressed with her that he granted her the land of Pennant as a perpetual sanctuary of refuge and protection. She lived there for a further thirty-seven years, establishing a small community of female hermits. During this time the wild hares used to visit her every day and came to be regarded locally as having the protective blessing of Melangell. One of the local names for hares is '*wyn bach Melangell*' (Melangell's little lambs).

The feast day of this pioneer hunt saboteur is 27 May. The little church of Pennant Melangell is dedicated to the saint. It contains her shrine, said to be the oldest Romanesque shrine in Europe.

The native hare of Britain was the Arctic hare, which was later replaced by the common brown hare, probably brought here by the Romans. Its gifts are rebirth, balance and intuition. In Celtic lore, the hare is a creature of the goddess, the night and the moon; at the same time it stands for the east, the dawn and bright light. It also represents the corn spirit and the harvest, and the two equinoxes. The cycle of rebirth which it brings in with the spring equinox is remembered today by the tradition of the Easter bunnies. It brings healing and transformation, good luck and fertility. It is the best animal shape-shifter and as an ally it helps you to draw on your intuition and inner guidance. The key attributes are intuition, rebirth and balance. All of this would have been well known to Melangell.

---

[1] Ray Spencer, *A Guide to the Saints of Wales and the West Country*, 1991, p.58

Saint Melangell

The Red Kite

A very modern symbol of conservation in Mid Wales is the red kite. The sight of a kite swooping down at feeding time takes your breath away! Once they were common all over Britain, but by 1989 only a handful clung on in Mid Wales. It took a decade of effort by a small and enlightened group of conservationists, helped by local farmers who were proud to have these magnificent birds on their land, to bring them back from extinction. The Nature Conservancy Council, the Joint Nature Conservation Committee and the RSPB decided to reintroduce the kites in 1989. By 1998 there were 163 breeding pairs in Wales, and kites from Spain and Sweden have been introduced in southern England, northern Scotland and the English Midlands. It is hoped that before long they will once again become a familiar sight in northern England also. What an inspiring story for a country which began its conservation with Saint Melangell.

By the year 2004, 500 breeding pairs reared more than 400 chicks in Wales. There were a total of 1,000 chicks fledged in the UK. They can be seen at close quarters at feeding time (2 p.m. GMT, 3 p.m. BST) at Gigrin farm at Rhayader (tel. 01597 810243), or at the Nant-y-Arian Forest Centre, near Ponterwyd, nine miles east of Aberystwyth on the A44 (Saint Melangell Walk, fifteen miles, map from tourist centres).

The red kite

The Windhover

To Christ, our Lord

I caught this morning morning's minion, king-
dom of daylight's dauphin, dapple-dawn-drawn Falcon, in his
　　riding
Of the rolling level, underneath him steady air, and striding
High there, how he rung upon the rein of a wimpling wing
In his ecstasy! then off, then off, forth on swing,
As a skate's heel sweeps smooth on a bow-bend; the hurl and
　　gliding
Rebuffed the big wind. My heart in hiding
Stirred for a bird, – the achieve of, the mastery of the thing!

Gerard Manley Hopkins,
1844–1889
Dedicated to the kestrel

Valle Crucis Abbey (Abaty Glyn-Y-Groes)

MESSENGERS FROM THE FOURTH DIMENSION

When we walked into the grounds of the abbey we were greeted by a whole cloud of swallows, swifts and martins flying around the building. We had never seen so many of these beautiful little birds before. It was an amazing sight. Immediately I was transported into the air, the ether and the next dimension – they took me with them. These are birds of the air and the ether. This is the domain of the angels and the ascended masters. Watching their perfect flight, appreciating their mastery of their element, it was clearly shown that this was their link with the angels and masters. We, too, can ascend. Our spirits are destined to soar. We shall achieve mastery.

A part of this building has a roof, and there is a small staircase to the upper floor. The swallows had built their nests in the rafters as they do in old barns. They flew up chimneys and in and out of windows and doors. They twittered at us with their silver

241

voices, singing their song of summer days. They are the emissaries of summer, of the sun and of the light. They are the messengers of the light and the fourth dimension, and they have the ability to transport us into this dimension while flying around these old abbey walls.

There is a rose window high in the west wall which is striking in its simplicity, because it has only eight petals. Eight is the number of this chakra after the crown. It is the number of infinity and perpetually moving energy. Were the Cistercians and the Druids before them aware that this is the eighth station of the Pathway of the Beloved? Because here in Valle Crucis, it is written in stone.

After completing the visit of the chakras up to the crown, a map of a grid of energy radiating out from the heart chakra was 'given'. It had eight spokes or petals. The area inside the circumference was called the 'sphere of influence of the heart chakra'.

The rose window at Valle Crucis

The Abbey of the Valley of the Cross: Valle Crucis

The cross referred to is the Pillar of Eliseg, a ninth-century memorial cross set up by Cyngen, king of Powys, to record the ancestry and ancient glories of his forbears. The remains of the cross-shaft stand on a small hillock, a few hundred yards to the north of the abbey. The Pillar of Eliseg stood on a mound which was a prehistoric barrow. It contained a coffin formed of large blue stones. This may have been the grave of one of the very early rulers of Powys. An early Welsh poem sees the graves of heroes as features in the Welsh landscape, and this may be one. Cyngen was the last king of Powys, who, as an old man, died on a pilgrimage to Rome in AD 845. On his death, the kingdom passed to the kings of Gwynydd.

The inscription records his descent from Brydw, son of Gwrtheyrn (Vortigern, associated with Merlin), and the grandson of the Roman emperor Magnus Maximus.

This emperor married Princess Helen Luyddog, and her Welsh kinsmen conquered Rome itself. Tradition blames Maximus for taking the Roman army away and leaving Britain helpless before the invading English. He and his wife are written about in 'The Dream of Macsen' in *The Mabinogion*. He had the title of Maximus Regis and Vor Tigern, which both meant 'great prince'.

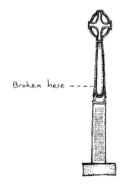

(Left) The Pillar of Eliseg, the cross that gave its name to Valle Crucis. Artist's impression of the cross, which is believed to have been 20 feet high.

THE INSCRIPTION ON THE PILLAR:[2]

1, Cyngen son of Cadell, Cadell son of Brochwel [he gave Saint Melangell land for her church and sanctuary], Brochwel son of Eliseg, Eliseg son of Gwylog.

2, Cyngen, therefore, the great-grandson of Eliseg, erected this stone in honour of his great-grandfather Eliseg.

3, It was Eliseg who united the inheritance of Powys (laid waste for nine years) out of the hand of the English with fire and sword.

4, Whosoever shall read this writing, let him give a blessing for the soul of Eliseg.

5, It was Cyngen (who united ... to his kingdom of Powys).

6, ...

7, (Cadell) the great (ruler) of Britain (son of) Cattegirn, Pasgen, (Maugan held) the monarchy (after him).

8, But Brydw was the son of Gwrtheyrn (Vortigern) whom Germanus blessed and was borne to him by Servera, the daughter of Maximus the King, who slew the Romans.

9, Cynfarch painted this lettering at the command of his king, Cyngen.

10, The blessing of the Lord be upon Cyngen and upon all his household and upon the whole land of Powys until (the Day of Judgement. Amen).

The History of the Abbey[3]

Valle Crucis Abbey was founded in 1201 by Madog ap Gruffudd Maelor, the ruler of Northern Powys. He died in 1236 and was buried in the abbey church. Like its sister abbey of Strata Florida, the abbey was pro-Welsh and suffered for it. In 1277, its abbot was one of the seven abbots of the Welsh Cistercian houses, who wrote to the Pope defending the reputation of Llywelyn ap Gruffudd against the charges brought against him by Anian,

---

[2] D H Evans, *Pillar of Eliseg*
[3] Jeremy K Knight, *Valle Crucis Abbey*, 1987, p.51

Bishop of Saint Asaph. This was the prince known as Llywelyn the Last, who was murdered at Cilmery near Builth Wells in 1282.

The abbey's estates became a target during the wars of Edward I (1272–1307), and it was one of several houses in North Wales to suffer damage, for which it received £160 compensation in 1284. By the end of this century the monks had become involved in literary activities, and this is where the already mentioned Brut y Tywysogyon was compiled during the years 1282–1332 (National Library of Wales, Peniarth MS 20, p.262b). In this way, its reputation was very similar to its sister, Strata Florida. A period of further building work was undertaken in the early part of the fourteenth century, but the Black Death, together with changing social conditions, led to a decrease in the number of lay brothers, which occurred in other Cistercian abbeys also. In 1419 the abbot petitioned the Pope, claiming that he had repaired the monastery, after its destruction by fire during the Welsh uprising under Owain Glyndwr.

The three abbots who held office between 1450 and 1518 earned a reputation as scholars, liberal patrons of the Welsh bards and collectors of Welsh literary manuscripts. They welcomed poets like Guto Glyn and Lewis Mon, and were praised by them probably as much for their lavish hospitality, as for their religious devotion. When the penultimate abbot, Robert Salusbury (1528), was appointed, there were only seven monks left. This abbot was removed to Oxford after being accused of perjury, robbery and seizure of property in three counties in 1534. In Oxford, he became a leader of a band of robbers until he was imprisoned in the Tower of London in 1535. The abbey was closed in January 1537, with all its fixtures and fittings auctioned off. Some of its bells found their way to the Shropshire churches of Baschurch and Little Ness.

Abbey Crucis is unusual in having some buildings with roofs, and for this we can thank a tenant, Edward Davies, who converted the east range of the cloister into a dwelling house.

Later in the eighteenth century, the chapter house became a farmhouse. A cottage was built at the east end of the church, a large house at the south end of the east range and another in the west range. The former refectory became a barn and a dairy was built outside the kitchen. To a large extent, this conversion into a dwelling house has fortunately preserved the abbey, and with it the energy of the place. The abbey is under the care of Cadw: Welsh Historic Monuments.

The Rose Window

The first 'flower window', complete with stained glass, was the 'rose' built at St Dennis by Abbot Suger.

The beautiful jewels of the rose windows enabled the Gothic masons to create a new Jerusalem on Earth. The eight-petalled window in Valle Crucis has an inscription above it in Latin:

ADAM ABBAS FECIT HOC

OPUS IN PACE QUIESCAT

AMEN

Abbot Adam carried out this work;

May he rest in peace. Amen.[4]

This abbot held office between 1330 and 1344.

Meeting Llywelyn, Our Last Welsh Prince

A STORY OF HEALING

In 1277, the abbot of Valle Crucis courageously wrote to the Pope in defence of this prince. Although this is not associated with any of the chakras and is not directly on the line, it is nevertheless a vital part of the history of Wales at this time, and was part of our present experience.

Llywelyn was a prince of North Wales, and was a visitor to Strata Florida Abbey, once staying at its grange. He must have met the Lord Rhys at that time. This story concerns the death of Llywelyn ap Gruffudd through treachery in 1282 at Cilmery near Builth Wells, Powys.

---

[4] Jeremy Knight, *Valle Crucis Abbey*

On a beautiful hot day in the summer of 2002, we were travelling down to the sacral chakra in Carmarthen and as we passed Llywelyn's monument, we decided to visit it. We climbed the steps and went through the little gate. Gradually we became aware of a feeling of deep sadness followed by a sense of heavy dark energy, like a great weight. It was gut-wrenching, stomach-churning despair. At the back of the monument were steps leading down to a beautiful clear stream, and there was a notice which said, 'Legend has it that this is the well wherein the head of Llywelyn ap Gruffudd was washed.'

Again this feeling of despair washed over me and I couldn't take any more of it and left. I was able to understand this feeling. This was the place where Wales lost one of its much-loved leaders… but this was much worse than that. This was the place where the nation lost its last and only hope against the Normans. Because of what happened here, the land of Wales became nothing more than a province of England. Even the Welsh Tudors did nothing to help them. The red dragon had not won; Merlin's prophecy was untrue. All was lost, or so it seemed.

Llywelyn's body was taken to the nearby Cistercian abbey of Cwmhir and buried near the altar, where there is now a slate memorial stone. His head was taken to the Tower of London.

A poet named Gruffudd ab yr Ynad Goch wrote an elegy expressing his despair at the death of the last dynastic prince of Wales. He describes how his heart is cold with grief at the loss of the king of Aberffraw. He rages against the English for doing such a thing and at God for taking him away. He asks how it is possible that we should not see that the world has come to an end. He wishes that the sea would rise up and flood the land, since there is no hope, no refuge, no one to guide or to give counsel. All of this I could feel as I stood on the grass. I had felt like saying to Llywelyn that there is no need for this any more. Wales is coming into her own at last. The sword is not a sword of battle but the sword of truth. The victory will be one of spiritual enlightenment which will link with our sacred places, and Merlin will be proved right in the twenty-first century.

Llywelyn's grave at Abbey Cwmhir

In January 2003 a friend from Builth Wells contacted me and I took the opportunity to ask her if she had been to this monument. She went to visit the field and sent a message to me to say that she had seen Llywelyn lying wounded on the grass. She spoke to him, saying that Wales no longer needed him, and that it was time for him to move on towards the light. She said that his face began to fade and she hoped that this was a good sign. We wished to offer our help if it were needed, so we sat in meditation with Dee and her husband. Llywelyn was still there, but was looking relaxed, leaning on his sword which he had stuck into the ground at the top of the mound. I said that he no longer needed to be there, and that there were people – his family and friends – waiting for him to join them. At the same time Dee was talking to him, asking him to remember Merlin, and that Wales no longer needed him because everything had changed. She said it was time for forgiveness, both for others and himself. He was listening but did not intend to desert his post. I thought of asking Merlin to help, and suddenly Merlin was there and Llewelyn knew who he was and followed him.

They seemed to walk to the back of the field and into the sunset. That was the last I saw of them because the next thing I knew I was flying – hedge-hopping over the fields. I knew that Merlin and Llywelyn were in front but I could no longer see them. Then I was hovering over a sacred building which glittered and was in the spiritual dimension of the light. As I looked down on it, I knew that Merlin had taken him inside, where his wife, daughter, parents, grandparents, comrades-in-arms, and fellow countrymen and women were being united with him, for which they had waited so long. Dee told me that they had both experienced the sense of terrible despair at the beginning of the meditation, and also that she had felt the great sense of relief of a great burden being lifted.

All of you will be aware that our planet cannot lift itself into the fifth dimension while there are still black holes like this on its surface. We will go to this spot to take some of the sacred water, say prayers and put flowers in the well as soon as we are able. If you pass this spot, would you stop and say a prayer for Llywelyn the Last, a man whose loyalty to his country transcended death itself? Thank you. The monument is about three miles from Builth, at the far end of Cilmery, on the A483 to Llanwrtyd Wells.

This is the story of Llywelyn ap Gruffudd and is taken from the *Brut y Tywysogyon* (*Chronicle of the Princes*) Peniarth MS 20 1282:[5]

---

[5] This was compiled as a continuation of Geoffrey of Monmouth's *Historia Regum Britanniae*. It starts with the death of Cadwaladr in the late seventh century and continues to 1282 (with a continuation to 1332). It is a Welsh translation of the Latin original, which is now lost. It was written not long after 1282. It is probable

Gruffudd ap Maredudd and Rhys Fychan ap Rhys ap Maelgwn (Rhys Fychan, son of Rhys, son of Maelgwn – great-grandson of Lord Rhys), on the feast day of Mary at the equinox, took the castle and town of Aberystwyth; and they burned them and destroyed the walls, but granted their lives to the garrison because of the imminence of the days of the Passion. That day Rhys ap Rhys ap Maelgwn gained possession of the cantref of Penweddig and Gruffudd of the commote of Merenydd. On Palm Sunday took place the breach between Llywelyn ap Gruffudd and Edward, king of England. And the autumn after that, the king and his host came to Rhuddlan. And he sent a fleet of ships to Anglesey, with Hywel ap Gruffudd ab Ednyfed as leader at their head; and they gained possession of Anglesey. And they desired to gain possession of Arfon. And then was made a bridge over the Menai; but the bridge broke under an excessive load, and countless English were drowned, and others were slain. And then was effected the betrayal of Llywelyn in the belfry of Bangor by his own men. And then Llywelyn ap Gruffudd left Dafydd, his brother, guarding Gwynydd; and he himself and his host went to gain possession of Powys and Builth. And he gained possession as far as Llanganten. And thereupon he sent his men and his steward to receive the homage of the men of Brycheiniog (Brecon), and the prince was left with but a few men with him. And then Roger Mortimer and Gruffudd ap Gwenwynwyn, and with them the king's host, came upon them without warning; and Llywelyn and his foremost men were slain on the day of Damacus the Pope, a fortnight to the day from Christmas day; and that day was a Friday.[6]

Brut y Tywysogyon starts with the death of Cadwaladr in the late seventh century and continues on to 1282, with a continuation to 1332. It is a Welsh translation of a Latin original which is now lost. Peniarth MS 20 and Llyfr Coch Hergest are versions of the *Brut* but are independent translations. The original work was probably written not long after 1282, and refers to the annals kept by Strata Florida Abbey where it was first written in Latin using texts from Saint David's (up to 1100) and Llanbadarn (1100–1175).

---

that the Latin original was written at Strata Florida, and the Welsh version at Valle Crucis (from Welsh history website, historical texts).

[6] From Meic Stephens, *The New Companion to the Literature of Wales*, University of Wales Press, Cardiff, 1998

The Peniarth MS 20, dating from the late fourteenth century, is the most complete version and is not always the most reliable, but is considered to be without the flights of fancy of Geoffrey of Monmouth's *Historia Regum Britanniae*.

Eleanor

There is a sequel to this story. It was not until September 2006 that I felt the need to go to Cilmery, although friends had visited and had assured me that the energy was changed for the better. We stood there quietly and heard the words 'thank you'.

Later that month, I was sitting on the seat outside my studio, enjoying the warm sun. Closing my eyes I became aware of a spirit lady coming down the drive towards me. She had a presence that indicated royalty. She was beautifully clothed in a gold taffeta dress, over which was a full-length coat that swept the ground at the back like a small train, so that she glided rather than walked. There was some ermine trimming on the front edges of the coat. Her hair was worn in a thick plait coiled round her head like a crown. Who was she and what did she want?

At that moment Bob came out of our house and I told him about her. 'Is she Welsh?' he asked. Dowsing revealed that she was connected to Prince Llywelyn. She said, 'My husband died a violent death; my child was orphaned, and I was displaced. Much healing is needed.' She was Princess Eleanor, the daughter of Simon de Montfort and King Henry's sister, also named Eleanor. There was a need to find out more about what she wanted from us, so I spoke about her to a friend who is a medium. She was able to relay this rather despairing message: 'Nothing has changed since my time. There is still betrayal, there are still political pressures and people are still being imprisoned and killed.' The healing she said she wanted was not just for her situation but for us, for our world and our time too.

Eleanor had been married by proxy in France in 1275, but had been imprisoned by the king at Windsor for three years on her arrival in England. They were finally allowed to marry in Worcester Cathedral when she was given away by King Edward who provided the feast.

In 1282, Eleanor died in childbirth and in June that year Llywelyn joined the uprising begun by his brother Dafydd. His baby daughter Princess Gwenllian was sent to the nuns at Sempringham in East Anglia, where she died in 1337, at the age of fifty-six.[7] I feel that she never knew who she was. It was after Eleanor appeared to me that two friends went to Sempringham on a pilgrimage of healing. They saw the stone to the memory of Princess Gwenllian, which has recently been erected. They found the energy of the place was tranquil, and they were aware that Eleanor's maternal energy was overlaying their visit. Sempringham has become a place of pilgrimage for Welsh people. (Healing prayers will work wherever you are; please ask for healing of old wounds and present times. Whatever your deepest desire is, you will attract those in the spirit world with the same desire. If you wish to heal, spirit helpers will help you.)

---

[7] Acres Twigg, *Llywelyn, the Last Welsh Prince*, 2001

*Chester Cathedral
and the Four Yorkshire Chakras:
Fountains Abbey, Ripon Cathedral,
Rievaulx Abbey and Whitby Abbey*

This is where we say goodbye to Wales and the Welsh section of this line. Our next visit is to Chester Cathedral as we travel into England and on to Whitby.

Chester Cathedral

The fifth-dimensional portal is connected to the Pleiades and the Pleiadean emissaries of light. This chakra is the link, or bridge, between the Welsh chakras and abbeys and the English ones. From here it crosses the Pennines to arrive at the tenth chakra which is Fountains Abbey in Yorkshire. I got to this cathedral on my third attempt, as I did when I found Llyn-y-Tarw on my third try. Perhaps it is to do with the number three and its significance for 2003. To the Celts, nine was especially sacred, multiplying three by three to make the thrice-sacred number nine.

The trinity stood for many things in their lives: mother, father, child, or air, sea and land, or the three aspects of Brighid. I had dreamed of a woman who had three daughters, and each of the daughters had three daughters, making nine granddaughters, with a total of thirteen women in all, the number of the chakras.

Three friends had visited the cathedral before me. They did not find it a happy place. They felt its darkness and there was a sense of depression and heaviness there. Pat and Dee went separately and both of them came away wondering if there was something wrong with them, until I was able to tell them how each of them had had similar experiences. Behind the cathedral, there is a beautiful little garden where Dee sat to ask, 'What is wrong?' It was here that she was made aware, through her etheric vision, of a tree temple. In the centre was the altar stone, a rough-hewn stone slab. It was the sacred place of the Druids, on which was built the first Christian church. We were later to realise that there was a blockage on the chakra line about forty-five miles away, and that this was having an adverse effect on the adjoining chakras, just as it does with our own bodies.

The spiritual guardians must be very concerned when mankind, in our supreme ignorance, creates this havoc in the Earth. When we have performed a ceremony, and have done something 'right', we feel an uplifting sense of happiness, we can feel their joy, and we know that somehow we have been able to help to right the wrong.

Chester Cathedral

Healing a Blockage on the Chakra Line

One day I received a phone call from a lady who was a medium, and she asked me what it was that I did. I told her about the discovery of the chakra line. She said that there was a blockage on it, but she was unable to tell me where it was. She said that she could see men with hard hats and JCBs. 'They don't know what they are doing,' she said. Thanking her for her help, we began to dowse along the line for this block. It was found at a village further to the north. Synchronicity was at work again, for it just happened that one of our dogs needed an operation, and we were going to take Dusty to a veterinary hospital the following week. After taking him to the hospital, we set off to find whatever it was that was causing the problem. I was looking for some kind of building site, and was totally unprepared for what it really was. It was a quarry that had filled with water. The quarrymen had left the road running through the middle of it, like a bridge that separated the two water-filled areas.

It was horrible, and it stank! I did not want to go anywhere near it, but I forced myself to walk down the middle of the road, stopping in the centre to consult my pendulum, although I already knew that this was the place. I walked to the end and saw a notice on the gate leading into one of the quarries. It said 'Danger of Death, blue-green algae'.

So we had identified the place and the problem, but did not know what to do about it. The stagnant, blocked energy pathway had created stagnant, poisonous water. Knowing there must be someone who could heal this place, I began to ask people I came into contact with if they were Earth healers or knew of anyone who was. Three months went by, when I had a letter from a man to tell me that he had been talking to a lady who mentioned my work of mapping the chakra system. They had talked about Earth healing, and he felt that he should write to me. He told me that he was an Earth healer, but he did not know why he had been directed to contact me; would I let him know what it was about?

He said that a bridge should be built in the etheric over the quarry, from one side to the other. This would carry the energy, and the problem would be solved.

He also said that he knew that something was going to happen because during that week, pictures of dragons had been appearing everywhere in front of him. Dragons, of course, are the spiritual signs of the Earth energy and the spirit of the Earth. I sent him a sketch of the quarry and he told me that we could do it between us; I would be the seer and he would provide the necessary healing energy. So we set to work. I saw this bridge as a rainbow bridge, and

Merlin came and stood on it. I felt that this was the kind of magic he enjoyed. Then I saw it as a solid stone bridge, which was suspended in the air over the quarry. I was puzzled by this because it was defying gravity, until the realisation dawned that I was being shown, in symbolic terms, that the bridge was now complete and it was as solid as stone.

My Visit to Chester Cathedral

Would there be any difference in the energy of the cathedral now, and would I be able to pick it up? We visited it on a Sunday in April, and it was easy to see why my friends had said it was dark. The old red sandstone was black in places, giving the facade a very gloomy look, but there was cherry blossom out on the trees around it, lighting up the whole edifice with the divine pink of unconditional love. Inside, a service was in progress, the organ music and singing lifting the vibrations of the whole building. The stained-glass windows were joining in the whole effect by singing with colour and light.

My feet seemed to lead me through to the back of the nave, where there was a shrine to Saint Werburgh. Standing before it, I felt that she had known of the feminine energy line passing underneath her church, and so asked for her blessing on the work to re-energise it. It is not an accident that this church's founder was female, and the last abbot of Saint Werburgh's became the first dean of the Cathedral Church of Christ and the Blessed Virgin Mary in 1541, when King Henry VIII gave the abbey back as a cathedral. The Mary energy was being recognised, although they were probably unaware of it at that time.

Saint Werburgh was born c. 650, the daughter of the Mercian King Wulfere. She became a nun, and eventually an abbess renowned for her reforms and holy life. She died at Hanbury in Staffordshire, and many miracles were reported at her tomb. In 907 during the reign of Ethelred of Mercia, his wife Queen Ethelfleda had the relics of Saint Werburgh brought to the city in order to protect the city from the Danes, who were settling in the Wirral. A Christian church or minster seems to have existed on this site which was then enlarged to house the saint's relics, so that th church became a place of spiritual pilgrimage as well as pastoral care. For 200 years it was known as Saint Werburgh's Minster.

The saint is associated with geese. It was believed that she had restored one to life after it had been stolen and killed by a servant. In the modern west window, the saint is depicted, together with Saint Oswald, Saint Aidan, Saint Chad, Saint Wilfred and Queen Ethelfleda. Outside in the garden, there is a Druidic emblem of an acorn. This is the emblem of the Cheshire Regiment. It is symbolic that this sign of the oak tree is still there where the tree temple once stood. It is a source of great interest how the energies of past ages sometimes linger in a place, unconsciously influencing people in the present. The memorial is a large rectangular block of stone similar to a stone altar. The official cathedral guide says that the garden is also known as the 'garth'. This is an English spelling of the Welsh word for garden, '*gardd*'. It was outside the east window that we poured chakra water on the grass, and linked with Valle Crucis Abbey, content in the knowledge that all was well.

Saint Werburgh

Saint Werburgh

The Story Ends in Yorkshire.

Chester Cathedral is the chakra which bridges Wales and England. It is from here that the line crosses the Pennines to arrive at Fountains Abbey on the North York Moors. The link is clearly demonstrated in the west window where Saint Oswald, Saint Aidan, Saint Chad and Saint Wilfred are shown.

As I mentioned, Saint Werburgh was the daughter of the king of Mercia. The kingdom of Mercia stretched northward to Northumbria and Whitby Abbey. When Saint Augustine arrived in Canterbury, Paulinus came with him. Paulinus accompanied Queen Ethelberga when she came to Northumbria in 625 as Edwin's queen. When Edwin was converted to Christianity, thousands followed their king to be baptised, but Cadwalla and King Penda soon defeated Edwin in battle and tried to stamp out Christianity in the kingdom. In AD 633 Oswald, Edwin's nephew, returned to fight them. Oswald had a vision of Columba assuring him of victory, and the next day, despite being heavily outnumbered, Oswald won. He had been educated on Iona and sent for a missionary from there to come to his kingdom and 'carry the light of Christ'. It was Saint Aidan who came with twelve companions. He was supported by Oswald who became renowned as a man of justice and compassion. It was he who gave his name to Oswestry in Shropshire. He died there in a great battle with the Mercians, and the soil in which he was buried was attributed to heal the sick, and it was noted that the grass was especially green and more beautiful than the rest of the field.[1]

Among those schooled in Christianity on Holy Island were two brothers, Chad and Cedd. They were made bishops and Cedd went to Mercia and later became bishop to the Saxons in Anglia. His brother Chad was sent to Ireland to study, and on his return became Bishop of Mercia, establishing his centre in Lichfield.

The Synod of Whitby hosted by Hilda in AD 664 brought to a head the struggles between the Roman insistence on absolute

---

[1] Stephen Smalley, *Chester Cathedral*, A Pitkin Guide; *Celtic Saints*, A Pitkin Guide; John Marsden, *The Illustrated Bede*, 1996

authority and conformity, and the Celtic desire for continuing autonomy and mutual respect. Colman, Abbot of Holy Island, Cedd, and Hild could not prevent the persuasive and politically astute Wilfred, Abbot of Ripon and supporter of the Roman tradition, from eloquently swaying the Synod in favour of Rome. Celtic monasteries in England were overtaken by the authoritarian disciplines of the Roman Church.

Chakra Number Ten is Fountains Abbey

In 1132, a small band of discontented Benedictine monks left Saint Mary's Abbey in York. They were dissatisfied with the worldliness of their house and sought a new life of greater austerity. They celebrated Christmas at Ripon as guests of Archbishop Thurstan. On 27 December, the monks travelled three miles west into Skelldale and founded Fountains Abbey on land given to them by the archbishop. They sheltered in caves and beneath an elm tree. In the following year, they were admitted into the Cistercian order and began construction of a timber monastery. The abbey flourished until its suppression by Henry VIII in 1539. In commemoration, there is an annual pilgrimage to Fountains Abbey from Ripon on Boxing Day. The size and state of preservation of the Yorkshire abbeys seems miraculous to us coming from Wales. Fountains Abbey has a connecting relationship with water; the River Skell not only flows around it but underneath as well.

This is a Cistercian abbey here and its name is Saint Mary of the Fountains, because of the abundance of water and springs. But it may also have got its name from its guiding spirit, Bernard of Clairvaux, who was also known as Saint Bernard de Fontaines. In this beautiful ruined building, I was both surprised and disappointed to find myself feeling sick and ill. We stayed only long enough to pour some of the chakra water in front of the altar, and send our love and energies through our feet and back over the Pennines to Chester Cathedral, creating the link in the grid system. Back at the hotel, dowsing checked that the link had not yet been made, so we did the meditation similar to the one used by the Fountain Group. On checking again, I found that the chakra was now functioning. On the next visit, we felt a change in the energy. It felt lighter and I no longer felt queasy. I had felt sick at the other chakras we visited and realised that this was because I was sensitive to the blockage in the energy. Once it was cleared and functioning, it was fine.

Ripon Cathedral is Chakra Number Eleven

Ripon is an impressive and interesting cathedral. On my first visit I felt ill and this was a lot worse than on my first visit to Fountains Abbey. We left the cathedral, did the meditation and poured chakra water outside the east window. As we walked back past the cathedral we saw a white dove looking down at us from the roof, which we took to be a sign of the acceptance of the water and the meditation. Returning the next day, the energy in the cathedral felt lighter and I was able to walk round the building without any ill effects.

The first monastery at Ripon was established around the year 675 by a Celtic monk named Eata. The following year Alhfrith gave the monastery to Wilfrid who relocated the church to its present site overlooking the River Skell. There, he set about the construction of a Roman-style basilica of dressed stone. The dedication ceremony was attended by Oswiu's successor, King Ecgfrith. Apart from Paulinus's cathedral at York, this was probably the first stone building to have been built in northern England since the Romans. The church was adorned with gold and silver and varied purples, while the high altar was vested in purple woven with gold thread. He also commissioned a set of illuminated gospels on purple parchment and a jewelled bookcase. The Ripon jewel is a rare example of such craftsmanship. Wilfrid's crypt survives, built beneath the high altar.

Wilfrid (born 634) was the son of a Northumbrian aristocrat and was one of the most influential and controversial figures of the seventh-century Church. He was educated at Lindisfarne, the Celtic monastery established by Saint Aidan. Aidan died in 651, three years after Wilfrid entered the monastery. It was here that Wilfrid developed a longing to go to Rome, which he visited three times. He fell in love with all things Roman, including the Catholic Church, to such an extent that he wanted to live there. Back in Northumbria he was granted the abbey at Ripon in 658 and it was six years later that he acted as Bishop Agilbert's spokesman at the Synod of Whitby. His forthright defence of Roman customs led to their imposition throughout the Northumbrian Church. His reward was to be made Bishop of Northumbria. He discovered that Chad had been infiltrated into the see, so he withdrew to Ripon and a series of further disputes meant that Wilfred spent a total of twenty-six years of his episcopate in exile. During this time he acted as a bishop to Wulfere, king of Mercia, and father of Saint Werburgh (of Chester Cathedral). Wulfere had a great liking for Wilfred and he was to spend more than ten years there. He died in one of the Mercian monasteries that he founded.[2]

Wilfrid is controversial because he has been blamed for the demise of the Celtic Christian Church. There is no doubt that he hastened its end. The instigator of its downfall was Saint Augustine who was sent to Britain for this purpose accompanied by Paulinus, the Roman Catholics' 'power behind the throne' at the Synod of Whitby. The downfall of the Celtic Christian

---

John Nankivell, *Saint Wilfred*

Church was inevitable, given the influence of the ruthless power-hungry Roman Church. The Celtic Church, with its emphasis on individual spirituality, has, however, now come into its own with our present-day search for the spirit within. We are all returning to that spiritual realisation. This is the historical lesson of this pilgrimage. That the time has come for the reawakening of Celtic Christianity and with it, the awakening of ourselves.

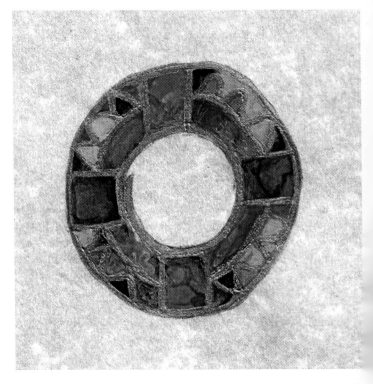

The Ripon jewel

Another Block is Found in the Line in Yorkshire

We knew that there was another block in the line because w~ were able to dowse it on the map. It came after Ripon and befor Whitby, somewhere on the moors. We still could not find th blockage because we thought that it may have been a quarry and we could not find one. We dowsed to find out where the crystalline grid had disintegrated and to my enormous relief we eventually found it. When we climbed up to it we found ourselves in the worst hailstorm we had ever been in, and as we parked the car there was a clap of thunder. It was very dramatic.

There was nothing more we could do that day so we went back to the hotel where we did a meditation to bridge the gap. This was done in the same way that the crystalline grid at the quarry had been restored. I had previously asked my friend, the Earth healer, how this could be done. He told me that I did not need to contact him, but simply to think about him and the energy provided by the red dragon with the golden breast. So this is exactly what we did, at the same time calling on Merlin for his help. I 'saw' the energy in three separate layers. At the top there were angels, in the middle was Merlin who was performing magic with his staff, and at the bottom level I saw the dragon. As I watched, the dragon flew up a shining pathway of light reaching to the top of the cliff. I saw him perch on the rock and I thanked him for his help.

'That's all right, my dear,' he said and flew off in a westerly direction. This was the end of the meditation.

The following day we checked by dowsing whether the etheric bridge was functioning and the energy flowing through. It was, so we continued on our journey.

Rievaulx Abbey is Chakra Number Twelve; Whitby is Number Thirteen

Rievaulx Abbey was the first Cistercian abbey in the north of England. Its greatest importance was during the rule of its third abbot, Saint Aelred 1147–1167, when there were 140 choir monks and 500 lay brothers and lay servants. It is a magnificent building. At first when we arrived I did not feel anything. But after fifteen minutes, I felt very cold. There was a very cold energy that is associated with negative energy. I then began to feel sick again. We put our chakra water into the ground before the altar and left. That evening we again did the meditation and dowsed to see if the energy was flowing. It was, so we were ready for our final trip to the thirteenth chakra at Whitby Abbey.

The chakra line travels across the North York Moors to Whitby and the only habitation on the line is the village of Rosedale. As we were passing, we decided to visit it on the way. There really was an abbey in this village; it was a priory, a nunnery which was founded under the Cistercian order by William of Rosedale in 1158. It was never a large community, having about nine nuns in the care of a prioress. The only visible ruin of the abbey is the tower in the garden outside the west door of the present church. The parish church of Saint Lawrence and Saint Mary was built on the foundations of the abbey chapel. If you look the other side of the altar rail you will see one of the old stone seats from the abbey; this is now the bishop's chair. In 1850 the village was expanded and the stone of the abbey was taken to build the villagers' houses, so that most of the abbey forms the present village. Since this is a feminine energy line, it seems appropriate that this nunnery was built on it. Leaving Rosedale Abbey behind, we set out across the moors to Whitby.

Since we had been in Yorkshire the weather had been showery, but on this day the heavens opened and it rained all day. The rain clouds rolled across the moors which were black and very forbidding. We passed Fylingdales which we had seen previously from Brimham Rocks near Pately Bridge, so we already knew that we had seen the chakra line as it ran north-east across the moors to Whitby. This had been another glimpse of the line's impressive scale.

We had arranged to meet two friends at Whitby Abbey who were going to join us in our final ceremony. The rain continued without letting up and the wind howled eerily through the abbey, seemingly trying to blow us over the cliff. This had driven any visitors away so that the four of us could perform our ceremony uninterrupted. We poured the chakra water in the abbey where Saint Hild's altar would have been, said prayers and did the final meditation.

We were later told that visitors were beginning to notice the change in the abbey's energies. I had been aware of a sense of pressure that the line was to be completed by that spring, but I did not know why. I was later given to understand that it was necessary to do it before the summer solstice. This became apparent when it was realised (but not planned by us) that Dee and John 'just happened' to be at Whitby on the day of the summer solstice when we would be at the other end of the line at Llansteffan. This proved to be a magical occasion when, at the appointed time, we once again linked up in meditation.

We were guided to send the energy through the crystalline grid into the ocean at the north-east and south-west ends of the line. The whales and dolphins were then asked to take the energy through the water and around the planet. This was concluding the task that had taken us three years to complete. We had carried it out to the best of our abilities, and I felt a deep sense of gratitude for the guidance that I had been given.

When visiting these ruined abbeys, floorless and open to the skies, it does seem sad to find them in this derelict condition. But when a sacred place is open to the Earth and the sky, it is functioning because of this fact. If someone decides to place a large building upon it, then the energies of the places can no longer function in the free and unrestrained way as they did when the ancients first held them sacred. So, sad though this may be from a physical point of view, from a spiritual point of view, it is glorious that the planet's energies are free once more. They have returned to their original free state.

The Roman Church sent out an edict that all sacred sites should be built on, in order to 'protect' them. This act of placing a building on these powerful energy lines hijacked this power for their own use. These energies were not lost but usurped. The Normans built taller, longer and larger buildings than had ever been seen before in Britain: they were symbols of power and wealth, used to bring the people into submission. So when an abbey is once again open to the sky, it regains its primeval function, with the added bonus of the energies contributed by the hundreds of years of prayers, singing and devotions of the monks. You only have to stand in these places to feel that this is true. We are all privileged to go to these ancient places and stand on this hallowed ground, knowing that people have been doing this since the beginning of time. Please remember to ask permission from the guardians to enter, and to thank them as you leave.

Historical Whitby

Visiting the chakras on this line, it is surprising how many were Bronze or Iron Age settlements. Archaeologists working at Whitby Headland have found the remains of a roundhouse, dating to the first or second century BC. The house measures eleven metres in diameter, and its entrance faces east, typical of Iron Age dwellings. This allowed the early morning sun to filter into the interior, warming the inhabitants. All that remains is a circular trench and post holes. The headland is eroding every year and much of this area will fall prey to the elements within the next couple of decades. It seems that the houses were situated along the present cliff edge with the industrial area some way back, divided by a trench to prevent the risk of fire spreading to the thatched roofs. They found iron slag, loom weights and even indications of glass vessel-making. This is the first sign of domestic settlement in this period.

After Oswald was defeated by Penda at Oswestry in 642, he devastated Northumbria. Oswald's brother Oswy in turn defeated Penda in 655. In gratitude for success, Oswy dedicated his daughter Aelfled to the monastic life. Two years later, in 657, Abbess Hild set up a new monastery at Whitby and moved there with Princess Aelfled. Bede describes Hild as coming from a royal family (she was the great-niece of King Edwin). After living a secular life for thirty-three years she decided to live in a monastery in Gaul, foreign exile being a common method of renouncing the world in this period. Saint Aidan did not want her to go and she was offered a hide of land near the River Wear. From there she moved to the monastery at Hartlepool and then to Whitby. Bede says, 'She taught the observation of righteousness, mercy, purity, and other virtues, and especially of peace and charity. After the example of the primitive church, no one there was rich, no one was needy, for everything was held in common and nothing was considered to be anyone's personal property.'[3]

In this respect Hild was following the ordered way of life that Columba developed for the monastery on Iona, which became a model for other Celtic monasteries. It required that the monks live

---

[3] John Marsden, *The Illustrated Bede*

only for God, praying constantly, offering hospitality to all, focusing their conversations on God and the Scriptures, owning no luxuries, eating only when hungry and sleeping only when tired.

According to Bede, the Iona community was characterised by 'their purity of life, love of God and loyalty to the monastic rule'. Women held a significant place in the Celtic church, for the Celtic Christians had been influenced by the Druid religion, and both men and women held authority in Celtic monasteries. Many communities were mixed, with monks and nuns living within conjoined enclosures, and some of them were married. A female abbot was always called upon to oversee these double monasteries. Under Hild's leadership Whitby became a centre for learning and the arts, but after the Synod these monastic traditions were crushed.

Saint Augustine is wrongly described as bringing Christianity to a dark and pagan land. What he actually did was to bring it to the eastern side of Britain, and Roman Catholicism to the rest. But it was Viking raids on monastic settlements which dispersed the wider Celtic Church in Britain. Many saw the Vikings as God's displeasure at their physical laxity, because not everyone was able to live the life of prayer demanded by the Celtic saints.

The Wild Goose, a Celtic Symbol of the Holy Spirit

Saint Werburgh's association with geese is a link with the crown chakra, where there are geese on the lake in springtime, together with the black-headed gulls. Saint Werburgh once raised a goose from the dead and Saint Brigid called wild geese to come to her. Geese make good guardians and watchdogs, as they once famously saved Rome by alerting the citizens to danger. They are fearless and are known to attack. It seems that if bulls are hoofed guardians, the winged guardians are the geese. The keynote of the goose is the call of the quest to legendary places. There are the childhood stories of Mother Goose, and they are mentioned in myths and fairy tales. Their migration stirs our imagination and makes us want to search out new worlds and dimensions. When flying, they constantly shift formation, creating wind-draught and easier flights for those behind them in the formation, which is a reminder that as individuals go on a quest, it becomes easier for others to follow.

They never fly directly in front of each other, so they do not obstruct each other's view, showing us that we should not enter into a quest without having a full view of what it entails. The V-formation is symbolic, reflecting a shape opening up to new possibilities, like an arrowhead pointing the way forward, but with one end open to reflect openness to new ideas.

This formation indicates a new path, and reflects a great fertility that should be acted upon if growth is desired. These birds have keen vision, and anyone who finds geese entering their lives will achieve a greater vision, both spiritually and physically.[4]

It would seem that these birds have come into this story for a purpose, to guard and inspire, and also as an aid to communication through the use of stories, because their feathers were used to make quill pens. For centuries, they were the only writing instruments known.

These birds mate for life, reflecting the belief that there is one special person for each of us, our soul-mate, and the ending without which no fairy tale is complete: 'and so they lived happily ever after.' They are associated with the number eight and the infinity symbol. It is appropriate that the goose should have appointed itself as the totem bird for this quest.

The Greylag goose is the only goose that breeds in Britain and is the ancestor of the farmyard goose. The ancient Celts preferred to keep their geese alive to produce eggs, in the same way that they kept sheep for their wool and milk rather than their meat. If we wish to keep the goose laying golden eggs, we have to keep the goose alive. This is an analogy for looking after ourselves to ensure our productive power. The goose feast occurred at Christmas and signifies renewal and purification, represented by the mid-winter solstice when the sun is reborn. The goose is a solar bird so that laying the golden egg is a symbol of this solar birth. The mother goose represents the mother goddess.

The Celts considered its fat to have healing properties. In Wales when I was a child, goose oil or fat was recommended for rubbing into the chest for colds or influenza. The goose represents a strong attachment to its family, as well as an ability to be at home in th

---

[4] Ted Andrews, *Animal Speak*

three elements of earth, water and air. As geese are able to fly extremely high and for great distances, they carry the quality of endurance. They show how it is possible to be grounded and spiritual at the same time, and as such they are a powerful symbol of the union of heaven and Earth.

On the day of our visit to Whitby Abbey the weather could not have been worse. The wind seemed to howl through the abbey and the rain washed over us. In spite of this, my sense of the energy of the place was of tranquillity. Serenity was the abiding feeling that has transposed itself into the picture, which was painted eight months later. This is an attunement to the original Celtic inhabitants of the abbey, of Saint Hild and her monks and nuns and Saint Aidan from Holy Island.

The goose as a spiritual symbol is one of mankind's most ancient, going back an amazing 30,000 years. This carving from mammoth ivory was found in a cave in the Swabian Jura mountains of Bavaria, and is one of the objects which makes up the oldest body of spiritual and figurative art in the world. It is the earliest known representation of a bird, and is 47 mm long and 13 mm high.

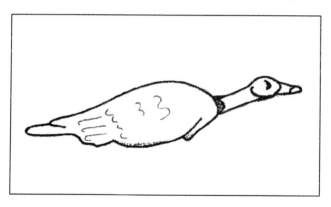

The energy from the Welsh heartland has been able to pulsate along the line to reach the thirteenth chakra at Whitby. A reconnection to the source, the heart chakra at Strata Florida. The picture has a power, not of itself, but because everyone who sees it will automatically transmit its image into the collective consciousness. This will help to uplift the energies. People should be aware that images have this power. Just think what negative images are doing to our planet's consciousness. If you are disturbed by a negative image, just surround it with light before you let it go.

My painting of Whitby Abbey is a recognition that this Celtic energy has returned to Whitby

We have reached the end of the Grail journey that began in Wales, which corresponded with a personal journey for each one of us. The Grail question pertinent to our time is: are we ready again to follow the wild goose? To go wherever this Celtic symbol of the Holy Spirit chooses to send us? Many people who are 'awake' have been, and will be asked to do just this, and direction will be given to them. To do so is so important for the future of our planet and ourselves.

It is so reassuring to know that spiritual knowledge can never be lost. Neither can it be destroyed, by time, people or even powerful institutions. But this was never a story about the past, because this past is our present and our future; it contains the stuff of our dreams and our ability to create our reality. We cannot cross the rainbow bridge unless we know who we truly are. There are Celtic spiritual treasures being rediscovered which touch the hearts of us all, causing us to ask: 'Where is the good way? Ask for the old path, and you will find rest for your souls.'[5] Many people in the past knew about the coming of the Golden Age of Aquarius and laid down a foundation in the very Earth itself. This is a two-way process:

> *As we awaken, so does the land.*
> *As the land awakens, so do we.*
> *The time is now!*
> *May the wisdom of the ancient ones be with you,*
> *And the blessings of the Celtic saints be upon you,*
> *as you walk your pathway of pilgrimage.*

---

[5] Jeremiah 6:16

Celtic Connections

The Pathway from the Past Leads to the Future

A little-known verse of the Celtic poem attributed to Saint Patrick, 'Saint Patrick's Breastplate', captures the ethos of the Celtic Church.

I bind unto myself this day
The virtues of the starlit heavens,
The glorious sun's life-giving ray,
The whiteness of the moon at even,
The flashing of the lightning free,
The swirling wind's tempestuous shocks,
The stable earth, the deep salt sea
Around the old eternal rocks.

(Left) A stone carving of a Celtic saint from
Kilpeck Church in Herefordshire

Some Celtic Christians travelled around the Celtic kingdoms of the British Isles and on into Europe, while others journeyed to places where Christianity had not yet been established. Their wanderings led to a separation from all they held dear, many pilgrims travelling for years and never returning to their homes. They were called by God to follow the example of Abraham and Columba, symbolised by the wild goose, a Celtic image of the Holy Spirit.

277

They were deeply connected with the Earth Mother and the spirit of the Earth. They truly understood that the spirit of their God moved and breathed in every living thing, in water, rocks, Earth and sky, and they lived in harmony with this spirit always. Although their times were very troubled, this connection gave them their strength. It gave them the courage to follow the wild goose wherever the spirit took them.

There is a Soul Plan for each Person; Each of Us Should Ask for Guidance

The Message Begins:

'There are many works on this planet which need to be done and all are as vital as the rest. This is about choices and about which to choose first. It is about priorities.

'This is so important, and again we come back to the flow. The priority is in the mainstream. The periphery, the edge, is not the priority, but it is so easy to enter a backwater if you are concerned with the wrong things. To find the right thing to do, you must ask your higher self for guidance. Ask in prayer and meditation and you will be given a sign which will point the way for you. This is a very important point in the lives of those on Earth. Much energy is wasted, sometimes whole lifetimes are wasted, because of a lack of understanding that guidance is only given if guidance is asked for. Teach people to ask, for it was ordained before they entered this life that guidance should be given, and no one is without this, for no one is alone. In order to get this planet back on its course, all those on the planet must receive guidance. This was part of the equation, an agreement that was entered into before they incarnated. There is a plan for each person here, and it is vital that each soul should freely enter into the plan.

'How else is the planet to vibrate in tune with mankind?

'All who entered this world entered into a contract with the planet and the cosmic spirit. This contract must be honoured.

'All the help you need is at hand. Go forward in the light. Honour your contracts, for you are all blessed.'

My Soul's Contract was to Reveal More of our Celtic Inheritance

The rediscovery of the Welsh chakra line was my soul's path, and I have been helped by a small group of people on this Earth, and by a much larger group in the spirit world. It just so happened that it really was a pathway, and I had constantly been 'told' by my spirit guides that I was going to shine the light on the path. I invite those of you who are inspired by it to follow it yourselves, or follow your own – whichever is right for you.

As we go on this pilgrimage, we follow our Celtic inheritance, seeking the sacred places that have lain dormant for centuries, and in these ancient places an old energy is being reawakened. When someone from the present visits an ancient sacred place, if they are able to see the past connections which that place has, or imagine how it might have been, then they are able to release it from its past and bring it into the present where it now belongs. If we see only the now, we are capable of condemning the past to remain in limbo, like a kind of island in a sea of time, which will never catch up with the present. The Earth is not just the present, it is the past and the future at the same time. Simply by acknowledging its history as we stand there, we can create a bridge, and the ancient timeline becomes our present and the future and all is well. It was a Druid from the old time who told me this; the past would appear to be an island in time.

The spiritual realities that the Druids and the Celtic saints knew are becoming increasingly relevant for us. We are being asked to remember and to honour their spiritual knowledge and practices, like those of the first Christians who made Britain their home long before Saint Augustine was sent to these shores. We are being asked to accept once more the wisdom and freedom of the individual soul to choose the way forward and accept that the responsibility is ours alone. We are being asked to understand that we are part of the overlapping worlds of the cosmos, and that the animals are our guides and teachers, showing us our soul's wisdom.

The Druids used animals, birds and insects as oracles, and they have presented themselves throughout our journey. In a connection with Taurus and the constellation of the Pleiades, there is a bull acting as the guardian for both the crown chakra and the third eye. At the crown chakra, the Canada geese are additional and noisy guardians. There are black-headed gulls nesting there also. Swifts and dragonflies and a red admiral butterfly were welcomed at our ceremonies. We always seemed to have an audience of sheep, and on our visits to Tregaron Bog and Strata Florida, we were greeted by red kites.

Celtic animals from Kilpeck Church

There is another area in which we need more understanding. We need to see trees as important beings who have memory, and if we know how to speak to them they are sources of the old wisdom. Some of them have medicinal properties and they are guardians of the wildlife and providers of homes for the nature spirits. They work with them to balance the atmosphere and maintain the soil. It is a part of our experience to understand the damage done by their displacement when their home in an oak tree was cut down. They attacked Dee in her home because they wanted their tree back, and although this was clearly impossible, nothing else would satisfy them. It was Merlin who stepped in to help us to right this wrong, by helping to create an etheric tree for them.

We are all guided on our pathway by an angelic presence. Working with this presence takes us to a far higher level than when we rely upon our limited human resources, raising our level of consciousness with angelic assistance. We must call on them as witness to any ceremony that is performed whenever there is a celebration of a sacred site. If we do not invite them to give their blessing, we leave a void which can then be filled by the influence of dark forces. Because this is the universe of free will, beings of light must be invited, but dark forces will come in whether invited or not. Angelic beings are always there to help us; we only have to ask. It is the responsibility of the Archangel Uriel to help us when there is any negative disruption in the energy of sacred sites. Archangel Michael can be called upon to assist us as well.

Some of the guardians of place are devas who are able to show themselves visibly to us in the shape of a bird or animal. At the crown chakra, a deva took the form of a red admiral butterfly which was at a height above sea level where these butterflies are not normally to be found. They behave differently from normal butterflies, going out of their way to draw attention to themselves. There is also a deva guardian in the form of a red kite which is often to be seen circling above our ceremonies at Strata Florida.

A Message about the Elements and the Elemental Beings

It is clear that we get the weather we deserve. This is a question of balance within ourselves because the nature spirits who work with fire, air, water and earth are directly affected by our attitudes and behaviour.

'I would like to speak to you about the weather which is changing on your Planet Earth. We are aware of the changes and the problems which it is causing. We wish only to say that the imbalance is inevitable, given the instability which is manifesting itself at this time. There are many changes in the vibration of this planet. There are changes in time itself. There have always been changes. The severity depends on mankind's wish and ability to work with the changes and participate in a more peaceful environment. Respect the Earth, respect the universe, and the cosmic forces which are coming into being in order to influence in the birth of Aquarius. It is a new dimension. At the beginning the Earth and its people will slip in and out of this dimension. This slippage will cause instability. It is more important than ever to hold onto your still centre, your centre of balance and harmony. Hold it – and teach others to hold it – that is all.'

Light a candle, say a prayer. If you can hold on to your still centre, you can help to hold the planet in balance.

Salamanders

One very hot summer day I 'saw' these fire elementals. They are salamanders, literally 'bright sparks'.

> *We are Salamanders.*
> *We are the light.*
> *We are the life force.*
> *Within our light is the universe held.*
> *We are the elementals of fire.*
> *We are love. We are heat.*
> *We are light. We are warmth.*
> *We bring all of these gifts. We are bountiful.*
> *We are splendid!*

I thought so too, and they were so full of themselves. They set fire to things through sheer exuberance – 'Oops! sorry, didn't mean to do that – just got carried away.'

Salamanders – fire elementals

It is important for each one of us to hold the balance of our own masculine and feminine energies. In doing so, we can help the elemental energies of the Earth to hold their balance and join them and the angelic forces, in co-creating a new harmonious planet. To be co-creators of the Earth, we need only to go about our daily lives with this awareness and understanding. We do not necessarily need to visit sacred sites, as the very act of walking on the Earth in a sacred manner is what Christ asked us to do: to walk in the light is to be awake to the reality of the spiritual realms of the planet. This is something we can all do every day, for wherever we go we leave an imprint.

The Angel of the Air

Acknowledge the angel, bring the angel into the centre of your awareness. Allow the colours of blue, indigo and violet to flow through you. Feel the kindness of this beautiful spirit. It feels like a gentle breeze; the colour is the cobalt blue of the sky. Link with its gentleness and kindness. This angel is linked to our breathing. We are breathing it in and out in every breath we take. Our connection is this close; and yet we are unaware and do not acknowledge it, although it sustains our every moment. Different coloured candles link with different angels. The angel of air links with purple or violet candles. You can link with it either through the element of air, or you can link first with the angel, and then with the element.

The Gift of Water

To me, water is a sentient being; it has a voice and a memory, it both speaks to us and remembers us. In meditation, I saw a water droplet – delicate, shimmering, a gift of water. I found myself meeting with the element of water as it comes from the heavens and the spirit of white light.

A Message from this Spirit

'We have always been concerned for the element of water. It is vital to this planet and its care transcends all other planetary care. Only if mankind understands this gift and this spirit can the world of men stand by their ancestors, who understood the gift of the elements. Respect and acknowledge this element wherever you find it.'

The Beautiful Family, the Fairy Realm

In the Welsh language the elemental beings are known as *Y Tylwyth Teg*, meaning 'the beautiful family'. This is a respectful title and we need to have more respect for them and their unselfish work. The Earth needs us to honour and work with the beautiful family because its survival depends on our ability to co-create with them. Although we may not be able to see them, we can sense their presence. They enjoy being with us if our presence is uplifting or creative. They are outside our cycle of life and death, and can live for many hundreds of years. At death they are absorbed back into the consciousness of their group, as the golden dragon of Tregaron Bog at the solar plexus chakra will be in time.

At the crown chakra, through my etheric vision, I have 'seen' hundreds of pairs of tiny wings like butterflies flying in the air over the lake. They manifested themselves in my picture of the rainbow crown, and this was reputed to be the last place in Wales where they could be seen.

The Christ Consciousness and the Feminine Energy Grid

In order to raise the vibrations of Planet Earth and ourselves, we need to know there is a network of energies which surround the Earth and which are linked to individual archangels. They can influence both ourselves and the planet through these networks. There are also cosmic energy fields coming from the various star systems, and our sun and moon. The sun powers the ley lines which were places of power known to the ancients, where the sun's energy was carried through the Earth's crust.

Another energy grid carries the Christ consciousness, bringing in the vibration of divine love. This vibration was guarded by the Daughters of the Moon, at the temples of their goddess Brighid, using their knowledge of the crystal kingdom. This was to carry the vibrations of love in order to bring about the combination of masculine and feminine energies which had separated into opposing forces, and whose balance was being lost. This grid contains two separate flowing energies, one masculine and the other feminine. These two bands of energies hold the blueprint of love which leads to a perfect balance in all the apparent dualities of our world. These lines gave rise to the Michael and Mary line in England, and others throughout the world. The Pathway of the Beloved is one of these negative (feminine) energy lines, bringing back the balance of the feminine influence to our planet.

When the Master Jesus walked the Earth, he carried this balance within his own body, so that he could bring us to a higher level of consciousness. 'And did those feet in ancient time, walk upon England's mountains green?' Yes, they did, because the Master's task was to earth this energy to enable the Christ spirit to materialise through this grid system. It was written that he 'with his finger wrote on the ground', and this was one of the ways in which he earthed these energies. He said, 'I am the light of the world: and he that followeth me shall not *walk* in darkness, but shall have the light of life.' The Holy Family considered that their work with the crystalline grid was very important, so the real reason for their coming here was to raise the planet's vibrations for future ages through this grid. If our Earth was so important to them, surely it behoves us to hold it in equal importance.

Along the pathway there were constant pointers to the past, and I wondered if it were really possible to go back that far. I am amazed to know that it does. The Master Jesus did not come to Earth solely to establish a religion. His mission was to unite the positive and negative Earth grids carrying the universal Christ consciousness, and to show us that the spirit lives for ever; only the body dies. He is the symbol of the everlasting life of the spirit through divine love. Through love of the Earth and an affinity with the Universal Christ Consciousness, we can raise the vibration of humanity and this planet, but we need to work with both.

Advice on Visiting Sacred Places

The most important thing is a sense of respect. Simply go to feel the energies, with positive expectancy – without expecting anything specific. If you expect something to happen, this will create a barrier in your mind. Just be open and ask for the light to protect and guide you.

Behave just as if you were visiting someone's house for the first time (which, in a way, you are). Be courteous. Introduce yourself and ask permission to enter the site (you do not have to do this aloud). You may leave a gift of some kind, remembering that as you give, so you receive. Thank the spiritual guardians and close an imaginary door on leaving. You will find that they will recognise you and welcome you each time you return. The word 'welcome' might even enter your mind. Courtesy and respect for the site and its ancient guardians are all that is needed.

A Celtic Blessing On Setting Forth

May the road rise to meet you;
May the wind be always at your back;
May the sun shine warm upon your face;
May the rains fall softly upon your fields.
Until we meet again,
May God hold you in the hollow of His hand.

The Celtic world is still accessible to those who are willing to search for it.

A section of carvings from Kilpeck

The Element of Water Has the Last Word

The Element of Water Has the Last Word

From the moment when this amazing adventure began in the year 2000, we have worked with the water element. I was asked to go to all the chakras and exchange the waters one with another. This was to link and energise the whole chakra line from the Scilly Isles to Whitby.

At all these sacred sites, prayers were said, and at the lakeside, flowers and rose petals were scattered on its surface. It was done intuitively with the feeling that it was the right thing to do. Certainly there was an awareness from the very beginning that the lake at the crown chakra was communicating with us. In 2002, Doctor Emoto's wonderful photos of water crystals came into the public domain and gave proof that prayers really did make a difference to the condition of water.

In 2005, we were acting as guides for a group of people at the lake. After they had performed a ceremony, Bob noticed that an amazing change had occurred on the surface of the lake. Parallel lines of foam had suddenly appeared, stretching east–west along the entire lake. There were sixteen people there to witness this. A lady from the group climbed to higher ground and took pictures of the phenomenon, and when they were enlarged we were stunned by the revelations.

Definite shapes had been created from the foam, taking the forms of elementals, animals and even humans. Two of the humans were swimming (of course). The element of water is communicating with us humans through writing on the lake, in a similar way to the crop-circles being communication through the earth element. Two of these shapes had a personal message and I feel that they were meant as confirmation for me. One of them, the pixie elemental, I had seen before in a painting by the Flemish artist Hieronymus Bosch, 1450–1516. It is a pixie with trumpets for ears (this was an artist who painted many weird creatures).

The second one was the body of a fairy with its face looking down.[1] Whenever I had seen fairies flying over the lake, and also when I painted them in my picture of the rainbow crown, I had

---

[1] See p. 21.

never been able to see the bodies between the wings. All I saw were pairs of wings. Now the lake was showing me the part of the elemental which I had not been able to see. This was confirmation indeed, and proof of the consciousness behind this message. We need no further proof that water can communicate with the people of this planet; it is already doing so, and now in pictorial form.

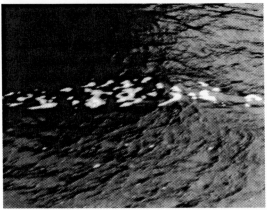

(Photos by Annie Henry)

PIXIE AFTER THE STYLE OF
HIERONYMUS BOSCH
FLEMISH ARTIST 1450 - 1516

BIRD

LITTLE FURRY ANIMAL
SHOUTING THE ODDS

FAIRY BODY [2]

A PIXIE RIDING
A BROOMSTICK

JUMPING
ELEMENTAL

'ASTERIX THE GAUL'
TYPE CARTOON
CHARACTER

A SCULPTED
LETTER 'M'

ELEMENTAL

SEAL WITH BALL

A GROUP

RABBIT RUNNING

MUSICAL
NOTE

EAGLE'S HEAD

TADPOLE

DOG / POODLE

DRAGON

WOMAN'S PROFILE
HAS A 1930'S CLARICE
CLIFF LOOK

HUMAN

SAME PROFILE TURNED
UPSIDE DOWN

HUMAN
SWIMMING

A WOMAN
SWIMMING
HOLDING UP
A BABY

Lake surface encryptions

[2] The Fairy body without wings, see illustration p. 21.

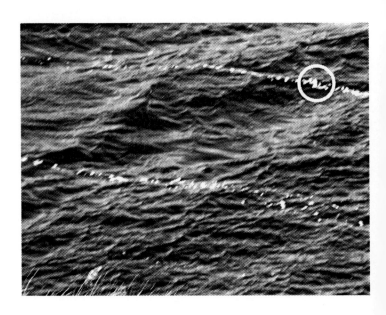

M for Merlin. The letter 'm' is composed of two horses' heads joined at the nose, with the head on the right complete with its body and a rider. Llyn-y-Tarw was very rough at the time.

Recommended Reading

Andrews, Ted, *Animal Speak*, Minnesota, Llewelyn Publications 2001

Baigent, Michael, *The Jesus Papers*, London, Harper Element, 2006

Blake, Steve and Lloyd, Scott, *The Keys to Avalon*, Dorset, Element, 2000

Bock, Emil, *Genesis, Creation and the Patriarchs*, Edinburgh, Floris Books, 1983

Bollard, John K (Trans.), *The Mabinogi*, Llandysul, Gomer Press, 2006

Carr-Gomm, Philip & Stephanie, *The Druid Animal Oracle*, London, Connection Book Publishing, 1996

Delap, Dana, and other partners of the Northumbria Community, *Celtic Saints*, A Pitkin Guide, 1995

Cooke, Grace, *The Illumined Ones*, New Lands, Liss, Hampshire, The White Eagle Publishing Trust, 1966

Cooke, Grace, *The Light in Britain*, New Lands, Liss, Hampshire, The White Eagle Publishing Trust, 1971

Courtenay, Edwin, *Reflections*, England, The Prince of Stars, 2004

Davies, J L (1944), E Jones (1947), D P Kirby & W J Lewis (1955), *Tregaron, A Journey Through Time*, Wales, Curiad Caron

Dawkins, Peter, 'Europa and the Bull', *The Grail Kingdom of Europe*, England, The Francis Bacon Research Trust, 1995

Earth, Melody, *Love is in the Earth*, Love Publishing, Colorado, 1995

Edwards, Lewis, 'The Pumpsaint Temple of the Stars', 1947, Morien Institute tribute to Lewis Edwards, http://www.morien-institute.org.uk/pumpsainthtml

Evans, D H, *Pillar of Eliseg*, Cardiff, Cadw, 1987

Fountain International, www.fountain-international.org

Gahlin, Lucia, *Egypt, Gods, Myths and Religion*, New York, Lorenz Books, 2001–2002

Gantz, Jeffrey (Trans.), *The Mabinogion*, Penguin Classics, 1979

Gardener, Philip and Gary Osborn, *The Serpent Grail*, London, Watkins, 2005

Grolier, Arthur Mee, *The New Children's Encyclopaedia*, 1981

Gwyndaf, Robin, *Welsh Folk Tales*, National Museum and Galleries of Wales

Hartley, Christine, *The Western Mystery Tradition*, Loughborough, Thoth, 2003

Heath, Robin and Michell, John, *The Measure of Albion*, St Dogmaels, Bluestone Press, 2004

Helliwell, Tanis, *Summer with the Leprechauns*, Llandeilo, Cygnus Books, 1997

Hoffman, Natasha with Hill, Hamilton, *The Standing Stones Speak*, USA, Renaissance, 2000

Jacobs, Alan, *The Gnostic Gospels*, London, Watkins Publishing, 2005

Kennedy, Mike Dixon, *Celtic Myth & Legend*, London, Blandford, 1996

Knight, Jeremy K, *Valle Crucis Abbey*, Cardiff, Cadw, 1987

Lynch, Francis, Stephen Alderhouse Green, and Jeffrey L Davies, *Prehistoric Wales*, Stroud, Sutton Publishing, 2000

Main, Laurence, *Camlan, the True Story*, Dinas Mawddwy, 1997

Main, Laurence, *The Spirit Paths of Wales*, Cumbria, Cicerone Press, 2000

Marsden, John, *The Illustrated Bede*, Edinburgh, Floris Books, 1996

Matthews, John Merlin, *Shaman Prophet Magician*, London, Mitchell Beazley, 2004

McGary, Gina, *Brighid's Healing*, Sutton Mallet, Green Magic, 2005

Melchizedek, Drunvalo, *The Ancient Secret of the Flower of Life Volume 2*, USA, Light Technology Publishing, 2000

Miller, Hamish and Broadhurst, Paul, *The Sun and the Serpent*, Launceston, Pendragon Press, 1989

Minehan, Rita, *Rekindling the Flame*, Sola Bhride Community, Ireland, 1999

Nankivell, John, *Saint Wilfred*, SPCK, 2002

Owen, Trefor M, *Welsh Folk Customs*, Llandysul, Gomerian Press, 1959

Pennick, Nigel, *The Celtic Saints*, New York, Sterling Publishing, 1997

Pettitt, Sabina, *Energy Medicine*, Pacific Energies, Canada, 1993

Phillips, Graham, *The Marian Conspiracy*, London, Pan, 2001

Pokorny, J, 'The Origin of Druidism', in J Matthews, *The Druid Source Book*, London, Brockhampton Press, 1997

Power, Rev. P, 'Life of St Declan of Ardmore', 1914, etext published by Irish Texts Society, London http://www.ccel.org/d/declan/life/declan.html

Poynder, Michael, *The Lost Magic of Christianity*, London, Green Magic, 2000

Rightly, Charles, *A Mirror of Medieval Wales, Gerald of Wales and His Journey of 1188*, Wales, Cadw, Welsh Historic Monuments, 1988

Robinson, David M, and Colin Platt, *Strata Florida Abbey and Talley Abbey*, Cardiff, Cadw, 1992

Simmons, Robert and Kathy Warner, *Moldavite: Starborn Stone of Transformation*, Vermont USA, Heaven & Earth Publishing, 1988

Smalley Stephen, *Chester Cathedral*, A Pitkin Guide, 1994

Spencer, Ray, *A Guide to the Saints of Wales and the West Country*, Lampeter, Llanerch Enterprises, 1991

Steiner, Rudolph, *The Goddess*, Sussex, Sophia Books, 2001

Stephens, Meic, *The New Companion to the Literature of Wales*, University of Wales Press, Cardiff, 1998

Stewart, R J, *Celtic Gods and Goddesses*, London, Blandford, 1990

Strachan, Gordon, *Jesus the Master Builder. Druid Mysteries and the*

Dawn of Christianity, Floris Books, Edinburgh, 2001

Straffon, Cheyl, *The Earth Mysteries Guide to Ancient Sites on the Isles of Scilly*, Cornwall, Meyn Mamvro, 1995

Street, C E, *Earth, Stars, the Visionary Landscape*, London, Hermitage 2000

Tabor, James, *The Jesus Dynasty*, London, Harper Element, 2006

The Complete Welsh-English, English-Welsh Dictionary, Y Geiriadur Gomer Mawr, Carmarthen, 1968

Thomas, W Jenkyn, *The Welsh Fairy Book*, New York, Dover Publications, 2001

Twigg, Aeres, *Llywelyn, the Last Welsh Prince*, Gomer, Llandysul, 2001

Welsh Annals (A Tenth-Century History of Britain in the British Library)

Wilson, Hilary, *Understanding Hieroglyphs*, London, Brockhampton Press, 1999

Wingfield, Megan, and Olive Hesketh, *Light is the Rainbow Bridge*, Llandudno, published by Megan Wingfield, 1998

MEGAN WINGFIELD is a native of Mid Wales and has moved house many times up and down the Welsh Border, from Ross-on-Wye in the south to Prestatyn in the north. She has a son and daughter, and now lives with her husband in North Powys. It is with the help of family and friends that this book has been produced.

A teacher who has trained both in healing and colour therapy, Megan considers herself primarily to be an artist. It was through painting that she found herself to possess the ability to 'tune in' to spiritual realms. Her first book, *Light is the Rainbow Bridge* came from pictures received in meditation and the spiritual guidance which accompanied them. It is a 'thought for the day' book, useful for divination.

Megan's attunement gives her the ability to 'read' the energy at sacred sites, translate it into pictures and take dictation from spiritual beings. This has led her and her friends and family on an odyssey which was both a physical pathway and a Grail journey. This is ongoing.

Megan's other main interests are in animal conservation and the rainforests' survival. She has bought many acres of forest and hopes to buy many more which are held in trust for perpetuity. She is a dog lover, with a particular fondness for Tibetan terriers.

Lightning Source UK Ltd.
Milton Keynes UK
UKOW04f0842260315

248566UK00001B/3/P